NOAA-15 RGB= CH(1,2,4) 08/29/2005 11:48 UTC

GOES-EAST AVNCOLOR IR CH. 4 - AUG 29 05 03:15 UTC

Katrina Ten Years LLC
Hattiesburg, MS

First published in August 2015

ISBN 13: 978-0-9967553-4-4 (Hardcover)

ISBN 13: 978-1-5173137-9-1 (Color paperback)

ISBN 13: 978-0-9967553-1-3 (B&W paperback)

ISBN 13: 978-0-9967553-2-0 (Epub)

ISNB 13: 978-0-9967553-3-7 (Kindle)

Please visit www.katrinatenyearsafter.com for supplementary information. There you can contact us for information about special discounts for bulk purchases, to book an event, or seek republishing rights.

Book design by Adam Robinson for Good Book Developers
www.goodbookdevelopers.com

Front Cover image by Betty Press. Back cover image by Mark Klinedinst.

Photographs in "Photo Essay by Betty Press" Copyright Betty Press

Katrina Ten Years After

The Rebuilding of New Orleans
and the Mississippi Coast

Mark Klinedinst

Laurence Hudson

Michael Marks

Coral Pogue

Betty Press

David Reynolds

and

Linda VanZandt

Katrina Ten Years LLC
Hattiesburg 2015

CONTENTS

EDITOR'S NOTE

THIS BOOK AIMS TO DESCRIBE THE AFTERMATH, TEN YEARS LATER, OF THE worst natural disaster to hit the U.S. Our aim is to tell the truth about the resiliency of the people of the area, buffeted by not only a storm but also by the Great Recession over the last decade. We look briefly at the area before the storm hit and then the rebuilding efforts up to June 2015.

No book can capture all the dimensions of a disaster of this magnitude. The best we can do is hope to offer a truthful description with all the warts and gems and with a sense of hope for an area that we cherish and would like to see thrive. We lived through this disaster and rebuilding. Our backgrounds go from economics, oral history, theater, private business, anthropology, and photography. We have done work over a number of years looking at the industries and people as they have tried to cope. We also supplement the data-driven parts with compelling interviews collected by a number of the authors, many of whom lived through the storm and continue to make this area our home. Our aim is to target a non-technical audience but also, through the use of appendices, offer something that a scholar may appreciate.

One of the distinctive features of our research is that it is the culmination of ten years of culling information and gathering data on this area's economy that in certain areas has no equal.

The rebuilding of the area is a reflection of who we are in the South. There was a great amount of generosity, but there were also conflicts between classes and ethnic groups over the spoils of aid funds. We start out going over a snapshot of the area before the storm hit, focusing on what types of people lived in the area, where they worked, what they did for cultural activities, and what makes them one of the most distinctive populations of the U.S. We then describe the scale of the storm and its destruction, unparalleled for natural disasters in the U.S. We have information on a number of the "stylized facts" about the immediate aftermath as well as some that have not been widely known. We can also disentangle the different responses in the states impacted, but we focus specifically on the New Orleans area and South Mississippi, where the greatest damage occurred.

Mark Klinedinst
August 2015

AUTHORS' NOTES

Author's Note (by Linda VanZandt)

As a history student in Vietnam the summer of 2003, I experienced Vietnam as a place, not a war. In a place of such exotic landscapes and handsome, smiling people, it might have been easier to forget the gnawing images of war. Surrounded by rubble and hovering helicopters on the east peninsula of Biloxi, Mississippi two years later, I could not escape the scene unfolding in my head as I sat with my tape recorder on a concrete slab in the immediate aftermath of Hurricane Katrina. I wondered—was the deafening whir of helicopter blades amidst dazed wanderers and crumbled buildings triggering difficult memories for my first interviewees Tong and Chien Nguyen? Tong and Chien were husband and wife Vietnamese survivors of war and now Katrina. How could I possibly ask them to tell, to give any more, when their losses were again so profound? It turned out they wanted to tell, and they were not alone.

The Nguyens would be the first of many first- and second-generation Vietnamese Americans I would come to know and record over the course of seven years along the Katrina-ravaged Gulf Coast. Concentrated primarily in East Biloxi (Point Cadet) and New Orleans East (Versailles), these Vietnamese communities' elders were people of the sea who had learned the fishing trade from their fathers and grandfathers along the shores of the South China Sea. They were the lucky few who survived perilous escapes by rickety boats from their homeland, landing in faraway and, later, U.S. refugee camps, and eventually on the Gulf Coast where the climate and waterfront felt familiar. Pooling their resources to build and buy boats with which to carry on the traditions of fishing and shrimping, as others had before them, was how they survived—they had families to support and spoke little English, a skill not required in order to make a living in the seafood industry. They were resourceful, close-knit, resilient people who, almost thirty years later, were once again forced to navigate new waters as the post-Katrina federal bureaucratic recovery climate was thick and left many lost in (lack of) translation.

My position as an oral historian at The University of Southern Mississippi's Center for Oral History and Cultural Heritage allowed me the time and resources to document the heroic and horrific stories of Katrina survivors, first responders, volunteers, and many others struggling to recover some sense of normalcy inside the Katrina zone. My life-changing trip with American veterans to the Vietnam of their youth rooted my desire to hear, in particular, the long silent voices of these Vietnamese communities, whom I imagined were quite used to being unheard. Stories collected focused initially on overcoming war, natural disaster, and fear of the unknown. Just five years after Katrina, which included setbacks due to the Great Recession, Vietnamese fisherfolk and small business owners were again drowning in the mire of a historic disaster, sharing their stories of the personal impact of the BP Deepwater Horizon oil disaster of 2010.

I share some of these personal stories, in their own voices, here—in honor of their struggles, their triumphs, and their legacies. As I write this introduction in 2015, the Gulf Coast recovery is ongoing and layered—concrete slabs and historical markers remain in place of historic homes. Oil spill claims remain in question. Also in question is the health and future of the Gulf Coast ecosystem and the most vulnerable industries and communities affected. The indomitable spirit and resolve of the people, however, remain inspiring. And for many, a renewed spirit grows from elders and youth joining together in collaborative projects for a brighter and more sustainable future.

A folklorist once said that out of shared telling and remembering grow identity, connection, and pride, binding people to a place and to one another. To this I can attest, and in this retelling I can hope. I will forever feel intimately bound to each and every one who entrusted me with their very personal stories during impossible times, and to the young and generous Vietnamese Americans who shared with me the impact they felt upon hearing these stories as they provided tedious and difficult translation, interpretation, and transcription. For these gifts I am eternally grateful.

Prelude and Author's Note: Bay Saint Louis (by David Reynolds)

MY MILITARY SERVICE WAS AS A PILOT. IN AVIATION, ATTENDING TO weather, in depth and in detail, is routine and compulsory. Long a civilian by 2005, I still kept the weather awareness habit, especially in summer, monitoring the tropical Atlantic and eastern Gulf of Mexico, where hurricanes consolidate and grow. Our 1880s home in Bay Saint Louis was a thousand feet away from Mississippi Sound, on safe ground at an elevation of 21 feet above high tide. The other dozen or so buildings on our block were all historical and on roughly the same high ground. The neighborhood had seen plenty of hurricanes, recorded for over two centuries. We knew what to do: provision, pick up, fasten down, cover-up, secure, protect, then listen to the wind, watch uneasily, sleep poorly, pitch in to care for others, and repair damage after.

By Thursday, August 25, my wife and I, and many others across southern Alabama and Mississippi, and southeast Louisiana—especially the Greater New Orleans metro region—took notice when tropical storm Katrina feinted toward the north Atlantic, turned abruptly left, and crossed the southern tip of Florida into the Gulf. Soon, the predicted track shifted northwest as Katrina widened and strengthened. On Friday, we brought out the plywood window and door covers and put them in place on the side facing the Sound. We checked provisions. On the 26th, barometric pressure, winds, and wave heights worsened in reports from the NOAA weather data buoy four hundred miles or so to the southeast. At dusk, frigate birds appeared, high up, in large numbers, as they do when things are not well offshore.

On Saturday morning, the 27th, I drove to New Orleans, where I managed The Green Project—a non-profit that acquired, conditioned, and sold for reuse salvaged and surplus building materials, components, and paints—to check storm preparations. Around noon, my wife called, anxious that we should prepare to depart inland in view of the predicted track and strength of the hurricane. I had grumbled about possibly being without power for a spell in the late summer heat and humidity, and worried about the great aged oak behind our neighbor's barn, close enough to put a good lick on our guesthouse if it blew down. I figured to stay though, as I had in previous storms. I knew the varied and brave sounds that our house made in high winds and wasn't much bothered, except for the added work, inconvenience, and discomfort.

In the meantime, my wife, who didn't have a lifetime of living on coasts and was of decidedly less of a mind to stay than I, followed the TV and Internet storm coverage. Friends in Birmingham called, inviting us. While I put on the more difficult west-facing plywood covers, left off the day before, a second weather buoy, much closer, reported a barometric pressure of 27 point something. I can't recall the decimal "something," only that the low number was alarming, not so far from becoming 26 point something, radically low. That was enough. We would leave in the morning (Sunday), and be back in a few days. Going without electricity when we returned seemed likely, and would be uncomfortable, but there would be gas for cooking, and we had lanterns, flashlights, candles, and neighbors who looked out for one another and who would enjoy visiting on porches in the evenings until our houses cooled inside.

On Sunday morning, things were quiet around town—a car going by once in a while, an occasional sound of sawing or hammering. We packed lightly: casual clothes, laptops, some vital documents, and, oddly, a few personal keepsakes. In a bureau drawer, I noticed my Coast Guard flight log, with its dates and notations of search and rescue at sea, and tucked it in my pack. The cat, uncooperative in most things and strongly adverse to transport, entered the pet carrier on her own, skipping the usual balking and hiding.

Author's Bay Saint Louis, Mississippi home prior to Hurricane Katrina

After Katrina

CHAPTER 1

The Story

"He reached down from on high, he took me;
he drew me out of mighty waters.
He delivered me from my strong enemy,
and from those who hated me;
for they were too mighty for me.
They confronted me in the day of my calamity;
but the Lord was my support."

——Psalm 18, 16-18, NRSV

THE STORY OF HURRICANE KATRINA, THE MOST EXPENSIVE AND ONE OF the deadliest natural disasters in U.S. history, is a story not just about the region where the impact was felt and lives either lost or often profoundly changed, it is also a story about our national culture and government. This book does not claim to cover all the intricacies of the storm's devastation and rebuilding, but it does try to give an honest and compassionate look at the successes and failures as this region tries to recover.

This book is a collective effort by all the authors listed in the title. The magnitude of the devastation, both physically and emotionally, that the storm brought makes the strength that a joint effort can bring to the task all that more compelling. Drawing on the strengths from a number of fields allows us to ferret out the truth that may go missing from a narrower perspective or an "official" description. As we write this book, we are aware of the really good books and documentaries already done on parts of this story (a number of them are mentioned in this book) and that there will probably be a number of accounts by politicians, academicians, and more, retelling what happened and forming a narrative that will shape the public's understanding. Our diverse backgrounds help us to tell the story not only from a macro overview of the systems that did and didn't work but also from a solid grounding learned from our own personal experience and numerous interviews (audio files of some of these are available in the book). The experience of collecting data on such an event can be quite mundane at times (e.g., gathering data from online sources and matching them up over time and across geographical or institutional boundaries), but often the best data collection is informed by interviewing the key actors that supplied the data, a practice that has been repeated over the last ten years. Small nuances in the data can only be explained at times by this close connection to the actual sources. An example experienced by one of the authors serves to illustrate this point well: when trying to understand company performance in Eastern Europe as those countries made the transition from centrally planned systems, there were entries that did not seem to make sense. After interviewing a number of employees and managers at the firms where the problem seemed to be, it was learned that the entries were masking payments made to different mafia groups. The long hours spent interviewing and the personal experience of many of the authors here will hopefully have helped to guide us in giving an accurate and compassionate account of one of the most interesting areas in the U.S., relatively free from miscalculations and cold hearted numbers.

While covering some details on the whole scope of the hurricane, we will focus on the areas hardest hit, specifically New Orleans and the Mississippi coastal area. This area is unique in the United States in its relation to the Gulf of Mexico, the Mississippi River, the diversity of people and cultures that resulted from rival sovereign claims (Native Americans, Spain, Britain, France, and the U.S.), some of the oldest cities of the United States, and the spawning of great musical and culinary lineages. Southern tradition and warmth, mixed with the joie de vivre of "Nawlins" (New Orleans), are the frosting over a past that included some of the darkest events of the U.S. The plantations of Louisiana near New Orleans and the brutal slavery they rested upon have been aptly described in the book and much later in the popular movie "12 Years a Slave" written by Solomon Northup (Eakin 2013). Commenting on Northup's 1853 text, Frederick Douglass claimed that "its truth is far greater than fiction. Think of it. For thirty years a man, with all a man's hopes, fears and aspirations… Then for twelve years a thing, a chattel personal, classed with mules and horses… It chills the blood…" (ibid., p.3). Hundreds of years of slavery and segregation have left pockets of hatred and bigotry that still stain this area, as in other parts of our country. When people in other parts of the country think of Louisiana and Mississippi in particular, they don't often think first of rich music, literature, beautiful landscapes, beaches, gardens, and Southern hospitality; instead, they typically think of scenes from the civil rights era and the motion picture "Mississippi Burning."[1] Probably some of the stigma that follows is partly due to the fact that Mississippi has the highest percentage of African Americans than any other state at 37% and Louisiana is second at 32%.[2] This history, the area's accompanying high poverty rates and low educational levels, and an unfamiliarity with the region probably combined with lingering racism might make some feel that this area was not deserving of the massive amounts of aid necessary to rebuild.

The belief held by some that the government should be tightly fettered also played a role in the tragedy that came over the region. Ideologically driven imperatives to "starve the beast" of the U.S. Federal government[3] (except for the programs you like) meant that the Federal Emergency Management Agency (FEMA) and the Army Corps of Engineers funding and staff had been scaled back.[4] The incorporation of FEMA into the new Department of Homeland Security in 2003 created tensions and lines of authority that were not always clear. FEMA had long had a dual role of protecting the country from natural disasters and also coordinating the efforts to keep the government running after an enemy attack (e.g., the hardened shelter of Mount Weather). The new department under the helm of former Pennsylvania governor Tom Ridge, who tried to coordinate the alphabet soup of agencies, privatized the creation of the "National Response Plan" (NRP) to the Rand Corporation. The Rand Corporation has been for many years a contractor for the government, especially the military, but their plan was not created by the people in the field who actually would be in the disaster zones, and FEMA's expertise in dealing with past hurricanes and other natural disasters was largely bypassed (Cooper and Block, 2006). This reshuffling, privatizing, and cutting back, combined with the point person in FEMA, Michael

---

1   The film centered around the town Philadelphia, Mississippi and the effort to capture the murderers of civil rights workers James Earl Chaney, Andrew Goodman and Michael Schwerner.

2   For Mississippi the figures are 1098385/2967297=.37 and for Louisiana 1452396/4533372=.32 from U.S. Census 2015.

3   A classic example by one of the supply side proponents is Milton Friedman's "I never met a tax cut I didn't like" (Friedman, 2003).

4   See Brinkley 2006, Horne, 2006 and Roberts, 2006.

D. Brown, having been previously the head of an Arabian horse sports association (Hsu and Glasser, 2005), seems to have created the necessary conditions for FEMA's failure when the storm hit. Tax cuts, spending on the wars in Iraq and Afghanistan, deficits, an emphasis on terrorism, and cut backs were all part of the mix that led to one of the nation's most unique cities and coastal Mississippi being unable to rely on the federal government in a timely manner.

Complacency about the threat of a "perfect storm" hitting New Orleans or the Mississippi coast came from the over thirty-year hiatus of a major storm hitting these areas. Hurricane Betsy had hit New Orleans in 1965 and Camille had hit the Mississippi coast in 1969. Both of these were strong storms, and Camille in particular was a category five hurricane that pummeled Waveland and Bay St. Louis just as Katrina would do. This long stretch of time since a large hurricane threatened the area and the many feints and turns at the last minute that ended up, in hindsight, costing needless evacuations left a number of people with the idea that another "hurricane party" might be called for as Katrina approached. The wetlands that had helped protect the coastal areas and New Orleans had been greatly reduced and helped the storm wreak greater havoc (Heerden and Bryan, 2006). Although Katrina was rated only a category three at landfall, its large size meant that the hurricane force winds and surge covered a much larger area than Camille and Betsy (Fritz et al, 2007).

There is some concern that the global rise in temperatures may lead to even more powerful storms in the future and may have helped to make Hurricane Katrina even more destructive (Stone, 2013). According to climatologist Aslak Grinsted, "we have probably crossed the threshold where Katrina magnitude hurricane surges are more likely caused by global warming than not" (Koebler, 2013). It seems our inattention to the clamoring by the vast majority of scientists that we must cut our carbon emissions has helped to make the likelihood of perilous storms for future generations a reality.

Strong hurricanes, earthquakes, fires, or terrorist attacks can all leave an area of our country on its knees hoping for the aid that we as a nation can afford and, out of compassion and gratitude, feel compelled to give. The experience of Hurricane Katrina gives us valuable lessons for preparing for the next disaster and serves as a cautionary tale that we have many problems to rectify if we want to make our country safe.

In the weeks and days prior to Hurricane Katrina's descent upon New Orleans and the Mississippi Gulf Coast region, what were the topics of discussion forefront in the media, and would these topics remain important in the weeks to come, or fall by the wayside after the storm's passing? In politics, the headlines addressed issues of judicial bribery (Judge Oliver Diaz and Paul Minor) in Mississippi (Lee, 2005), and other forms of corruption within the government were brought to light when Federal agents issued a raid on U.S. Representative William Jefferson's home in Louisiana and seized large amounts of cash from his freezer. However, there were claims that this cash was stored away in preparation for hurricane season (Elie, 2005).

The casino industry was in an era of expansion, welcoming the Hard Rock Casino, which was on the verge of opening and predicted to bring much prosperity to the Mississippi Gulf Coast with big headlining entertainment acts (Wilemon, 2005). In New Orleans, Harrah's Casino was a few months out from opening its new 450 room hotel (Mowbray, 2005). Along with the casino industry, the high rise condominium business was expanding. The condo boom was happening, and Mississippi Gulf Coast city officials were scrambling to find ways to slow down this development (LaFontaine, 2005). In New Orleans, there was even talk of Donald Trump showing interest and buying into the condo boom (Thomas, 2005). The arrival of Hurricane Katrina would surely slow down these advancements, and for a while this type of development would be moved to the backburner.

Just before this catastrophic storm's arrival, some gulf coast residents would be remembering Hurricane Camille's impact upon the Mississippi Gulf Coast because August 17-18 would mark her 36th Anniversary (Bergeron, 2005). Many others, however, may have been more focused on offshore drilling that would affect the gulf coast region, rising gas prices (Sayre, 2005), and the war in Iraq (Maute, 2005), which was still a very important topic in the media.

It was officially hurricane season and FEMA had put out a memo that stated, "Uncle Sam will gladly pick up the tab, even if it's not the weather that kills you" (Hiaasen, 2005), and New Orleans, on the verge of a fiasco, was still hashing out issues with the federal government concerning disaster funding from the repercussions of Tropical Storm Cindy (Grissett, 2005); however, they were soon going to have much bigger issues at hand.

Before (East Biloxi, by Linda VanZandt)

IT WASN'T THE FIRST TIME VIETNAMESE RESIDENTS OF POINT CADET IN East Biloxi looked to their boats to save their lives. During a packed Sunday morning mass at the Church of the Vietnamese Martyrs Catholic Church on Oak Street, Reverend Phan Duc Dong (known as Father Dominic) strongly cautioned parishioners to prepare and evacuate the Point that afternoon, less than twenty-four hours ahead of Hurricane Katrina's predicted arrival. Father Dominic had practiced as a spiritual leader in difficult times—he had been a chaplain for the South Vietnamese Army during the Vietnam War. After the collapse of South Vietnam's regime in 1975, he offered spiritual guidance aboard the first fishing boat to flee by a new escape route to the Philippines, rather than Thailand, across the South China Sea.

Father Dominic, in white t-shirt under umbrella, as young priest on Saigon River dock

Listen: "Father Dominic of Biloxi: Escaping from Vietnam"

I escaped by fishing boat. Small one, like in Back Bay here. Eighty-two people. And it was so crowded, so crowded! Small one, not big one. Engine single one. Not only one mile, not only one hundred mile, not only one thousand mile, thousands mile on the China Sea. Single one. They didn't come for rescue. No compass. No computer. No radio, no radio! We had some fishermens, young one. They knew very, very well. But we could not imagine how far away. If we just [had] big wind, we die -don't care about hurricane or thunderstorm. So we are so lucky. We face challenge, we face challenge, challenge!

The challenges they faced once they landed on Filipino shores were mitigated somewhat by shared religious connection. "Easy for us because they were Catholic," Father Dominic noted. Through each major dislocation and setback—war and resettlement, Katrina, and the BP Deepwater Horizon oil disaster—Vietnamese residents of the Gulf Coast drew strength and comfort from religious organizations and close family networks—these were their social safety nets, which supported a strong, resilient community.

Next door to the Catholic church, also on the Sunday before Katrina's early Monday landfall, the Van Duc Buddhist temple was celebrating its official grand opening after years of limited operations as a communal space for Vietnamese-American Buddhists. The Catholic church, temple, popular Vietnamese-owned Le Bakery café, and a few other small businesses and restaurants were anchored primarily on Oak Street and intersecting Howard Avenue. This was the heart of the community where celebrations like the beloved Vietnamese New Year "Tet" marked the importance of continuing cultural traditions. Mostly modest homes, many which decades ago were owned by French and Slavic seafood workers, were within an easy walk to the commercial shrimp boats moored at the docks. Towering casino hotels sandwiched the working docks along the perimeter of Back Bay to the north and the Mississippi Sound and gulf to the south. Seafood processing plants stood staffed and ready along the Back Bay to service the larger boats with fuel and ice, while unloading, processing, and delivering the product—wild caught seafood from the sea.

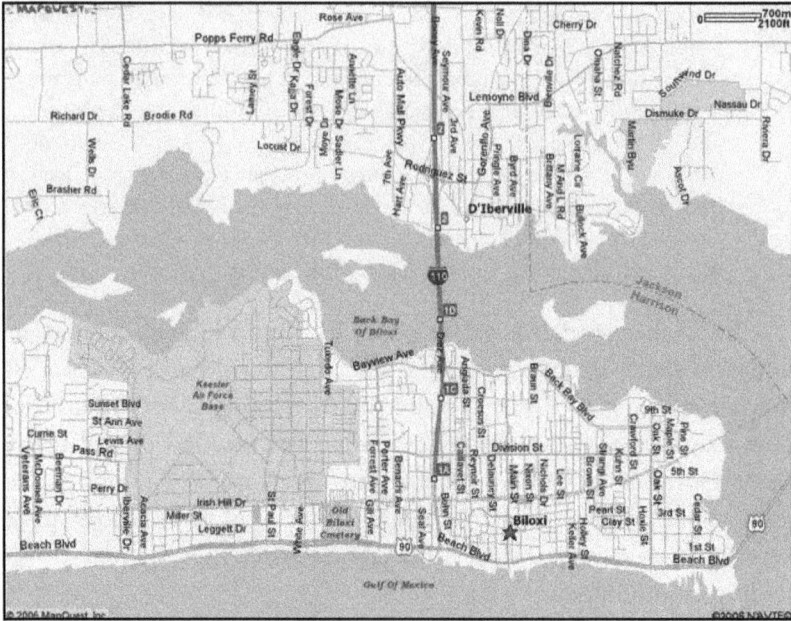

Map of East Biloxi

East Biloxi has been unique in Mississippi for its vitality of ethnic diversity and heritage and its blending of cultures. Transformed by the seafood industry at the turn of the twentieth century, Polish, Slavic, Austrian, Louisiana French, and Cajun laborers laid the foundation for Biloxi to become the "Seafood Capital of the World." Since the late 1970s and 1980s, when Vietnamese families resettled across the United States, East Biloxi's Vietnamese population reached a few thousand within two square miles and comprised the majority of the Mississippi Gulf Coast's shrimping fleet. They participated marginally in coast-wide celebrations like the Mardi Gras Parade and, to mark the beginning of shrimp season, the Blessing of the Fleet. Richard Gollott, president of Golden Gulf Coast Packing Company on the Back Bay harbor, expressed his respect for Vietnamese seafood workers. He helped them settle and they helped his business and the industry thrive.

Vietnamese shrimp boat, Biloxi

Listen: "Richard Gollott: "Bringing First Vietnamese Oyster Shuckers to Biloxi from New Orleans"

Mr. Mao Van Nguyen was the first family that actually moved to Biloxi. And what I did, I got him a house in the Biloxi Housing Authority… and he brought his family to Biloxi from New Orleans and started shucking oysters every day. And then he asked me could he bring some more people…and the first thing you know I think we had about 3000 in Biloxi like this (snaps fingers)! And at that time a lot of Americans didn't want to have anything to do with the Vietnamese but Biloxi pretty much welcomed them…but the Vietnamese actually saved the industry in Biloxi. It was going down. The younger people didn't want to work in the industry anymore and the Vietnamese stepped in and they started filling these gaps up.

Prior to Katrina, with the growth of a casino-led tourist industry, the aging out of immigrant fisherfolk from the seafood industry, and virtually no second-generation family members carrying on the family tradition, many saw on the horizon the inevitable death of the seafood industry. Though the work was physically demanding and the income unpredictable, most Vietnamese fishermen spoke with a smile when they described their love of life on the open sea—the quiet space, watching the sun rise and set, and seeing so many different species of marine life. They did not take as well to land-based, nine-to-five vocations, and most planned on continuing to fish as long as their health and boats held up.

Shrimper Tung Nguyen, who works with his wife and father-in-law on their two boats, expressed his attachment to the trade and the sea saying, "I came here in [19]86 until now. I never move anywhere because I'm a shrimper, so I like it."

Evacuation prior to Katrina was not a consideration for Tung, his extended family, and many others in the East Biloxi Vietnamese community. Material preparations were made, but nothing could prepare them for what was about to come. Tung and his family lashed their boats to almost 200 other shrimp boats to ensure a maximized, coordinated effort using the engine power of all the boats moving in concert in one direction once the waves arrived. As Tung recounted to me this part of his story, I couldn't help but appreciate the metaphorical significance of this close community of fishermen relying on the bonds of shared experience, collective ingenuity, and culture to weather yet another storm. It was ordinary practice during a storm to work together to protect their most important assets, which meant staying anchored near home. But this was no ordinary storm. Ricky Mathews, publisher of the *Sun Herald* newspaper during Katrina and a Biloxi Back Bay resident, described a prophetic moment in the newsroom two days prior to Katrina's landfall.

Listen: *"Ricky Mathews (Sun Herald): Preparation Before Katrina"*

We had a meeting in the newsroom on Saturday. And we brought all the newsroom people together. And I had told them from what I had seen, from the research I'd done on the internet, I told them to go ahead and start making arrangements to cover this story because it's gonna be one of the most fundamentally important stories in the history of this newspaper. And that, I hope that I'm wrong, but I think I'm not, that our community is going to be destroyed. I actually have a picture of that meeting in our newsroom up in my office to remind me that it is so important as leaders to stay on top of issues like this so that we know how to best direct our people. And when you look at the faces of the people that were in that meeting on Saturday, many of the people who were in that picture actually lost their homes. So it was a really prophetic moment. I wish, you know, we had been wrong about what we saw was going to happen, but it prepared our newsroom for one of the most important stories in the history of South Mississippi, and got them thinking about, you know, how are we going to go about covering this in the aftermath. And as you know now the Pulitzer was awarded us as a result of our work so it was an important time—the reflection and the planning we did before the storm.

While many Vietnamese boat owners, like Tung Nguyen, retreated to the Industrial Canal in wait, deckhand Tong Nguyen and his wife Chien heeded Father Dominic's advice and their own desire to gather family close, and left their Point Cadet rental home to retreat a few miles north to their pregnant daughter Kim's home in D'Iberville. This was higher ground where they thought they would all be safe from rising waters. They not only awaited Katrina's arrival but also were awaiting the arrival of their first grandchild.

Before (New Orleans East, by Linda VanZandt)

ABOUT EIGHTY MILES WEST OF EAST BILOXI'S VIETNAMESE NEIGHBOR-hood is the neighborhood of Versailles in New Orleans East, home to one of the largest concentrated settlements of Vietnamese in the nation. You will know you are in Versailles by a few telltale signs—South Vietnam-ese yellow with red-striped flags waving proudly beside American flags; a street named Saigon Drive; a pagoda-style stage behind the Catholic church; and thriving vegetable gardens perched along the banks of the bayous.

Photo of Mary Queen of Vietnam Church with American and South Vietnamese flags

The majority Catholic, many residents of Versailles were born in neighboring villages in North Vietnam before fleeing communism and religious persecution to South Vietnam in 1954, after the Geneva Pact divided the country in two. Initially, close to one thousand Vietnamese Catholic refugees were resettled in New Orleans East in 1975 with the help of the Catholic Church. Versailles is named after the Versailles Arms Apartments where the first Vietnamese refugees were housed. Over the years here, some residents had progressed from meager beginnings in public housing to become middle-class homeowners. Some relocated early on for work in East Biloxi, as Richard Gollott described, and returned only to visit extended family. It wasn't until I drove to this residential suburb in search of the priest of Versailles' Mary Queen of Vietnam Catholic Church (MQVN) that I was convinced I would begin documenting this unique community, in-between trips to East Biloxi.

Similar to Point Cadet's Vietnamese community, but much larger in population and geography, pre-Katrina Versailles was a neighborhood spiritually and culturally centered around the Catholic church, Buddhist temple, and a mix of Vietnamese-owned small shops and restaurants primarily located along Alcee Fortier Boulevard off Chef Menteur Highway.

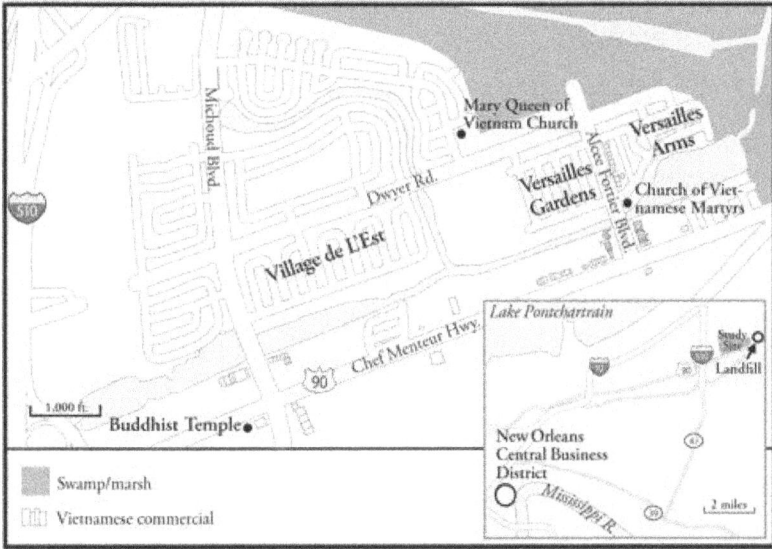

Map of New Orleans East Versailles neighborhood

This was a community, for the most part, well insulated and invisible to the rest of New Orleans. I will never forget, on one of my first drives into the neighborhood, suddenly stopping for an elderly woman carrying loaded baskets balanced on each end of a long pole across her shoulders; another wearing the traditional conical hat pushing a shopping cart down the street in front of the church. I was immediately taken back to the bustling markets on the streets of Vietnam. In fact, each Saturday morning at 5:00 a.m., local gardeners spread out, on tables and blankets, fresh produce, live chickens, rabbits, and ducks. Vietnamese pop music provides the soundtrack to this popular weekly event. Many vendors drive over the few blocks from church just as soon as early morning mass lets out.

My first meeting with Father The Vien Nguyen, the priest of MQVN Catholic Church, happened several weeks *after* Katrina-induced flooding devastated New Orleans. In the chaotic post-Katrina environment, having this few minutes to meet was unexpected, and I appreciated what time he could spare. He was as eager to start an oral history project involving his parishioners as I was. But it was not until 2010, after Father Vien's energies were focused on fueling a historic fight against a toxic Katrina debris landfill near the neighborhood, that I could begin documenting the community of Mary Queen of Vietnam. And in a cruel twist of fate, my success in carrying out this bilingual oral history project was due to yet another historic disaster heaped disproportionately upon the Vietnamese communities of both East Biloxi and New Orleans East—the BP Deepwater Horizon oil disaster, just five short years after Hurricane Katrina.

CHAPTER 2

The Storm (the "Sto-wuum")

"And that was pretty shocking, because I expected to see people wandering around or dogs or animals floating in the Bay or somebody that—I ran search-and-rescue boats. I thought there'd be somebody to rescue, and there was just nothing. And then by this time, I'm looking from the east to west, and the sun is starting to go down, and so the sun is shining through what remains of these trees with no leaves, and I'm thinking, 'This is what Hiroshima looked like.' But then for added insult, there were curtains and people's clothes and rugs up in the tops of trees that had flowed through and got caught. And so it's like Hiroshima, and then the gods had toilet-papered the town just for added insult."

—Congressman Gene Taylor (former, February 21, 2008).

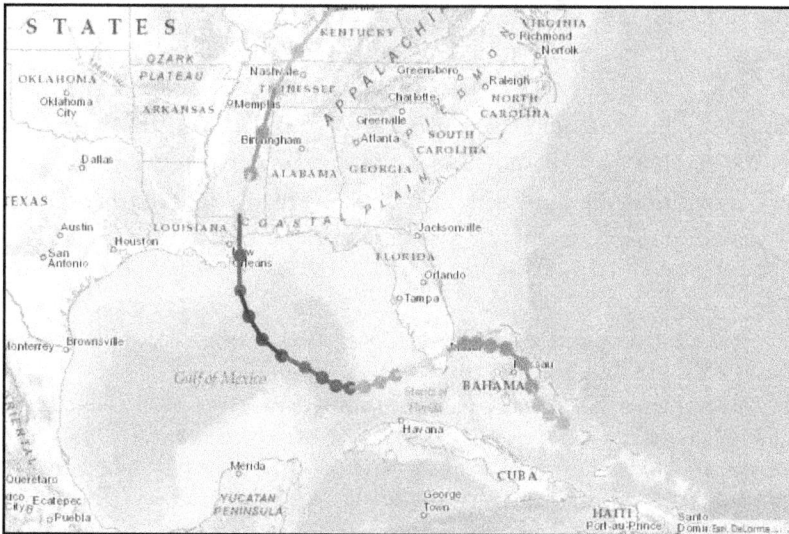

Path of Katrina: Yellow Category 1 Hurricane to Purple Category 5. Graphic from ESRI, DeLorme and USGS.

THE STORM STARTED IN THE NORTH ATLANTIC NEAR CLARENCE TOWN IN the Bahamas as a tropical depression on August 23rd, 2005 (see picture graphic above). To those of us near the ocean in the southern United States, a tropical depression developing nearby is a newsworthy event, especially in late August when the water has had a chance to warm up.

Hurricane Katrina had a profound effect on New Orleans and Mississippi. For those who lived through the most destructive natural disaster to hit the United States, the passing or recording of time in this part of the country is often described as "before-Katrina" or "after-Katrina." Other states felt the wrath of Katrina (e.g., Alabama and Florida in particular), but this study will focus on the hardest hit areas, New Orleans and the Mississippi coastal area. The destruction spread across such a wide area that it would encompass the country of Great Britain.[5] A tragedy of this magnitude allows for a rare glimpse into the best and worst behaviors of which people and institutions are capable. Hurricane Katrina's death toll, according to scientists at the National Hurricane Center (Knabb et al. 2011), was estimated to be 1,836.[6] Although this figure is not as high as in other natural disasters to have hit the U.S., the damage to the economy is without parallel. A good part of the damage to New Orleans could be argued to be an "unnatural disaster" due to the failure of leadership and institutions to provide proper levees to keep back the long expected storm surge.[7] In the hardest hit areas, there were 22,000 businesses and over 350,000 homes destroyed, with another 137,000 buildings that sustained significant structural damage. It was estimated that the storm led to the greatest U.S. diaspora, with the exception of the Civil War and Reconstruction, causing over 1.3 million people to flee (DeParle 2005). A year after the storm, only 53 percent of the pre-Katrina residents had

---

5   Katrina was estimated to have damaged over 90,000 square miles versus Great Britain's 88,745 square miles (Horne, 2006).

6   The real amount will probably never be known. For example, how should people be counted who died due to the lack of electricity in intensive care wards or the lack of dialysis, or who died a few days later after the stress of the storm? There tends to be an element of boosterism that gives a bias towards a smaller count.

7   Though some may view damage to the New Orleans area as an "unnatural disaster," Francesca Nicosia describes the discourse used by government officials to discuss victims of Hurricane Katrina as "expected losses of a natural disaster," in comparison to rhetoric used after 9/11 where casualties were looked upon as "innocent victims of a terrorist attack." According to Nicosia, this obscures the central role of government policy in the lead up to and the outcomes of the disaster (Nicosia, 2009).

returned to New Orleans, and non-black residents were more likely to be among those who came back (Sastry and Gregory 2014).

Among the better things to come out of the storm was an appreciation of neighbors and community. Neighbors who rarely met when the air conditioning and televisions were on joined together and helped to pull trees off homes and pooled their food from their disabled freezers (the electricity in some areas did not return for weeks). Volunteers from the area and from across the globe came to the South and helped, distributing food and water and assisting to clean and rebuild.

Hurricane Katrina was not the first storm to place New Orleans in the national spotlight. In 1965, the city experienced Hurricane Betsy. In its wake, 165,000 homes were flooded and it killed 76 people.[8] Betsy highlighted the poor levee system surrounding the city when it flooded 165,000 homes and led to the passing of the Flood Control Act of 1965 that authorized a project by the U.S. Army Corp of Engineers to construct a new levee system for New Orleans. The Lake Pontchartrain and Vicinity Hurricane Protection Plan, as it was called, was projected to cost $85 million and estimated to be complete by 1978. When Hurricane Katrina made landfall on August 29, 2005, that project was still under construction.[9] More alarming, depending on the location of the 125-mile levee system, construction ranged anywhere from 60-90% complete,[10] and even "completed" sections were subpar with some levee walls built three feet short of their original design.[11] The project was created as a joint effort between federal, state, and local governments, with 70% funding from the federal government and the remaining 30% from the state and local governments (GOA 2005). Over the years, responsibility for the project became tangled between the Army Corp of Engineers and the local levee districts, leaving a puzzled picture of who was responsible for the failures at the time of Katrina.[12] In 2015, U.S. Court of Federal Claims Judge Susan Braden declared in her ruling that "the Army Corps' construction, expansions, operation, and failure to maintain the MR-GO caused subsequent storm surge that was exacerbated by a 'funnel effect' during Hurricane Katrina and subsequent hurricanes and severe storms,

8   (Michel-Kerjan 2010).
9   (Derthick 2007)
10   (GAO 2005)
11   (Derthick 2007)
12   (Derthick 2007)

causing flooding on Plaintiffs' properties that effected a temporary taking under the Fifth Amendment to the United States Constitution."[13] The devastation Hurricane Katrina had on New Orleans was directly related to the levees' capacity to hold back the storm surge from the city.

When the danger of Hurricane Katrina was fully realized in New Orleans on August 27th, a mandatory evacuation was issued, and a traffic system called "contraflow" was implemented that turned highway exit lanes into one-way roads. It is estimated that 1-1.2 million of the 1.4 million people in the Greater New Orleans area safely fled the city two days before the storm hit. While the contraflow plan and mandatory evacuation were successful in evacuating most of the city's residents, it is estimated that over 70,000 people remained in New Orleans.[14] The fault in the evacuation plan is that it assumed that people could provide their own mode of transportation to a safer area even though 27% of New Orleanians did not own a car at the time of the storm.[15] Income and race played a large role in who evacuated and when. Low-income households evacuated much later than higher-income households, and some of these low-income families even evacuated during the storm. African American non-evacuees were much more likely to have stayed because of their inability to leave.[16] The greatest concentration of devastation caused by Hurricane Katrina and the ensuing levee breaches was highest among African Americans.

Despite knowing that a storm like Katrina would have devastating effects on the city of New Orleans, there was not a response strategy in place to sufficiently deal with the destruction that Katrina had left in its wake. The failures of the immediate response to Katrina are widely known, both because they were hardly immediate and not nearly adequate enough to handle the catastrophe. Poor communication between and within organizations is partly to blame. FEMA was in control of the supplies that were needed, but in order to get them to the governmental and volunteer organizations on the ground, the Red Cross had to process requests for supplies before they could be distributed. This task proved overly difficult given that not all of the officials in charge were aware of

---

13   MR-GO is the acronym used for Mississippi River-Gulf Outlet channel. A short cut to the Gulf. See Schleifstein 2015.

14   (Derthick 2007)

15   (Watkins 2007)

16   (Thiede and Brown 2013)

the order or procedures that were necessary slowing down the process (Koliba et al. 2011). To make matters worse, at the time FEMA had a 15-20% vacancy rate with only 2,500 full-time employees on hand (Derthick 2007). The question of what to do with those who were rescued or remained in the city further exacerbated the response efforts shortcomings. All 113 shelters in Louisiana were at capacity. The superdome was ill-equipped to handle the number of people brought in from the city, and the Ernest N. Morial Convention Center lacked food, water, medical treatment, and protection from the National Guard for the thousands that sought refuge there (Derthick 2007). People needed to be evacuated out of the city, but FEMA first needed to contact private bus contractors across the country and have them driven to New Orleans (Koliba et al. 2011).

The areas hit by the storm are among the poorest in the U.S. Table 2.1 shows that the poverty rates for Louisiana and Mississippi are about 50 percent higher than the national average. The African-American population in the two states is almost triple the percentage found in the country as a whole.

Table 2.1
Socio-economic Stylized Facts about Katrina Impacted States
Louisiana and Mississippi (U.S. Census Bureau 2014 figures)

	LOUISIANA	MISSISSIPPI	UNITED STATES
Population	4,649,676	2,994,079	318,857,056
Land area in square miles, 2010, sq. miles	43,203 (69,528 sq. km)	46,923 (75,515 sq. km)	3,531,905 (5,684,050 sq. km)
Median household income, 2009-2013	$44,874	$39,031	$53,046
Persons below poverty level, percent, 2009-2013	19.1 %	24%	15.4%
White alone, percent, 2013	63.5 %	59.8 %	77.7 %
Black or African American alone, percent, 2013	32.4%	37.4%	13.2%
Hispanic or Latino, percent, 2013	4.7 %	2.7%	17.1 %
Bachelor's degree or higher, percent of persons age 25+, 2008-2012	21.4%	20.0%	28.5%

Parts of the Katrina impacted area also suffered over this period from the downturn in business brought about by the British Petroleum oil spill in April 2010, layoffs from the Great Recession, tornadoes, and lately from lower oil prices.

Besides insurance and government funds, private philanthropy—estimated at approximately $3B within three months of the storm (Lawrence 2006)—played a crucial role. The Insurance Information Institute estimated that the insured losses for Katrina were 47.6 billion versus 23.9 billion for the 9/11 attacks (both measured in 2013 dollars, Insurance Information Institute, 2014). Insurance payouts on deposit helped the combined assets of credit unions and banks in the affected area to increase by 27.6% in the year following the storm. A number of credit unions were merged or closed within a couple years of the storm, and almost all of these were in New Orleans. Trying to rebuild after such devastation is a herculean task on its own, but this effort was made even more difficult by the British Petroleum Gulf of Mexico oil spill and the worst national economic downturn since the Great Depression. The economic downturn that many cite as beginning just a little more than two years after Katrina in December 2007 meant that the pull the rest of the country could have had on raising this area's economy was noticeably absent. The BP oil spill happened about half way through the ten years following the hurricane on April 20, 2010. This spill compounded the hardship for the tourist and seafood industries struggling to rebuild.

The trauma of the storm and the lack of quick response in New Orleans and the Mississippi coastal areas by parts of the federal government left great numbers of people homeless, without proper medical treatment, and without basic necessities. The death toll from Katrina has been typically cited at over 1,836 for all states impacted by the storm (Zimmerman, 2012). There are a number of people who question the reliability of these numbers, and the true number may never be known. David Brinkley spoke of this imprecision when, in his excellent account of the storm, he claimed, "there will never be exact statistics about the damage and death toll inflicted by Katrina. Were a looter shot by the NOPD or an old man who died of a heart attack victims?" (Brinkley, 2007). These imprecise statistics leave the subject of the death toll in a hazy fog of smoke, and as stated by Henry Giroux, "death, therefore, becomes the ultimate mechanism for the politics of disposability, where the lives of certain people are privileged over the lives of others" (Giroux, 2006). Given the time people spent without basic necessities, wading through a toxic soup in sweltering heat, and anecdotal accounts of a number of deaths that didn't seem to be counted, the real impact of the storm and our lack of proper preparation was probably much more costly than the 1,836 lives commonly stated. Was the elderly person without proper medicine who died a causality? Were the people in numerous hospitals who died when the power went out in the intensive care wards across many counties and parishes victims of Katrina? There are numerous stories, and many deaths that have been left unaccounted for in the death toll. For instance, in the case of several nursing homes that failed to evacuate in the New Orleans area, residents drowned in the flood, while others died in the hours to follow due to extremely harsh conditions. According to the Houston Chronicle, which conducted interviews with nursing home administrators, residents, family members, and investigators, though some of these deaths were reported, others remained unidentified until months after the storm (Khanna, 2005). These are tough questions, and, as David Brinkley and others have pointed out, there may never be a precise answer, but there is also a number of people who would like to keep the numbers low. Keeping the numbers low is understandable from a boosterism standpoint, and as people who have raised families here and are fond of the area, we certainly would like to boost the prospects of people and businesses that live in this area. There is also a question of liability for the deaths that would propel many to attribute them to "natural causes," or accidents not related to the storm directly. In the years following the storm, liability would prove to be an issue. As demonstrated in court cases, doctors, nurses, and hospital facility administrators were put on trial for deaths relating to an array of offenses, including power outages and lethal injections administered by nursing staff to patients who were not terminally ill. Though some families were awarded compensation for the death of loved ones due to loss of power and backup generator failure, specifically in the Memorial Hospital lawsuit (Fink, 2013), those involved in the lethal injection case were not convicted, but admitted to "comfort care," administering of drugs to keep patients comfortable (Lugosi, 2007). It would certainly not be in the interest of FEMA or the Bush Administration to admit that the death toll from Katrina on their watch was higher than that of 9/11.[17] The emphasis on scaling back FEMA and other government programs that may have been of assistance would appear, in the wake of Katrina, as short sighted.

Another contributing factor to having an imprecise count on fatalities is that the Center for Disease Control has no reports for New Orleans from September 2005 until 2013.[18] What reports are given for the state show an increase in 2005 of 2,140 deaths compared to 2004 (see figure 2.1 below, a jump from 42,215 to 44,365) with the crude death rate per 100,000 people going up 4.5 percent in a year (from 927.3 to 969.2).

---

17   The death toll from the 9/11 attacks was 2,977 (CNN, 2015).

18   See for example http://wonder.cdc.gov/mmwr/mmwr_1995_2014.asp?mmwr_year=2006&mmwr_week=26&mmwr_table=4A&request=&mmwr_location=New%20Orleans,%20La.

Figure 2.1
Louisiana Deaths from 1999 to 2013[19]

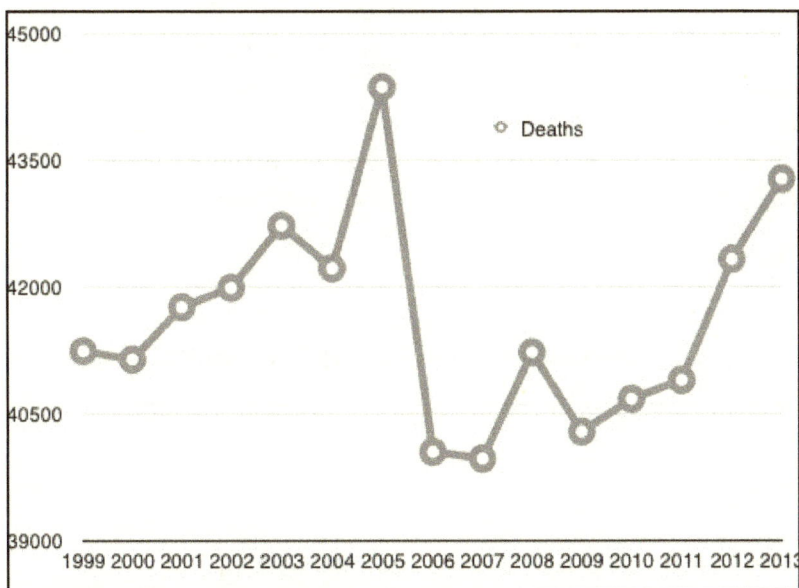

The data for Mississippi do not clearly show a dramatic increase in 2005, as seen in Figure 2.2 below. Mississippi shows only an increase of 1,325 from 2004 to 2005 (29,196—27,871= 1,325) with the crude rate per 100,000 persons going up 4.1 percent, and like the Louisiana data, the highest rate for the period 1999-2013 (from 964.7 to 1,004.7). This data, with a combined increase for just Louisiana and Mississippi of 3,465 deaths for 2005 (1,325 plus 2,140= 3,465), a number of evacuees in poor health, those not fully accounted for in other states, and those known missing and never recovered, imply that there is "smoke" of a higher death toll. Another bit of "smoke" was that the *Times-Picayune* also carried about 25 percent more obituaries in January 2006 versus January 2005 (Brunsma, Overfelt and Picou, 2007). Some have estimated the death toll at over 4,000 if the missing residents, collapse of the health care system, contamination, and increased impoverishment are taken into account in the months following the storm (Heldman, 2010 and Stephens, 2007). The death toll among the elderly, whether evacuated or not, remained higher for months after the storm (Dosa et al, 2010).

19   Source is the U.S. Center for Disease Control: http://wonder.cdc.gov/controller/
datarequest/D105;jsessionid=AD46DCBFB0FF64450E72401A5F6C8087

Ezra Boyd found in his Ph.D. dissertation that: "While most of the flood victims were elderly African-American males, the most prevalent victim overall were displaced elderly Caucasian females," (Boyd, 2011). Those of us who continued to live in the area noticed that the storm's impact lingered and appeared to age many people considerably. Higher mortality rates are often correlated with income inequality (Yang et al, 2012), and the large numbers of poor and elderly people in the affected region would point to higher susceptibility of a number of individuals.

Figure 2.2
Mississippi Deaths from 1999 to 2013[20]

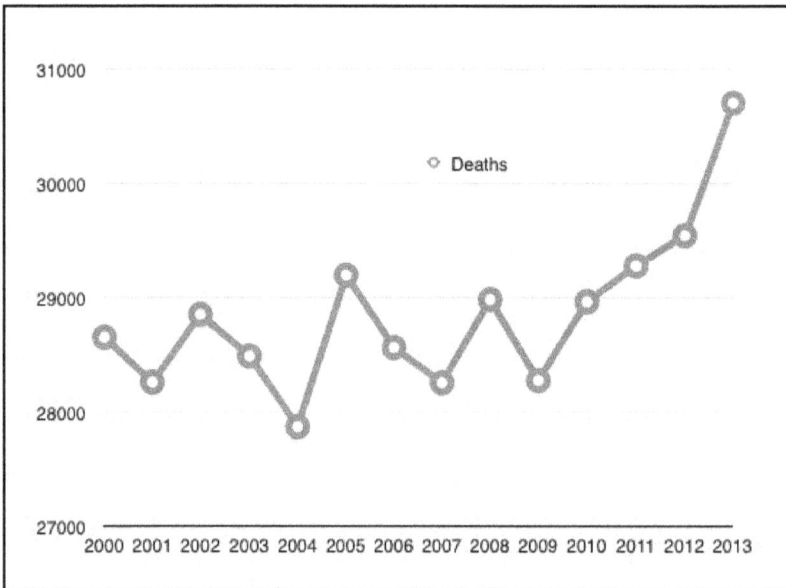

20   Source is the U.S. Center for Disease Control: http://wonder.cdc.gov/controller/
datarequest/D105;jsessionid=AD46DCBFB0FF64450E72401A5F6C8087.

During (East Biloxi, by Linda VanZandt)

TRINA TRINH KNELT WITH HER FOUR YOUNG CHILDREN. SHE TOLD THEM to make the sign of the cross and prepare to go to heaven. Hanging onto each other, they climbed higher and higher in their Point Cadet bungalow ahead of the rising tide of Katrina. But now they were in the attic with no place else to go. There was a small window at one end of the attic but none of them knew how to swim. Still it was their only chance. Despite the rain, pounding wind, surging tide, and fearful protestations from her children, Trina managed to get them all onto the rooftop. Just as they were losing their hold on the roof, Trina felt a tap on her left shoulder—it was an angel, she would later tell me, drawing her attention to an empty boat coming toward them. She still had to find a grip on the boat while somehow hoisting her traumatized children inside to its cabin below. Trina was one of over two hundred trapped East Biloxi residents who frantically called 911 during the raging storm, but it was too late to dispatch responders. Though it wasn't clear to her at the time how this would end, it was clear that, once again, a boat was there to save her.

Listen: "Trina Trinh: Calling 911 and Saved by a Yacht"

I called 911 and the lady, she was yelling at me, "Did I tell you to evacuate? Did we tell you to evacuate?! And you didn't leave? We can't get out there, it's too windy. Once the storm calm down we can go out there and help you." I said, I don't know when it's going to stop, probably never, probably five more hours, that's what I'm thinking. And I didn't know if my kids would survive…first of all, it's cold, soaking wet, hungry. And suddenly I felt like someone patting me and telling me, "Trina, look in the back, look in the back." I looked once and thought, imagine that, there's a yacht on my roof! "Justina! There's a yacht on our roof!" And everybody look like, "Mommy! There's a yacht!"

As Katrina made landfall, a record 30-foot storm surge inundated the low-lying peninsula of East Biloxi where Trina's house was located. Katrina's winds continued to pound the Mississippi coast and areas inland for 12 hours without relief. Trina's "angel yacht" spun and shook in the waves while her children—lips turning blue, soaked, and exhausted—fell asleep in the shelter of the cabin below. When the Coast Guard came to their rescue hours later, after the water had receded, they found the boat resting against a telephone pole. When I first met Trina, two weeks after her family's rescue, it was while I was walking past her shell of a house with the boat perched against it. We agreed to meet later to record, in her neighbor's words, her "Hollywood-worthy" story, but right then she was focused on inscribing a note, to whomever was the owner, with permanent marker on the side of the boat. She wanted them to know their boat had saved her children's lives.

Trina Trinh and "angel yacht" next to her house, Point Cadet

When Trina and I sat down to record her story just three weeks later, her matter-of-fact manner and the excitement in her voice seemed consistent with the first stage in mental health disaster recovery called the "heroic" phase, which occurs in the period immediately afterward when all emotions are strong and direct. She had survived, saved her children, and everything else at this point paled in comparison to this triumph.

Trina Trinh's decision to ride out the hurricane at home was a gamble, but for many, there were plenty of reasons to avoid leaving town ahead of a storm, some of which were the hassle of packing and traveling with children (and for some, pets), the risk of leaving their homes unattended, and the expense to evacuate (hotel stays, gas, eating out). It was the end of the month and bank accounts were low. They were willing to gamble. Trina rode it out with the children at home, while her husband helped man the shrimp boat in the Industrial Canal.

Also gambling on safety in the Industrial Canal, Tung Nguyen, his wife, and their young children prayed together as their shrimp boat rocked violently. As Tung began telling his story to me, in English that seemed to be limiting him, it was as if the waves he recalled swelled into a tidal wave of grief when he revealed his feeling of helplessness witnessing the drowning of a family. He began speaking in Vietnamese describing the nuances of his horrifying situation, then fought back tears as he reverted to English to convey the tragic ending, raising his voice. Later and deeper into the bilingual interview project, I would pay particular attention to this language switching to convey intricacies and emotion of the narrator's story.

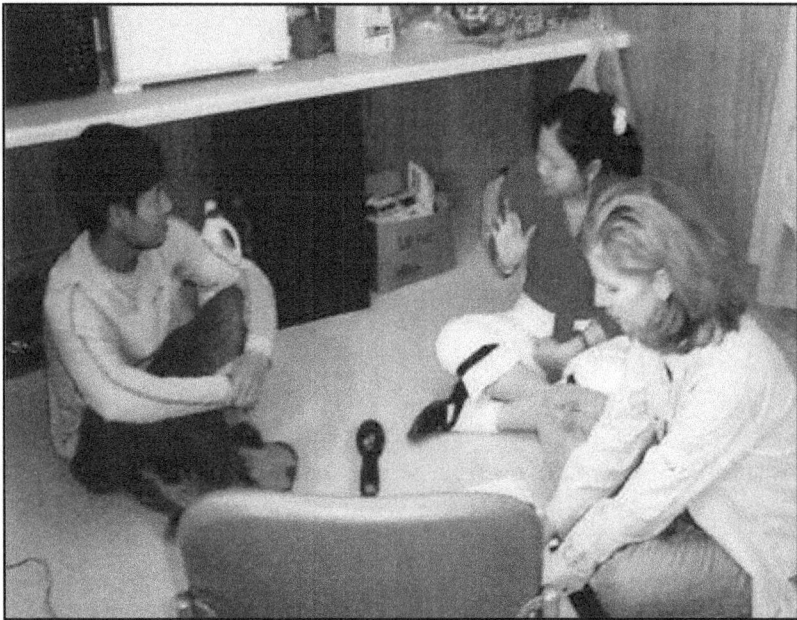

Tung Nguyen, translator Von Nguyen, and Linda VanZandt, Back Bay Biloxi

Listen: Tung Nguyen: "Witnessing to Tragedy from Hurricane's Force"

> The day before the storm we get everything on the boat, we prepare everything. And then we stay on the boat. Like every boat come together and tie up the line. During the Hurricane Katrina, a lot of wind, a lot of rain, then the boat (speaking Vietnamese) shaking. (Translator— some other boats, the tie, it was broken and then it floated and hit to the bridge and sank) And we saw, we saw people die! But I can't, you know, and so (crying)—I'm sorry, I'm sorry.

Disasters are often portrayed as events that affect everyone equally, but research shows that children can struggle particularly hard. Evidence suggests that children who experienced Hurricane Katrina will have a more increased risk of emotional and psychological changes than adults. This is because younger children may not have the ability to process the events they witnessed, and so may not be able to cope with the destruction in the wake of such a disaster. I have wondered over the years not only about Trina and Tung, but also about how their young children have fared since Katrina.

The displacement and disruption of so many survivors made it difficult and sometimes impossible to maintain contact in the early months after the storm. In the immediate aftermath, however, it was the young adult children of first-generation Vietnamese survivors I would come to know who, after now experiencing their own profound loss as adults raised in America, had a better understanding of what their parents had experienced at least twice before. These young adults quickly formed new grass roots community organizations—Asian Americans for Change (AAC) in East Biloxi and Mary Queen of Vietnam Community Development Corporation (MQVN CDC) in Versailles—and staffed local offices of the national organizations of Boat People SOS and National Alliance of Vietnamese American Service Agencies (NAVASA). This was crucial to helping lead the recovery and bridge the language and cultural gaps that presented daily struggles for the Vietnamese living in the Katrina recovery zone. This new spirit of intergenerational connection created a foundation of emotional support when there were suddenly few foundations left standing.

Aftermath: Bay Saint Louis (by David Reynolds)

NONE OF THE BUILDINGS ON OUR BLOCK WAS SUBSTANTIALLY INTACT BY the night of August 29, 2005. We were not there to see it happen. People died in wind, storm surge, and building collapse, or survived, frightened and wet, in attics, in trees, and on roofs. It took until 2011 to clean up, clear, and groom the property again. I drove the 375 mile round trip from Jackson countless times, in our small pickup, down and back in a day, in all seasons, getting in six or more hours of site work. In 2013, we built a small, comfortable cottage on one side of our property and retreat there often on weekends as I write this in 2015. The buildings on our block now are fewer, all residential, and all new. Around town, some names and faces are as before. Others came after Katrina. We all love Bay Saint Louis: happily, gently, and, for some of us, sadly and fiercely.

CHAPTER 3

Riots and getting to know your neighbors (the Good and the Bad, Philanthropy, Altruism)

"There's a lot of people in America see this happen along the Gulf and say 'Well, we don't have these kind of events here.' Yeah, but events like this can happen anywhere and it's a disaster, where the local government loses control of the ability to secure and take care of your people, and that can overwhelm any local government."

—Lieutenant General Russell Honoré (Retired commander of military relief in New Orleans and Mississippi, August 4, 2010)

THERE WERE MANY ACTS BY INDIVIDUALS THAT SPAN THE FULL SCALE OF human emotion, from life saving attempts to murder for little reason. The time without modern conveniences also allowed people that are usually "plugged-in" a chance to meet others and see a night sky unimpeded by city lights. The response by some communities was to "circle the wagons" while in others it was a helping hand. We will illustrate how poor planning and ineffective communication between governing/emergency officials led to inadequate resources and manpower on the ground in the immediate aftermath of the storm in New Orleans and in Southern Mississippi. We will also show that much credit is due to nonprofit, volunteer, and religious groups for their service.

Thanks to warnings issued by the National Weather Service and the National Hurricane Center, many people had left the soon to be ravaged areas. The "contraflow" traffic routing (all lanes reversed to one direction) began Saturday at 4 p.m. for the MS coast and New Orleans. This evacuation went fairly smoothly but was not without glitches and long delays. "The problem was that not everyone knew about the storm or had the means to get out of the city. Among difficulties faced by state and local planners was that more than 100,000 New Orleanians, principally the poor, mostly black residents without cars, together with the elderly, disabled, and infirm, would be unable to evacuate themselves. In the face of this certain knowledge, government officials failed to provide public transportation, leaving tens of thousands of residents to fend for themselves" (Center for Progressive Reform, 2006). Without a clear way out, many poor, elderly, pet owners who often weren't welcome in shelters, and those mistakenly believing that they were safe since they had weathered hurricanes in the past (hurricanes Betsy in 1965 and Camille in 1969) stayed in place to ride out the storm. The U.S. Senate described the New Orleans evacuation:

> As Mayor Nagin took the unprecedented step (albeit with some hesitation) of calling for a mandatory evacuation of New Orleans. Both President Bush and Governor Blanco actively encouraged that step. There was no question that evacuation before landfall was the highest priority. While the widespread support for mandatory evacuation is laudable, it is unfortunate that the federal government did not take a greater interest in the practicality of that evacuation in a city widely known to have made no arrangements for evacuation of the thousands of its citizens lacking personal transportation. Federal officials had participated actively in the Hurricane Pam exercise [See Chapter 8], which predicted that some 100,000 New Orleanians would lack means of evacuation. Federal officials did not need to wait for a request before offering help. Although time would not have been on their side in the last two days before landfall, the DHS had a window—however slim— within which to act. But it does not appear that DHS leaders asked about what the state and the city were doing to evacuate the 100,000 people without transportation. (U.S. Senate, 2006 p. 258)

The U.S. House report reiterated the same findings as the senate when they stated, "The failure of complete evacuations led to preventable deaths, great suffering, and further delays in relief" (U.S. House Report, 2006). Mayor Nagin's evacuation order did not include New Orleans' hospitals, leaving the hope that they could be of assistance but also leaving many very ill people to cope with the storm. As Sheri Fink described, "an emergency response leader from the US Centers for Disease Control and Prevention alerted several colleagues to the problem in an e-mail hours later. 'It is assumed that many of the hospital generators will lose power given the expected height of the water.' He reported that around

2,500 hospital patients remained in New Orleans as Katrina advanced on the city" (Fink, 2013). Given that there remained people who in many cases were disabled, aged, or without means to leave, the loss of life when the levees broke, the storm surge washed through, and the tornadoes struck should be of little surprise. For those left when the storm passed, survival for themselves and their loved ones became a priority. Hanging from trees or stuck in an attic or on a roof were just some of the horrific places people found themselves. Heroes came from next door, and emergency services personnel put their own lives at risk to help others. The stories of self-sacrifice and courage were found in every county and parish where the storm hit. James P. Smith, in his excellent telling of the Mississippi experience of Katrina, describes "...at least one of these heroes is known. Sgt. Joshua Russell of the Mississippi National Guard lost his own life trying to rescue an elderly couple in Harrison County. As his commander stated in tribute to Sgt. Russell, 'He died facing forward to the enemy, in this case a natural disaster.... His last moments on this earth were spent helping others at the risk of his own life'" (Smith, 2012). Jed Horne, in his compelling look at the "Big Easy" (New Orleans) after Katrina, tells the story of another person, hazardous materials specialist Ukali Mwendo, who put the needs of others first by doing his job of rescuing people and finding food: "Mwendo, like most first responders, stayed on the job...Mwendo's twenty-four hours were due to end Sunday, but then the governor declared a state of emergency and he was ordered to stay on the clock, as he would for eight days straight...'I love New Orleans. Working every day, this is my contribution'" (Horne, 2006).

People—scared, exhausted, and without clean supplies for themselves or their families—resorted to "provisioning" for food in places that often would have rotted anyway. There was some looting and stealing, but some of this provisioning was, if not semi-officially sanctioned, not unexpected given the dire circumstances in which people found themselves. New Orleans has had one of the highest levels of violent crime in the country, and given the chaos in the wake of the storm where people met others in strange conditions and with different lifestyles, instances of rape, murder, and looting, often mistaken, were reported (Thevenot and Russell, 2005). Sometimes this prompted officials to delay sending in relief for fear that rescuers would be put in harm's way. Officials at Charity Hospital, a hospital that was used to not having great resources and relying on their "make it work" know how, coined a phrase to help stop panic and misdirection of resources: "You can only say it if you've seen it" (Fink, 2013).

As we will discuss in later chapters as well, the vast majority of people in the wake of the storm tried their best to survive and help others, often complete strangers. The generosity shown over and over by neighbors and the outpouring of volunteers from around the country and the world shows that "radical hospitality" is alive and well.

After (East Biloxi, by Linda VanZandt)

LIFE CAME TO A SCREECHING HALT. SURVIVORS EMERGED FROM HIDING, battle-weary, to walk the littered and broken streets in dazed confusion. No landmarks left, cars crushed under crooked houses—it was as if houses had been plopped down in a new Land of Oz, except devoid of color and sound. When Tong and Chien Nguyen made their way to Point Cadet to see if their home was still standing, like so many others they found it in a thousand pieces with what was left of their belongings strewn for blocks.

Tong Nguyen in front of the remains of his rental home on Point Cadet

Listen: "Tong and Chien Nguyen: Losing Rental House on Point Cadet"

Translator speaking: This rent house they just rent about four days (before Katrina). (speaking Vietnamese) They hadn't paid the rent yet. That's not good luck.

As Trina Trinh drew comfort in having saved her children, Tong Nguyen recounted to me his relief and pride in saving his daughter Kim Uyen from drowning in her D'Iberville home, where they had evacuated. Kim was seven months pregnant at the time and couldn't swim. Tong was able to lift her, covered in ant bites, onto a neighbor's roof keeping them afloat using a trampoline pad that floated by. Like Trina, they were later saved by a boat that floated within reach. In 2009, on the fourth anniversary of Katrina, I visited Tong, Chien, Kim, and her now *two* children just after Tong and Chien had moved into a long-awaited MEMA cottage. This move came after brief stays in their car, on friends' floors, and in a cramped, one-bed FEMA trailer. The MEMA cottage wouldn't last long either, but the renewed spirit of connection I mentioned earlier would have deep and long-lasting roots. Unexpectedly, Tong and Kim candidly shared how Katrina had changed their lives and father-daughter relationship since we first met four years before.

Linda VanZandt, Tong and Chien Nguyen, Kim Uyen and children in front of MEMA cottage

Listen: "Kim Uyen: My Daddy Loved Me"

Kim translates for her father, Tong: He says, "It's better [since the hurricane] because it's a start over." I guess what my dad's trying to tell is that, he doesn't take a lot of things for granted. You have to almost lose everything to realize what's really of value. Took that day to realize that my daddy loves me (shy laugh), because you know Asian culture, you ask anybody, a lot of them will tell you that their parents aren't very (pause) intimate with their children. So my dad, he only said what he needs to as I was growing up. But that day I really—it made me see that you don't need words to show that you love somebody. That day he loved me; I could tell.

In the immediate aftermath of Katrina, Tong lost his job as a deckhand because the seafood industry was reeling from the loss of boats and entire infrastructure that supported them and the product they provided. The east peninsula where many Vietnamese lived was wiped clean, and the value of waterfront property around East Biloxi reached a new premium that threatened the rebuilding of affordable housing, as well as seafood industry rebuilding. With boats and docks damaged, and fuel, ice, and processing plants no longer available, the future looked especially dire for commercial fishermen, seafood processing workers, and plant owners. To make matters worse, rising fuel prices and an influx of cheaper, imported seafood further threatened, and continues to threaten, the viability of the commercial fishing industry. Uncertainty was the order of the day again, which made any long-term planning challenging.

Bright spots and important recovery service providers amid the debris-littered landscape of Point Cadet weren't governmental organizations like FEMA—who weren't prepared with Vietnamese-language representatives or materials—but the Church of the Vietnamese Martyrs and the Buddhist temple next door where a Burning Man group from California set up a supply distribution center around a donated giant red geodesic dome tent.

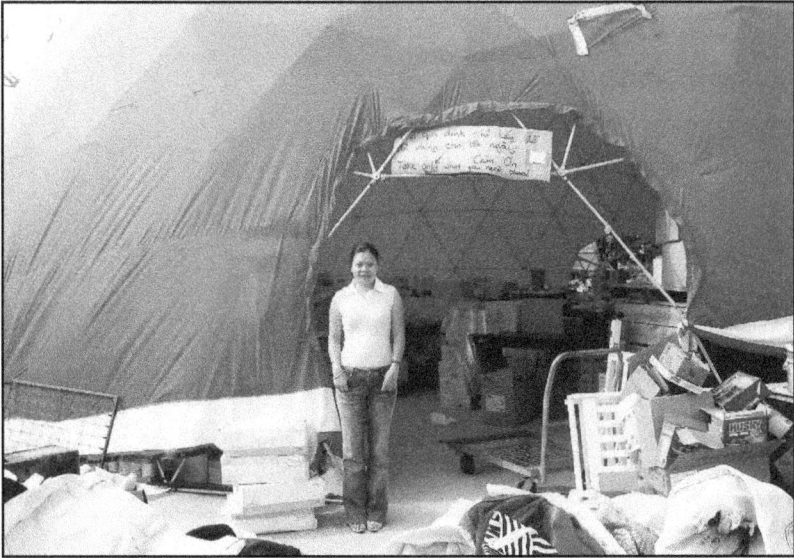

Translator Von Nguyen in front of dome supply center at Buddhist temple

Prayer at Buddhist temple—FEMA tarp and Katrina Relief t-shirt

Vietnam veteran FEMA rep with nuns at Vietnamese mass

Le Bakery café was the first Vietnamese-owned business on Oak Street to open in the aftermath. Located just down the street from the church and temple, it was a welcome place to rest, get news, and enjoy traditional Vietnamese food, which was a challenge to find in the early days. Owner Sue Nguyen-Brown expressed her hopes for the future of her Biloxi community.

Listen: "Sue Nguyen-Brown: Keeping Biloxi's Character"

I am hoping that Biloxi doesn't lose its character in the sense of the people that built this city, a lot of the immigrants that came to this area, you know, and you go back and you think about whether it's the Yugoslavs to the French to the Vietnamese community. I just hope it doesn't fade away, and that people just remember that the casinos were (not the only things) here. And you know, we did have a large fishing and shrimping industry, things that built Biloxi, and I'm hoping Katrina didn't wash that away.

In the months and even years of governmental recovery fund red tape that followed Katrina's wrath, countless hours of translation and consultation services were provided by young Vietnamese staffers holding information sessions, computer services (once power and internet communications were restored), legal and health clinics, and serving as intermediaries between agencies and individuals. They were the eyes, ears, and voices for much of the elder Vietnamese community when interaction with governing agencies was required. Many of these support services would continue to assist community members through another round of red tape and advocacy after the BP Deepwater Horizon oil disaster.

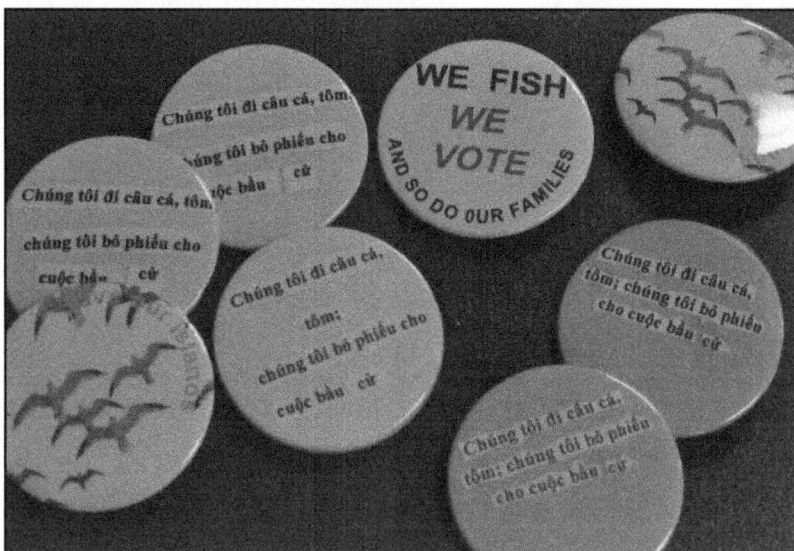

Bilingual buttons displayed at oil spill conference

After (New Orleans East, by Linda VanZandt)

SIMILAR TO THE VIETNAMESE' EXPERIENCE IN EAST BILOXI, IT WOULD BE easy to chalk the New Orleans East Vietnamese community's resilience in Katrina-related recovery to "model minority" traits, like strong work ethic and identity, but the community was, even more, deeply rooted in shared refugee experiences and memory and a particular history of shared community and religious roots during their youth in North Vietnam. It was extraordinary to think that some members had known one another and attended church together almost daily for over fifty years, but Katrina's floodwaters in New Orleans East tore them from their church and community roots and scattered them to the winds, mainly to large cities in Texas and California where extended family lived. Father Vien later lamented to me his belief that the traumatic dislocation caused a number of his parishioners' health to deteriorate. Several passed away within a short period of time.

As important as shared community and memory were to residents struggling through yet another catastrophic loss, the strong leadership of Father Vien was equally important. His fierce determination to bring residents back home from far-flung places resulted in Entergy, the utility company that powered the city, restoring power in mid-October of 2005 after he secured five hundred signatures from residents pledging to return. New Orleans East then became one of the first areas to have power restored after the storm. Within two years after Katrina, 90% of residents had returned home (not dependent on affordable rental housing that wasn't coming back). Tuan Nguyen and his then fiancée Mary (they have since married) were second-generation Vietnamese parishioners who came back early and became instrumental in the community's remarkable recovery through the creation of the Mary Queen of Vietnam Community Development Corporation (MQVN CDC). Tuan recalled the CDC's origins and important role early on, including addressing language barriers with FEMA representatives:

Listen: *"Tuan Nguyen: Origin of MQVN CDC and FEMA Shortcoming"*

I remember coming back early and, my wife's house had a lot more work to do, but she started volunteering with the church and Father Vien. At the time CDC wasn't born yet. And she started volunteering doing a lot of important supply distribution, you know, cleaning supply, food. He was the one who actually recruited my wife Mary. She was applying for pharmacy school…and she said, "Well, I'm just going to do it temporarily." Doing a lot of FEMA assistance because a lot of the language barrier and all that. FEMA's really horrible at having that. It just wasn't there, even when they hired some folks that could speak the language, they were the FEMA reps, they weren't community members. You get what I mean? In other words, she was a community member trying to help another community member.

In a city struggling to entice residents' return, the church and the new advocacy organization helped build a bridge for the Vietnamese community in the easternmost reaches. Suddenly they found new political leverage and a collective voice that proved loud enough to face down Mayor Ray Nagin and win the closure of the nearby landfill mentioned earlier.

Four years after the landfill crisis, I was settling into a small room in the MQVN CDC office finally preparing to meet my first interviewee, Mrs. Xuyen Pham, a talented gardener, oyster shucker, war refugee, and Katrina survivor who was one of many elder residents now out of work and caught up in the uncertain aftermath of the BP Deepwater Horizon oil disaster. While still processing Hurricane Katrina oral histories at the Center for Oral History, in 2010, the Center was awarded a social resiliency grant from the National Oceanic and Atmospheric Administration (NOAA). The grant would fund the collection of oral histories of Gulf Coast fisherfolk affected by the oil disaster. Because of the relationships I formed during my Katrina work, my part of the NOAA project would be with the Vietnamese communities of the coast. I would be remiss if I did not mention the contributions of Khai Nguyen, a Versailles resident and staff member of MQVN CDC, who arranged and provided translation and interpretation for the interviews we would conduct in this community still in recovery mode.

Xuyen Pham spoke volumes, through smiles and tears, about her lifetime of experiences. Afterwards, she offered to show me the garden she and her husband planted in an empty lot where their home was lost to Katrina. I followed her in my car and spent time with her and her husband talking about vegetables and taking photographs inside her chain-linked paradise where her future and the future of many of her community members was taking root.

Xuyen Pham and husband in their Versailles garden

Mrs. Pham also took me to her home to meet one of her daughters and show me her seed bank and backyard plantings—her focus since being laid off from oyster shucking after the oil disaster decimated oyster reefs. Her daughter was learning too as she walked with us.

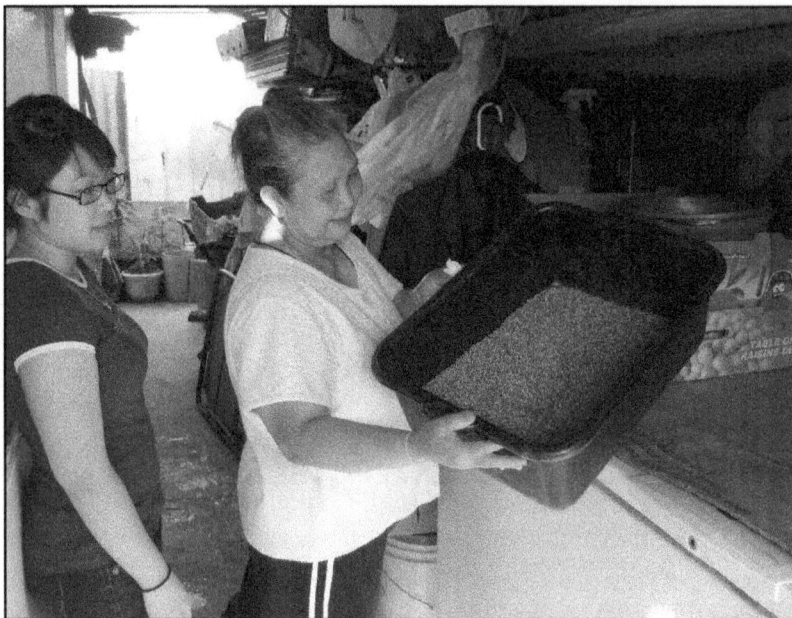

Xuyen Pham, daughter, and seeds for the garden

Listen: "Xuyen Pham: Seafood Industry Dying, Children and Garden"

Translator: She thinks her and her husband will be the last (in the seafood industry) because her children are focused on going to school and learning different professions. Sometimes some of her children would go fishing but it would just be like to catch fish to give to her to eat and that would be it, you know. She says she has a garden and would take vegetables to cook and eat but her children wouldn't even know what kind of vegetables she's growing in there (Mrs. Pham chuckling).

Within a year of my first interviews with Versailles residents in 2011, MQVN CDC staffers Khai Nguyen and Daniel Nguyen had helped organize Mrs. Pham and other elder and youth community gardeners and cooks into a new collective they named VEGGI Farmers Cooperative. Created originally to help supplement reduced incomes after the oil disaster, the cooperative has since grown in its reach to sell not only at the local farmers market but also to an A-list of restaurants in the city, like Emeril's and John Besh's latest. I followed Khai on one of his first pick-ups and deliveries from Versailles into the heart of New Orleans and witnessed the delight of such accomplished chefs receiving Vietnamese specialties like lemongrass and Thai basil, as well as soymilk and tofu produced, just a short drive away, from farmers who'd learned from their parents in Vietnam.

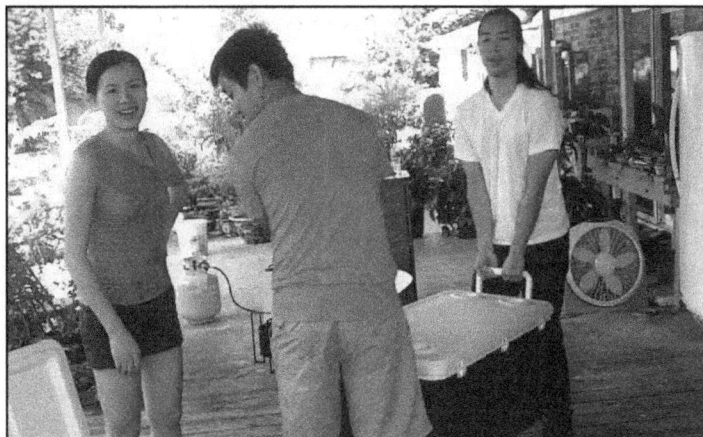

Daughter of local tofu maker, Khai Nguyen and Daniel Nguyen picking up tofu for delivery

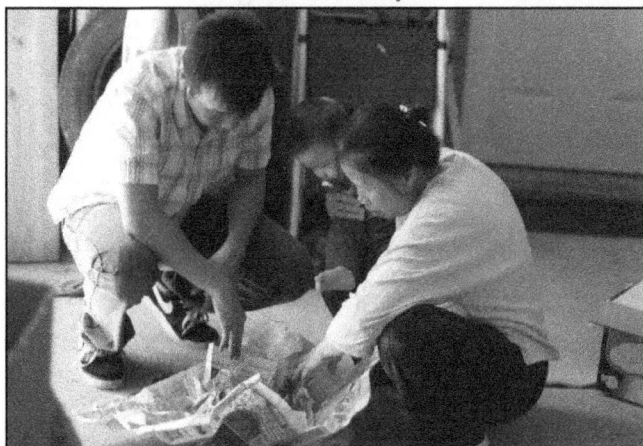

Khai Nguyen inspecting fresh produce from local grower with grandchild

The community has also finished collectively building several back-yard aquaponics systems, the first of which I had the privilege of documenting just before the Tet celebration in January 2012. Almost seven years after Katrina and two years post-oil disaster, there was indeed something to celebrate in this photo below. Once again, neighbors were helping neighbors and elders and youth were working together with humor, hope, and pride in something they were building for the future.

Daniel Nguyen, right, collaborating with local residents on a backyard aquaponics build

Since Katrina, some have found healing in their growing and building. One has found healing through writing. Just a few months before I attended the first build, I recorded the story of another elder survivor of Katrina and out-of-work fisherman, Kha Van Nguyen. Mr. Nguyen presented to me an autographed copy of a Vietnamese-language book he had written about his experiences during and after Hurricane Katrina, which included time at the nightmarish New Orleans Convention Center shelter. During our interview, he shared one of his darkest moments during the raging winds of Katrina.

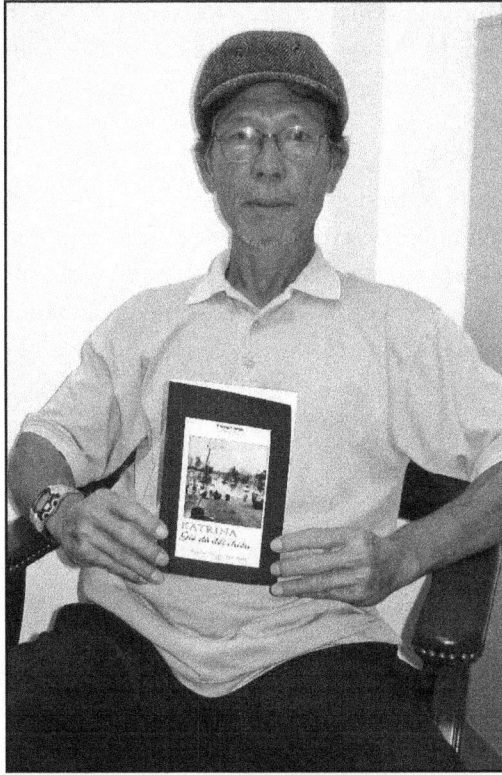

Kha Van Nguyen holding book he wrote about Hurricane Katrina in Versailles

Listen: "Kha Van Nguyen: Vision of Mother Returns Durings Storm's Fury"

Translator: On one of the worst nights of the storm he went back home but he was stuck at home because of everything that was going on around. And it was one of the worst nights because he didn't know what was going to go wrong. But then in his dreams he saw his mother and she was very soothing and was able to calm him. And she made him feel like things were going to be okay. (Mr. Nguyen speaking Vietnamese) The image of his mother comes to mind because when he was in Vietnam, when he was four years old, his mother was protecting him from the bomb, so when Katrina happened and the winds were strong, and around his house was falling down, he had a vision of his mother and he feels like she kept him safe. Mr. Nguyen: I believe that.

Living through multiple catastrophic events in a lifetime can have a profound effect on the character and identity of individuals as well as communities. As Rebecca Solnit states in her essay *The Uses of Disaster: Notes on Bad Weather and Good Government*, "Disaster makes it clear that our interdependence is not only an inescapable fact but a fact worth celebrating." Interdependence was key to recovery among the Gulf Coast Vietnamese communities in the wake of Katrina and the oil disaster. I would add that independence and some manner of control over one's circumstances and outcome was also key. When I asked interviewees which was worse, Katrina or the oil disaster, all answered the oil disaster. With Katrina, they explained, you could pick up a nail and hammer and get to work. With the oil disaster, you just had to sit by and wait, not knowing when or if you would be able to get back to work and life as you knew it. Daniel Nguyen of MQVN CDC added his observation.

Listen: *"Daniel Nguyen: Defining Dates / Katrina vs. the Oil Spill Disaster's Impact on Community"*

There are a couple of dates that define the community's stay here. Nineteen seventy-five when they first came over, and then 2005 of course with Katrina, and then now with the oil spill. So Katrina, you know, it hit everybody pretty hard but most people, especially the fisherfolk you talk to will say the BP oil spill was probably worse than Katrina, just because Katrina came and went and the community knew when they could start rebuilding again. But with the oil spill, they're uncertain about how long it will last and they're not able to go back to work and this is something tangible or not completely tangible but within their control that they can fix themselves. So this is one of the big issues with the BP oil drilling disaster is people's ability to self-determine is mostly taken away.

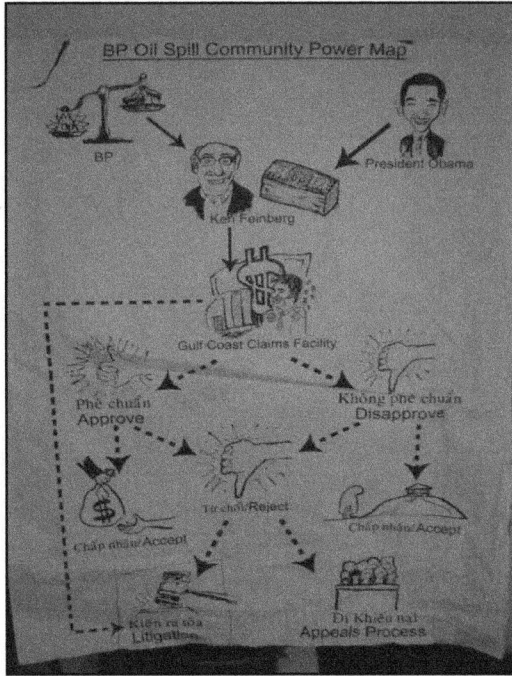

BP Oil Spill Community Power Map at MQVN CDC fisherfolk meeting

A similar refrain was expressed in East Biloxi as in Versailles regarding the oil disaster and future uncertainty. Dac Truong is a veteran fisherman and beloved community member of Biloxi's fisherfolk who exercised his voice in leading community meetings post-oil disaster and participated in surveillance of waters after the spill. His final few words in this excerpt, I believe, accurately represent a common attitude and outlook of most Vietnamese of these two hard-hit communities of the Gulf Coast who have had to tackle the challenges as they come—day by day.

Listen: "Dac Truong: BP Oil Spill, Vessels of Opportunity, and Uncertainty"

Translator: We've been pretty much a surveillance boat for BP. We go out there to see if there's any oil on the surface. (speaking Vietnamese) I see oil on the surface of the water. (speaking Vietnamese) Five, ten miles from shore, oil everywhere. No, he doesn't know how long he'll be able to participate in the program. It's just day by day.

Young Dac Truong after Vietnam escape, Malaysian refugee camp

In the summer of 2015, as the ten-year anniversary of Katrina and the height of hurricane season approaches, I have moved to the Gulf Coast and settle to watch shrimp boats trawl the Sound at sunset and families enjoy time together on the beachfront. There is much to be thankful for but also much work still to be done on the road to environmental and economic restoration for a more sustainable Gulf Coast future. A long-term and focused commitment will help us in this effort, and we will work together, day by day.

Photo Essay by Betty Press

THE THOUGHT OF KATRINA STILL MAKES ME QUAKE. WE EXPERIENCED the storm in our home in Hattiesburg, 60 miles from the coast, and that was traumatic enough with all the trees going down around our house. Fortunately they didn't fall on top of our house. But the real brunt of the storm was on New Orleans and the Gulf Coast.

I didn't get down to the Gulf Coast until five weeks after the storm. The University of Southern Mississippi (USM) gave me a security pass and encouraged me to document what happened to the Gulf Coast Campus and the surrounding areas.

I was shocked when I arrived on my first trip. The area was blocked off with security points manned by the National Guard and police. That in itself seemed strange. The water looked tranquil, not capable of such fury. But bits of debris, like bent pieces of metal along the beach or floating in the water, were reminders that all was not well in this normally idyllic place.

The roads were barely open, so driving around was a little scary. Debris was scattered everywhere. Boats, shipping containers from the shipyards, and cars were not in their normal place. The summer trees had no leaves. Only concrete steps or slabs remained of many houses located close to the water. Others a few blocks away from the water were very badly damaged. Owners were seen picking through what was left... finding odd things, like an unbroken porcelain teacup or a line of ties on a rack, or a slab with only the toilet left! They seemed to be still in shock and wandering aimlessly about wondering where to start.

The most surreal images were next to the shopping mall and businesses next to the water. All the merchandise that was in the stores like Wal-Mart was now scattered over the nearby area or lodged in trees. Strips of clothing and plastic bags hung like Christmas ornaments in the denuded trees decorating the ravaged landscape. Only the bolted down Waffle House stools stood like monuments to what was there before.

The USM campus buildings near the Gulf were stripped bare and appeared rather ghostly with their insides spilled out. The venetian blinds at the windows were twisted into dangling contemporary art sculptures. The Friendship Oak was damaged but still standing and managed to survive.

I made several trips to the coast after that first trip. People were beginning to leave their mark with signs on their properties. Many were prayerful, grateful for help, patriotic, and even humorous in a very trying situation. Others were disgusted, complaining that the cleanup and recovery was taking too long. The days were sunny and rainless for weeks after the storm. It was too hot and humid to work.

My last trip to document the coast was early Spring 2006, six months after the storm. Many organizations and volunteers were on the scene helping as best they could. Prayer messages were left on the bulletin board of God's Katrina Kitchen. Meals were being provided. Donated clothes and goods were being handed out. Many people were living in trailers or camping out on their properties. A few more businesses were open. Land was for sale. Signs of resilience, like "Together we rebuild," were prominent. There was a sea of blue tarpaulin covered roofs on the homes that had survived but had not yet been repaired.

When we stopped to talk to people now they were pretty upbeat. More properties were being rebuilt, just higher off the ground. More people were going about their normal lives. The empty properties had been cleaned up and were returning to nature. The live oaks, which had been stripped bare after the storm and had appeared to be dead, were showing signs of new leaves and growth. There was still a long road of recovery ahead, but it was beginning to happen.

On one of the empty slabs, with only the steps remaining, someone had a placed a statue of The Thinker. As Rodin explained, "What makes my Thinker think is that he thinks not only with his brain, with his knitted brow, his distended nostrils and compressed lips, but with every muscle of his arms, back, and legs, with his clenched fist and gripping toes." All of this was needed in the Katrina recovery process. It was a perfect metaphor for the resilience and determination of the people affected by Katrina as they have struggled to rebuild the Coast.

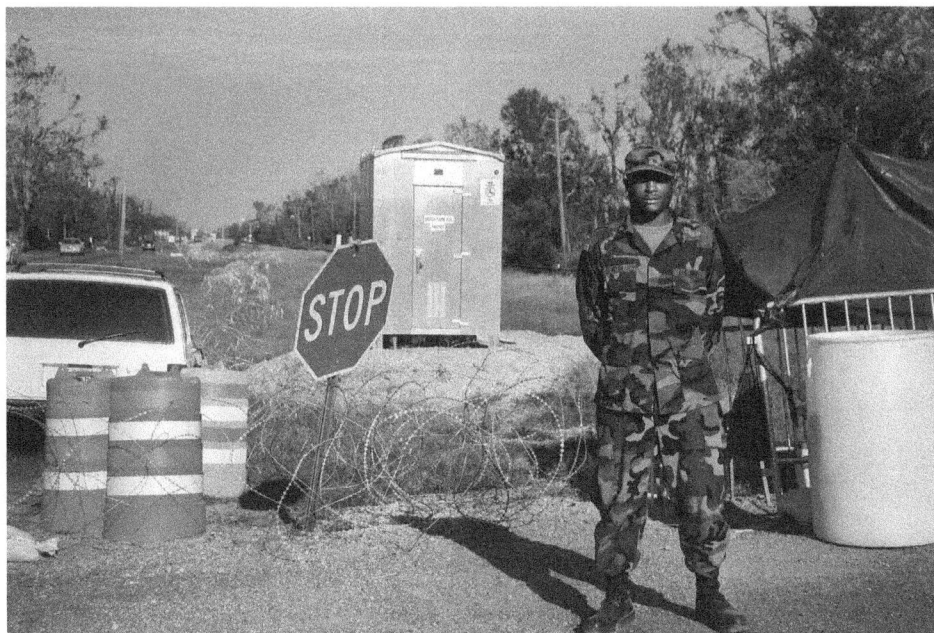

National Guard Checkpoint, Long Beach, Mississippi

Houses were wiped away by Katrina leaving only foundations and steps,
Long Beach, Mississippi

Debris from the large box stores was washed into the nearby area. Long
Beach, Mississippi

Kermit the frog surveys the scattered debris. Long Beach, Mississippi

Lloyd Hall of the University of Southern Mississippi, Gulfport campus, was badly damaged as well as many of the other buildings. Long Beach, Mississippi

Damaged house with flag. Long Beach, Mississippi

People spent hours going through the debris of their homes trying to find personal items. Pass Christian, Mississippi

This "Pray for us" sign reflects how the owners felt after the storm. Long Beach, Mississippi

Only a toilet is left on the slab of a destroyed house. Long Beach, Mississippi

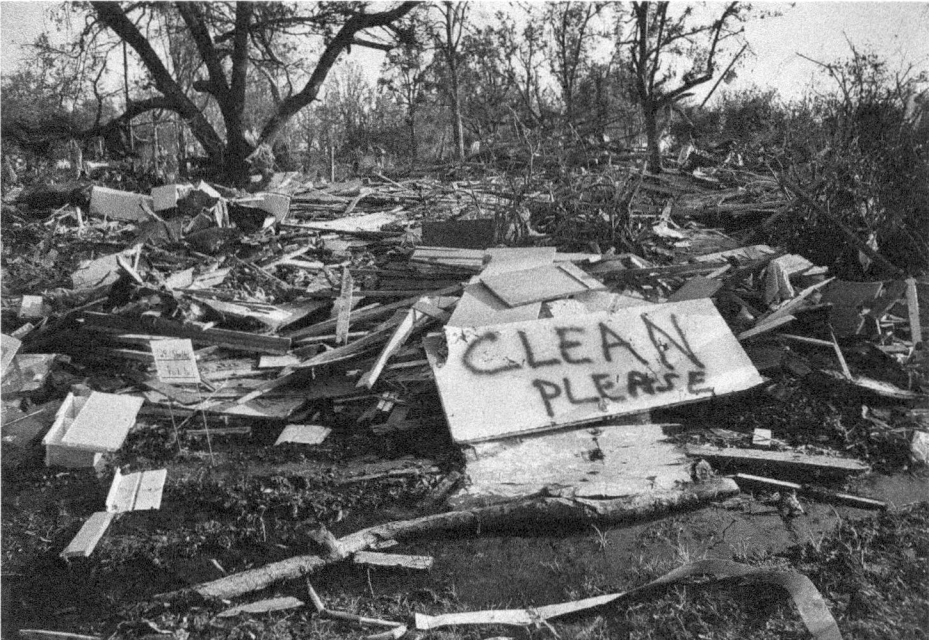

This polite sign "clean please," suggested that the owners were ready to have the debris removed from their lot. Long Beach, Mississippi

This family started to clean up their property and put out a "no dumping" sign among the debris. Long Beach, Mississippi

A Vietnamese family saved themselves in this boat during the storm. Biloxi, Mississippi

"Living for Jesus," part of the remains, of a Sunday School room, Baptist Church, Long Beach, Mississippi

The Methodist congregation put out a sign to save the toppled steeple of the church. Bay St. Louis, Mississippi

Magruder and Peggy Corban's home was badly damaged in the storm. In the debris they found an undamaged teacup. Long Beach, Mississippi

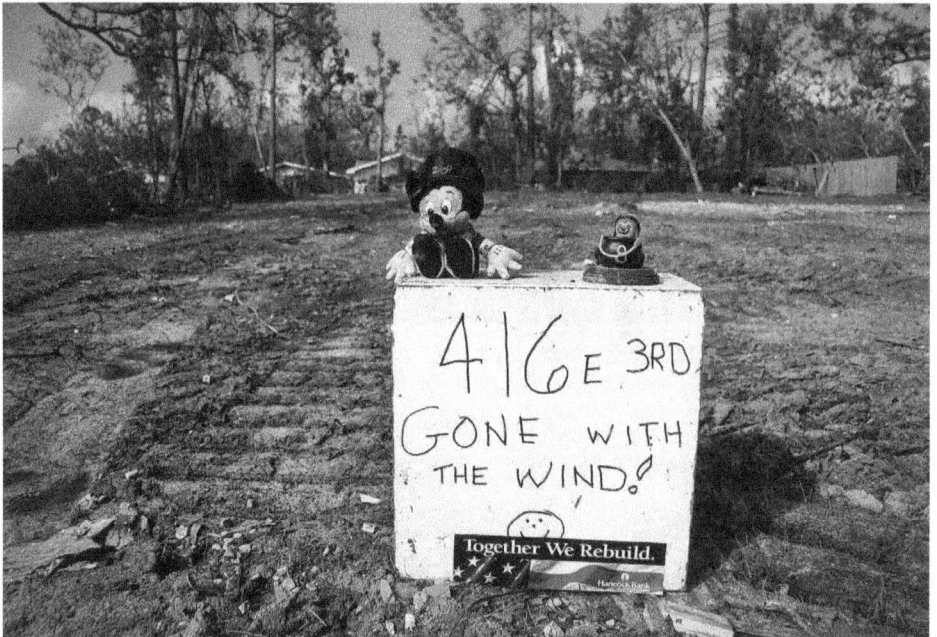

This lot has been cleaned up and the owner placed a sign saying "Gone with the wind" and "Together we rebuild" sticker. Long Beach, Mississippi

Waffle House. Long Beach, Mississippi

Waffle House. Long Beach, Mississippi

Donated clothing was left for people to take after they lost all their belongings. Black Creek, Mississippi

Prayer requests left at God's Katrina Kitchen, Pass Christian, Mississippi

Blue tarpaulins were provided to homes with damaged roofs. Bay St. Louis, Mississippi

The Red Cross provided thousands of meals and assistance to volunteers and residents. Long Beach, Mississippi

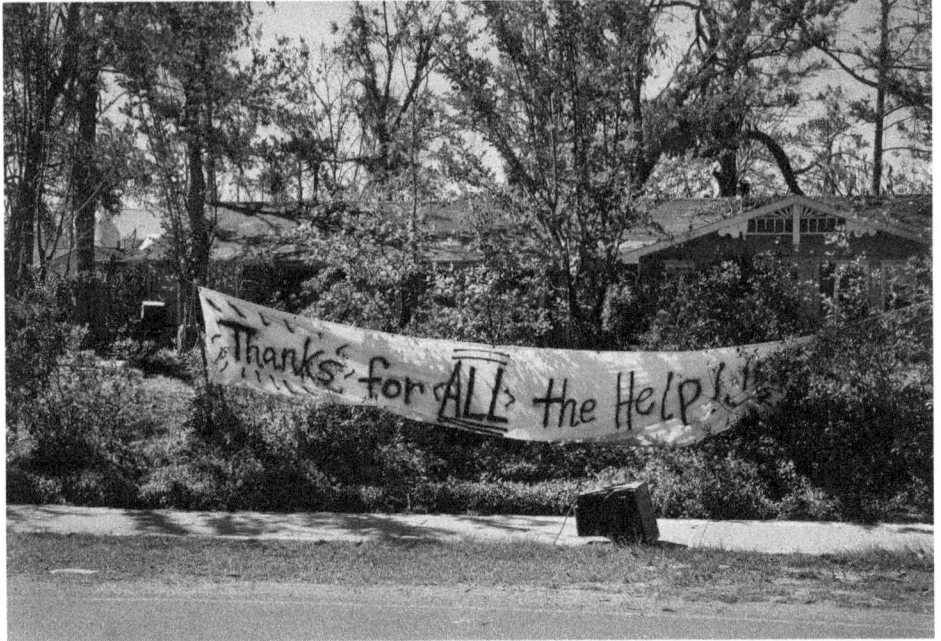

One family's response to the help they received. Bay St. Louis, Mississippi

Children playing in front of the trailers where families were living after losing their homes. Biloxi, Mississippi

This Thinker statue was placed on the steps of a home that was washed away. Bay St. Louis, Mississippi

CHAPTER 4

Where are the People

"The floods have lifted up, O Lord,
the floods have lifted up their voice;
the floods lift up their roaring.
More majestic than the thunders of mighty waters,
more majestic than the waves of the sea,
majestic on high is the Lord!"

—Psalm 93, 3-4, NRSV

"I'll just tell a very quick story. I went into my home. By the time I finally got into my neighborhood where I know at least ten out of the twenty-two people were in their attics as the water was lapping at the attic door, some of them people in their seventies. As I'm wandering down my street, and I see some of my neighbors wandering around the street like zombies, I had a woman about seventy-five years old, who was one of those people in the attic during the storm with water probably up to her ankles and got an ax to go through the roof, who said to me, "Dave, let me know if there's anything I can do for you." "Dave, let me know if there's anything I can do for you." I was a forty-eight-year-old, able- bodied, old-fashioned, white man, and here's this seventy-five-year-old woman who looked like she had just been through it all—and she had—asked me if there was anything that she could do for me."

—David Elliott (WLOX television reporter, August 31, 2009).

THE FLIGHT FROM THE STORM, BOTH BEFORE AND AFTER LANDFALL, LEFT many people in distant parts of the nation. This was the greatest diaspora in American history due to a natural disaster (Brunsma, Overfelt and Picou, 2007). Of the more than one million people who left the areas directly hit by the storm, most tried to find refuge in Louisiana and Mississippi, but others ended in up spread out across all 50 states (DeParle,

2005). Baton Rouge initially took on 250,000 refugees, though by the end of 2005, 100,000 of those people had returned to New Orleans (Dyer, 2006). In Texas, there was an arrival of 230,000 evacuees, according to Gov. Rick Perry; however, other New Orleans evacuees, rescued from the flood, were air-lifted to places far from anything familiar: Colorado, New Mexico, Utah, and Oklahoma (Egan, 2005), states with climates and landscapes contrasting to the humid air and luscious green scenery of the Gulf Coast. High rates of poverty and disadvantage among the pre–Hurricane Katrina population of New Orleans were likely to have affected evacuation destinations, displacement locations, and the likelihood of return for disadvantaged families compared with non-disadvantaged families (Sastry, Narayan, and Gregory, 2014). One year after the storm, 70% of those displaced were African Americans (Green et al, 2013). According to Stringfield, many analyses have specifically focused upon the plight of impoverished African American populations and their ability to return to their pre-hurricane residences. The amount of focus on this population group is at least partially attributable to the disproportionate amount of flooding and damage in historically African American dense neighborhoods located well below sea level, in addition to long-standing polarities in socioeconomic status between poorer African American populations in these areas and white populations in less flood-prone areas (Stringfield, 2009). Orleans Parish suffered the greatest population loss (219,094) followed by St. Bernard Parish (49,015, Hori et al. 2009). A number of variables come into play that affect the decision to remain in evacuated areas or to return home, such as housing, how much damage was inflicted upon the home or a particular neighborhood, whether or not the evacuee owns the home or renting properties, and how far some had to travel for evacuation. Another factor contributing to the decision of returning was "sense of place" (connection to culture and roots deeply embedded in a particular space). And even though there may be a strong connection to home, there was still the issue of job availability in the disaster area, or lack of job opportunities (Landry, Bin, Hindsley, Whitehead, and Wilson, 2007). In Stephanie Simon's interviews with Katrina evacuees in Aurora, CO, some people shared that their move was an opportunity to start a new life after emerging from poverty stricken areas (Simon, 2005).

Table 4.1 (Appendix A) has population figures for the U.S., Louisiana, and Orleans Parishes and similar figures for Mississippi and the three Mississippi coastal counties. New Orleans (Orleans Parish) saw a dramatic 55 percent drop in population after the storm but has come back strong with an 84 percent growth rate from 2006 to 2014 (the latest available figures)! The Mississippi coastal counties, which took the brunt of Katrina's storm surge, saw a much smaller drop in population in the period right after the storm and have actually grown in population since 2004. The chart in Figure 4.1 below, "Movement From Areas Prone to Flooding," shows that in the Mississippi coastal counties, people moved inland to an area typically beyond the railroad tracks that run along the coast and act as an impromptu levee (which was actually considered in the rebuilding to be reinforced to act as a proper levee, see Strout, 2015).

Figure 4.1

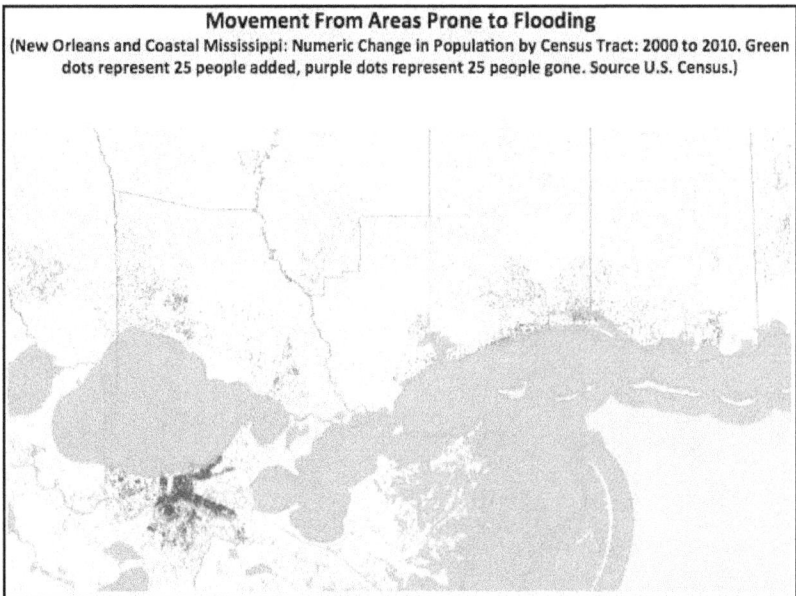

Movement From Areas Prone to Flooding
(New Orleans and Coastal Mississippi: Numeric Change in Population by Census Tract: 2000 to 2010. Green dots represent 25 people added, purple dots represent 25 people gone. Source U.S. Census.)

In New Orleans after the storm, almost all ethnic groups saw their population decline by double digits, with African Americans showing the largest drop of 59 percent by 2006. From 2004-2014, this group was still down 31 percent and now makes up about 60 percent of the city's population (229813/384320= 0.598). All groups have seen strong growth since 2006, with Hispanics having the highest growth rate of 91 percent. Hispanics also showed high growth rates along the Mississippi coast.

Part of the reason that some people who left did not return, besides the obvious hurdles of rebuilding a devastated home, was that many found people in other places quite hospitable and local economies that were strong. Uprooting families who have settled with children in school to go back to an uncertain future led many individuals to stay where they had landed. The slow response to rebuild and the undesirability of living in FEMA trailers that were found to be unfit with high levels of formaldehyde (45,000 people were still in those trailers in Louisiana in 2007) also contributed to some residents deciding not to return (Women of the Storm, 2015 and Eggers, 2010).

Table 4.1
Demographic Profile
Comparing the U.S., Louisiana, Orleans Parish and Mississippi Coastal Counties
See Appendix A

CHAPTER 5

Businesses, Jobs and Corruption

"... In Washington (D.C.) they speak of Wall Street and Main Street— well we know what Wall Street is, we know what happened there, and Main Street is people with jobs. If you think about people with jobs or recently lost their job, but they're still in the system and they've got the ability to get a job. But we've got a third of our population that absolutely require government assistance for the survival of day to day people, and that's the people who I say live on Railroad Street. It's not just a metaphor, it's an actual place because in most places, if you show me where the railroad passes, and I'll show you where the property is cheapest, I'll show you a place where the police have to visit a lot and it's underserved by education, health care and public service, and, it's like that Ninth Ward that's in every city—that's what I refer to as Railroad Street. Because when we have a disaster, the government is going to have to focus on Railroad Street first."

—Lieutenant General Russell Honoré (Retired commander of military relief in New Orleans and Mississippi, August 4, 2010)

"My thoughts turn to all who are unemployed, often as a result of a self-centered mindset bent on profit at any cost."

—Pope Francis (May 2, 2013)

"Well, again, even before FEMA could find this area—and this is the absolute truth. FEMA couldn't find Hancock County to deliver water, fuel, food, but the insurance industry found Hancock County. They went out and hired extra people, and within days of the storm, they were going from lot to lot, telling people, 'You had a homeowner's policy; it does not cover flood.' And there are trees down in every direction, clearly tornadic activity. The Navy says we had four hours of hurricane- force winds before the water ever got here, but the insurance company had been primed to say, 'Blame it all on the water.' To walk you through it as quickly as I can, under the National Flood Insurance Program, we hire the insurance companies to sell the policy. Not a bad idea; we don't have to have a huge force selling the po[licy], and they get a commission. We also count on them to adjust the claim after an event, and they sell the flood policy. They also sell the homeowner's. We count on them to do a fair adjustment of the claim; if it was indeed water that caused the damage, blame it on water, bill the government. But if the wind did it, then blame it on the wind and bill your company: State Farm, Allstate, or Nationwide. One of the flaws in that is that we give them total discretion. So imagine yourself, you're not college kids, you're out of school, you're moms and dads. You got responsibilities. You got a mortgage to pay, and you're a claims adjustor. And you're sent out to adjust that claim. You've already been told by your manager— and we have got copies of these internal memos—'Whenever wind and water occurred, blame it all on the water.' Now remember, they have a contract with America to have a fair adjustment of the claim, but their internal documents are saying, 'Blame it all on the water.' You got a mortgage to pay; you got kids to put through school, you got mouths to feed, you're thinking about your next promotion. Are you going to do the right thing, or are you going to make your company happy? So in every instance, they went on the property, mind made up, 'If there's any water at all, I'm going to blame it all on the water.'"

—Congressman Gene Taylor (former, February 21, 2008)

THERE SEEMS TO BE QUITE A BIT OF MOMENTUM IN SOME AREAS TEN years after, but some of the same problems that plague the country as a whole are seen in the Katrina ravaged areas. Using Table 5.1 (Appendix A), we can see that, even in the presence of the Great Recession and the BP Oil Spill, since 2006 until 2014 (the latest data available) that real gross product (or income) has grown in Orleans Parish (19 percent) and the three Mississippi coastal counties, Hancock (12 percent), Harrison (9 percent), and Jackson (16 percent). This growth compares favorably with the overall U.S. rate of 11 percent over the whole period. It is clear by the growth rate from 2004 to 2006 that New Orleans had the biggest shortfall to make up (19 percent) and overall, from the period before the storm used here, 2004, that it is still down slightly (3 percent) and that, except for Jackson County, lag the U.S. overall income growth. Bringing this area-wide income growth down to the personal level with real median household income (also in Table 5.1), we see some differences from the national downward trend in Orleans Parish's rise of 11 percent from 2004-2014 versus a decline for the nation as a whole.

Table 5.1
Economic Performance
Comparing the U.S., Louisiana, Orleans Parish and Mississippi
Coastal Counties
See Appendix A

The increase in poverty by 24 percent for the whole country is dramatic and due in large part to the economic downtown (i.e., from 12.7 in 2004 to 15.8 in 2014). Orleans Parish actually had a drop over the same period, but Harrison County's growth in poverty at 34 percent surpasses the increase seen nationally.

The Supplemental Food Assistance Program shows this increase in poverty that often hides behind the gross income figures for a state or county. For the whole U.S., this figure goes up 75 percent from 2006 until 2014. December 2007 is the beginning of the "Great Recession," which resulted in a skyrocketing of food assistance. Orleans Parish in this period had a 140 percent increase but was actually down from its 2004 levels, suggesting that those with lower incomes returned to the city at a later date than 2006. The counties in Mississippi, already higher by about third in their poverty rate than the national, saw an increase similar to the U.S. for the 2004-2014 period, with Harrison, again, showing a larger increase (note some of this could be due to differences in date of the most recent data) and all MS counties showing a much higher increase after 2006.

Looking at the number of businesses, also in Table 5.1, demonstrates that Orleans Parish is still down about 24 percent from 2004, but shows a strong 23 percent growth from after the flood. A similar pattern is seen in the two MS counties that took the brunt of the storm with much less decline and rebounding. Jackson County shows growth that parallels the overall U.S. growth and is ahead of the state figure.

The employment consequences of the storm were devastating, as Figure 5.1[21] shows. Employment was down before the storm, but since the hurricane, employment in New Orleans has continued to be stagnant. Although there was a rebound after the storm, the onset of the recession seems to have wiped out those gains. Figure 5.2 shows that except for the years 2005 and 2006, the Katrina micro area unemployment mimics to a large degree the national unemployment trends, but with higher unemployment.

---

21   No accurate figures are available for New Orleans for 2005 and 2006.

Figure 5.1

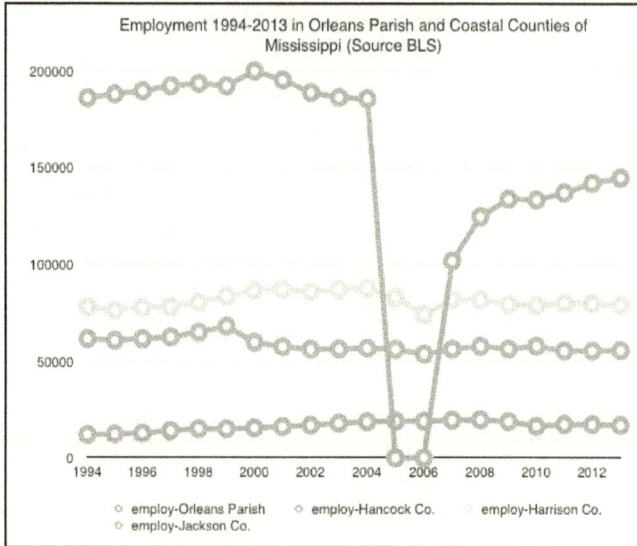

Employment 1994-2013 in Orleans Parish and Coastal Counties of Mississippi (Source BLS)

○ employ-Orleans Parish   ○ employ-Hancock Co.   ○ employ-Harrison Co.
○ employ-Jackson Co.

Figure 5.2

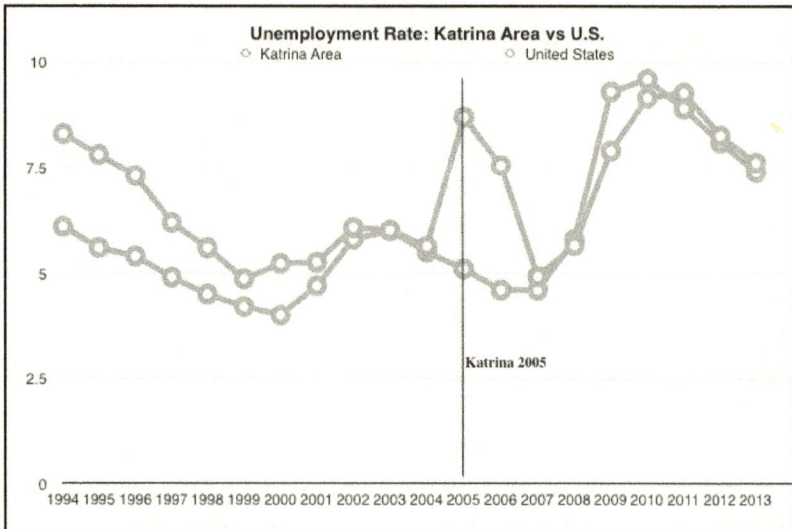

Unemployment Rate: Katrina Area vs U.S.
○ Katrina Area   ○ United States

Katrina 2005

Figure 5.3 demonstrates that quite a few counties and parishes in Mississippi and Louisiana experienced negative growth. Orleans Parish and all Mississippi counties on the coast had negative growth as well (see caption to Figure 5.4). New Orleans's growth of 66% since the storm (up until April 2015) is a hopeful sign that we are on a positive trend.

Figure 5.3
Employment Changes from 2004 to April 2015[22]

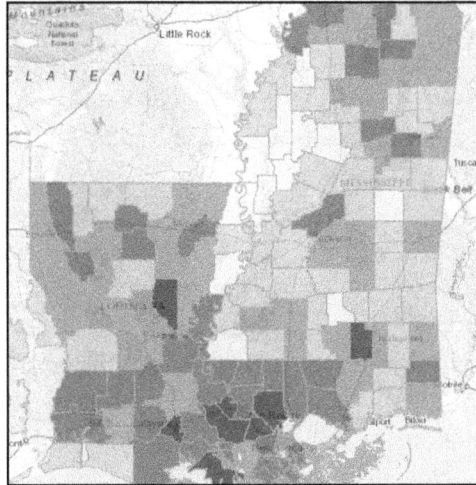

Figure 5.4
Employment Changes from 2004 to April 2015
Blow up of Coastal Area[23]

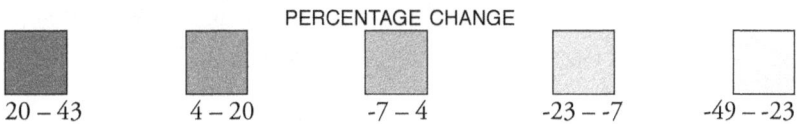

PERCENTAGE CHANGE

| 20 – 43 | 4 – 20 | -7 – 4 | -23 – -7 | -49 – -23 |

New Orleans: -0.09, Hancock County: -0.12, Harrison: -0.10, Jackson: -0.04

---

22 Percentage change, Bureau of Labor Statistics, residence based.
23 Percentage change, Bureau of Labor Statistics, residence based.

For 2006 to April 2015 the figures are: New Orleans: NA (0.66)[24], Hancock
County: 0.05, Harrison: 0.07, Jackson: 0.02

The New Orleans metro area saw a 19% decrease in employment
from 2004 to 2006. Orleans Parish saw a 38.5 percent decrease in wage
and salary employment (see Table 5.2, Appendix A). The New Orleans
industries that were significantly impacted by employment loss between
2004 and 2006 were Education and Health Services (-28%), Leisure and
Hospitality (-30%), Information (-28%), Financial Activities (-22%),
Service-Providing (-21%), and Other Services (-30%). On the positive side, proprietorships, real estate, and professional employment saw
increased employment over the entire period. The growth in proprietorships and small "indie" businesses help create local demand and offer
the resurgent tourism and convention industry attractions to offer visitors (Brancaccio, 2015). Also, a number of fields showed strong positive
growth from 2006 to 2013. On the Mississippi Gulf Coast, the only
industry to come close to the New Orleans area losses from 2004 to 2006
was Leisure and Hospitality (-21 percent) and other fields related to the
loss of the casinos, such as accommodations and arts and entertainment.
These same sectors and industries related to the oil industry came back
well over the whole period in employment and many industries showed
significant growth from 2006, with Jackson County having the highest
growth. Jackson County not only was furthest from the highest storm
surge and highest winds but also has oil refining and ship building to
help anchor employment (Berry, 2015).

Table 5.2
Industry Employment Growth
See Appendix A

The recovery has been thwarted in part by both the size of the devastation and the Great Recession, which has meant that demand, or potential demand, for the area's products is diminished. Figure 5.3 shows the
real Gross Domestic Product for Louisiana and Mississippi from 2004 to
2014. As noted earlier in Table 5.1 and can be seen in Figure 5.3, both
states show positive growth over the period while also showing anemic
growth since about 2010. The country as a whole has grown much faster

---

24   For New Orleans, if the first year of available data after the storm is used 2007,
then the growth from that period to April 2015 is 66 percent (169115−101687 /
101687= 0.66)!

at 17 percent versus Louisiana at six percent and Mississippi at seven percent for the same period, 2004-2014. How much of the slow growth is due to the devastation and how much is due to state policies that may impede growth? Both states have Republican governors (Bobby Jindal in Louisiana and Phil Bryant in Mississippi) that have conspicuously gone against policies that many economists consider useful in promoting economic growth. One of those policies is the acceptance of the federal subsidies for implementation of the Affordable Care Act (ACA) of 2010. Governor Bobby Jindal rejected Obamacare, claiming it would have a negative impact on the Louisiana economy, including small and large businesses (State News Service, 2013). He states that the expansion of Medicaid would also cost tax payers up to $1.7 billion dollars over a 10-year period, but by rejecting the Affordable Care Act wherein the federal government pays 100 percent for the first three years and 90 percent in later years, some estimate that the state would lose billions in federal funding (Alpert, 2012).

Mississippi Insurance Commissioner, Mike Chaney, a Republican and friend of governor Phil Bryant, took steps in 2011 toward complying with the Obama healthcare reform by creating an online exchange market. Research shows that if this had been implemented, 230,000 low-income residents would have been able to receive tax credits totaling $900 million a year. However, Governor Phil Bryant rejected this exchange market in a defiant act against the Affordable Care Act. Rejection of the Medicaid expansion for the ACA was estimated to have cost $426 million of federal money in just one year (Steenhuysen, 2013).

Governors Jindal and Bryant are not alone in following this strategy against the ACA and in raising revenue to support infrastructure and assistance programs. Governor Sam Brownback of Kansas has probably been one of the most out-spoken on favoring tax cuts rather than revenue, which has led to cut backs in many programs, including education (Cooper, B., 2015). The cutbacks in programs to support tax cuts has not had a stellar record on employment in the states that have tried this, and typically many of these states have had lower growth rates relative to the nation as a whole (Leachman and Mazerov, 2015). As a recent article by the Chicago Political Economy Group put it, "Over the entire period 2008-2014 real GDP first fell and then rose. The economy has been forced to wait on the slow expansion of the private sector, now up only 3 percent in real terms since the beginning of the recession. State and local expenditures have been left to lag far behind this sluggish recovery" (the Chicago Political Economy Group, 2015). Louisiana and Mississippi have both seen declines in their real budgets, from 2009 to 2014 the decline was over $71 million and $27 million respectively (see Figure 5.4). As an example, Mississippi public school teachers had a 6.2 percent decline in their real salaries from 2002-2013 (NEA, 2014). During this same period, the Public Employees Retirement System of Mississippi, representing about 96,000 retirees and 300,000 public employees, also took a huge hit from the recession on its investments and also lost money to mortgage investments with Goldman Sachs, recovering approximately two cents on the dollar (Bernstein et al, 2012).

Despite the massive losses from the storm and sometimes from their incomes, teachers and administrators along the coast and in Louisiana often acted in heroic fashion to get their schools up and running again, often in very trying conditions. Schools all over the coast and in New Orleans often sustained heavy damage if they were not totally ruined. In the town of Pass Christian on the Mississippi coast, where the storm surge was 28 feet high, school reopened six weeks after the storm (Strout, 2015 and Smith, 2012). Volunteers, trailers, and donations made many of these openings possible. In New Orleans, public school enrollment went from 66,372 in 2004 to just 25,651 in 2006, but by 2011, enrollment was back up to 42,657, and private schools over the same period also increased students from about a 1,000 to nearly 19,000. Critics maintain that the storm provided an opportunity to dismantle a large public school system in New Orleans and use privatization methods, such as vouchers and charter schools, that would perpetuate racial and class antagonisms (Akers, 2012 and Burkett, 2008). Along the Mississippi coast, where some of the best schools in the state were located before the storm, scores on the ACT (entrance exams for college) for county public schools compare favorably with scores in 2004 (Mississippi Department of Education, 2015).[25] Along the Mississippi coast, enrollment in county public schools is also above pre-Katrina levels.[26]

Corruption is a problem that has plagued the area for a while, as in many parts of the country. Before the storm, the levee boards in New

---

25   Composite ACT scores in 2004 in Hancock, Harrison, and Jackson County were respectively 20.2, 19.8 and 20.2 and in 2013 were 20.3, 19.7 and 20.9. The state average for 2013 was 18.6.

26   Enrollment in the 2004-2005 school year in Hancock, Harrison, and Jackson County were respectively (4,324), (13,170) and (8,431) and in 2014-2015 were (4,497), (14,472) and (9,384).

Orleans acted more as political payola rather than as rational protectors of the city. Bob Harvey, a former president of the Orleans Levee Board, stated that he had witnessed large sums of money given to members so that contractors could do sub standard work (Horne, 2006), and even Mayor Ray Nagin ended up going to prison (Hall, 2013 and Grimm, 2014). Questionable priorities seemed to propel the levee board, such as "$15 million spent on two overpasses that helped gamblers get to Bally's riverboat casino" (Meyers, 2005). Even though many police officers went beyond the call of duty helping victims of the storm, some police corruption and shootings by officers in New Orleans have also raised concerns (Perlstein and Lee, 2005).

Mississippi has also had a reputation for corruption long before Katrina, as the FBI's Operation Pretense of the 1980s showed (Crockett, 2003). A recent study has named the state as the most corrupt state in the nation (Matthews, 2014). Concerns about corruption and the spending of massive amounts of aid to help the region rebuild put the area under the spotlight as spending commenced. There is some "smoke" that has arisen both immediately after the storm and over the long-term use of the funds that were designated for the area. This concern, although with some justification, often meant a mountain of red tape impeded quick rebuilding of homes and businesses. Auditing assistance was given to state agencies, but local government agencies and individuals had to absorb large costs in terms of effort and delays to comply with the mountain of paperwork (Smith, 2012).

The insurance companies that were liable for some of the tremendous damages that businesses and individuals suffered used both paperwork and their anti-trust exemption in U.S. law to delay payments. The McCarran-Ferguson Act, passed in 1945, allowed insurance companies, if state regulated, immunity from federal oversight (Macey and Miller, 1993). This has allowed insurance companies to set up oligopolistic control over provisioning everything from healthcare to wind and flood insurance. In 2007, former U.S. Senator Trent Lott of Mississippi spoke to the U.S. Senate when he found out about the enormous clout insurance companies have (Lott, 2007):

> I appreciate this opportunity to address the Committee on this issue that I believe is vitally important to my constituents. As I have stated before, it wasn't until after Hurricane Katrina that I gained a true understanding of the fact that the insurance industry had a blanket exemption from our antitrust law. And as I witnessed the reprehensible behavior

of the insurance industry in their response to Katrina, I became curious about the history, rationale, and wisdom of such a broad exemption from federal oversight.

In his 2010 book "Griftopia," Matt Taibbi showed the divergence among states when an industry can control the regulators:

> Despite that fact and despite the fact that in larger, better-regulated states like Louisiana insurance companies paid out huge claims to homeowners for wind damage, in Mississippi the local insurance cartel—in this case an ad hoc union of State Farm, Allstate, Nationwide, USAA, and many others—decided en masse to deny all claims for wind damage except for those that the homeowner could demonstrate took place separate from flood damage.

> ... That helps explain why in 2005, despite the fact that it was blindsided by Katrina, one of the biggest natural disasters in American history, the property/casualty industry made an after-tax profit of $48.8 billion—a new record, beating out the previous year's record of $40.5 billion.

When insurance was available, the rates were three to four times higher than before, making it hard on individuals and businesses to get going again (Jervis, 2008). Some providers, like State Farm, stopped writing policies (WLOX, 2009) leading the state of Mississippi to offer a "Wind Pool" insurance fund to struggling individuals and businesses.

The U.S. taxpayer helped the region with over $125 billion dollars in aid. It is hard to get a firm estimate on the massive outpouring of aid to help the region from the U.S. and all over the world. Some of it was turned down due to bureaucratic red tape and inefficiency. According to the Washington Post (Solomon and Hsu, 2007):

> And while television sets worldwide showed images of New Orleans residents begging to be rescued from rooftops as floodwaters rose, U.S. officials turned down countless offers of allied troops and search-and-rescue teams. The most common responses: "sent letter of thanks" and "will keep offer on hand," the new documents show.

> Overall, the United States declined 54 of 77 recorded aid offers from three of its staunchest allies: Canada, Britain and Israel, according to a 40-page State Department table of the offers that had been received as of January 2006.

The tremendous amount of aid offered to many was humbling. Even though FEMA was often late in coming, neighbors helped neighbors and volunteers poured into the area. The informal and formal social networks that people were a part of made the difference for many. A study by Richard Forgette, Bryan Dettrey, Mark Van Boening, and David Swanson, published in 2009, found that friends, family, and religious organizations played the most significant role in getting out aid, with federal and state organizations having a much smaller role. Rita Duffus, in a letter to the editor to the *Sun Herald* (Duffus, 2007), which was widely circulated, said the words that summed up what many felt: "the whole world came and we were thankful. They came and suffered with us. They came and lived in tents, slept on the ground, but they came and we were thankful. They clothed us and fed us. They sheltered us and tended our wounds." This tremendous outpouring of assistance and volunteers from around the world is something that a social scientist will find difficult to measure, but it made a huge difference in the ability of the region to restore their lives and businesses. How do you measure the friends and relatives, neighbors and strangers who offered a hand (how many distant relatives reached out like one of the authors' poor aunt who sent a $500 dollar check)? Two years after the storm, it was estimated that already over 1,150,000 volunteers had come to assist the area (Corporation for National and Community Service, 2007). There were many heroes from the U.S. Coast Guard, local fire and police, hospital and nursing home staff, Louisiana Department of Wildlife and Fisheries, and others never caught in a photo or press article. The slow deployment of federal resources made these volunteers all the more important. As the Rand Corporation stated in their assessment: "The single most important problem was the speed with which the nation's local, state, and federal civilian organizations were overwhelmed" (Davis et al, 2007).

Once the aid started to flow in from federal and state organizations, there was often a tradeoff between getting things done and closely monitoring all expenditures. One of the most questionable ways that money was spent was for large contractors, often well connected, to get a contract for debris removal or putting "blue tarps" (meant as a temporary roof cover that to this day are still visible in some places) on homes, and then turning around and paying subcontractors, who might then re-subcontract to a local company. This multi-layered payment system showed that the largesse that went to those top companies was often times what the ultimate cost was. Gordon Russell and James Varney of the *Times-Picayune* uncovered a number of such cases. One of the most egregious were payments of $175 dollars to the Shaw Group of Baton Rouge to cover a 100 square foot section of roof that was actually put on by a contractor several layers down for $2 (Russell and Varney, 2005). Governor Phil Bryant of Mississippi, who was lieutenant governor in 2010, stated that the amount of fraud was less than one percent involved in the monies that Mississippi controlled (James P. Smith, 2012). Sue Sturgis and others reported on connections to the former governor Haley Barbour and to his relatives when there was found fraud and possibly kickbacks from companies donating to Republican candidates and lobbyists (Sturgis, 2011). Some have raised concerns about the slow pace of reconstruction and red-tape. Five years after Katrina, Geoff Pender reported that of the $20 billion of aid from the Department of Housing and Urban Development for "Community Development Block Grants that were earmarked in hurricane relief funds for Gulf Coast states after the 2005 storms. The answer: about $5.4 billion, comprising $3 billion of the $13 billion earmarked for Louisiana and 2$ billion of the $5.5 billion for Mississippi" (Pender, 2010). Do some people have an incentive to slowly spend the money, if at all, since there may be fees earned or priorities may be changed to fit well placed interests? Governor Barbour also wanted to improve the Gulfport harbor by diverting $600 million in funds that were designated for housing, angering housing advocates and prompting Reps. Barney Frank, D-Mass., and Maxine Waters, D-California to note that, according to FEMA, as of November 2007 there were still 40,897 Mississippians not back in their homes with just a fraction of the money being used to benefit low and moderate-income residents (CBS News, 2008). Mississippi's relatively quick comeback compared to New Orleans's made some question the amount of federal aid that went to Mississippi. Even former FEMA director Michael Brown said, "Unbeknownst to me, certain people in the White House were thinking we had to federalize Louisiana because she's a white, female Democratic governor and we have a chance to rub her nose in it" (Kromm and Sturgis, 2007). According to the Public Affairs Research Council of Louisiana, "Louisiana suffered 67 percent of the major and severe housing damage and received 62 percent of the CDBG funding, while Mississippi suffered 20 percent of the damage and received 33 percent of the funding" (CDBG stands for Community Development Block Grant; Pike, 2007).

Bill Quigley gives a sober assessment of how New Orleans is faring given the priorities and statistics mentioned above. He titles his article

"New Orleans Katrina Pain Index at 10: Who was left behind" (Quigley, 2015). There are bright spots for sure, but those on the bottom half of the income distribution are having a hard time still. The tremendous out-pouring of generosity from neighbors, faith-based and volunteer orga-nizations, and what seems unevenly from the government have helped many people and businesses get back on their feet. Journalist Roberta Gratz correctly stressed recently "It's a matter of supporting the locals who know the community and who are engaged in the aftermath of a disaster" (Gratz, 2015, p. 323). Educational support seems uneven, but there are indications, especially on the Mississippi coast, that progress is being made, while in New Orleans the number of students is still down and the city has implemented a controversial reorganization. The increase in poverty throughout the coastal area and the lack of jobs shows up in increased SNAP payments. The efforts to increase jobs since 2006 has met with some success, but the area still has a way to go to be back to the level of pre-Katrina.

Figure 5.5
Real Total Gross Domestic Product by State for Louisiana and Mississippi
(2009 Dollars, Annual, Not Seasonally Adjusted)[27]

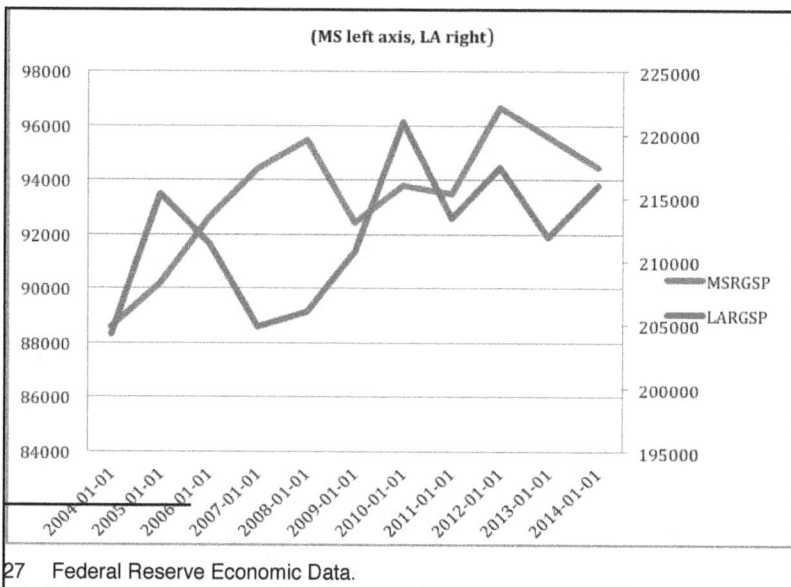

27   Federal Reserve Economic Data.

Figure 5.6
Real Budget Appropriations by State for Louisiana and Mississippi
(2009 Dollars, Annual)[28]

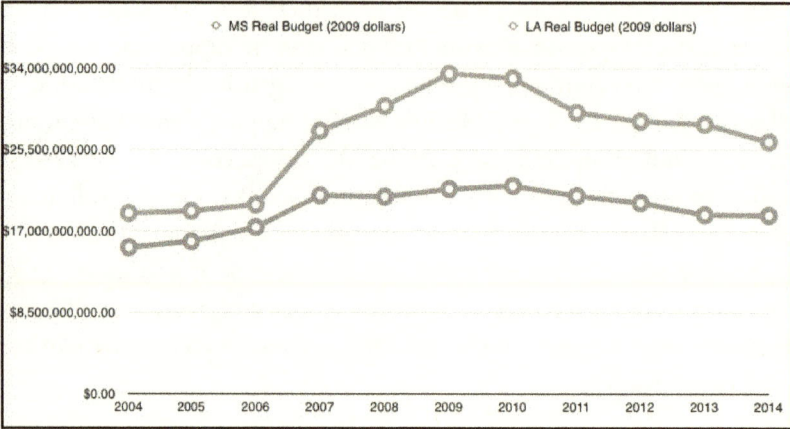

28   Sources include the Federal Reserve, Louisiana Division of Administration and Transparency.Mississippi.gov.

CHAPTER 6

Banks and Credit Unions

"Credit unions have always lived by a very simple credo: 'people help-ing people.' While that philosophy animates America's credit unions everyday, it is especially valuable to our members at times like these. Because of the member-owned, cooperative structure of a credit union, we are uniquely positioned to provide essential financial services to those effected by this disaster. While no one welcomes this disaster, we are doing what credit unions do best: serve our members …

"The credit unions along the Gulf Coast are challenged, to say the least, to provide their own members with the most basic financial ser-vices. Nonetheless, their members are, or will soon be, in need of their credit unions.

"Myriad efforts are underway across the broad spectrum of the credit union system to assist the victims of Hurricane Katrina, not just with access to financial services, but also with life's necessities of food and shelter."

—Charles Elliot (President & CEO of the Mississippi Credit Union Association, September 14, 2005).

CREDIT UNIONS ARE THE MOST COMMON FINANCIAL INTERMEDIARY IN the U.S. What sets credit unions apart from other financial institutions is that they are financial cooperatives, and every depositor (typically by opening a $25 savings account) can vote for the board of directors at the annual meeting. Each depositor has an equal vote, no matter how much money they have deposited. Figure 6.1 below shows the number of credit unions, commercial banks, and saving banks in the United States. Credit unions reached a peak of 23,866 in 1969 and have steadily fallen to stand at 6,687 in 2013 (see Table 6.1). Commercial banks reached a peak of 14,483 in 1984 and have also fallen to 5,885. Saving banks have followed a similar trajectory. This reduced number could be due to efficiency gains from consolidation, institutional life-cycles, high interest rates, deregulation, and idiosyncratic causes (e.g., Wilcox and Dopico 2011, Goddard et al. 2008, and U.S. Senate 2011). Even though the number of institutions has been declining for decades, the number of members in credit unions has actually been increasing over time (47.3 percent from 1994-2013), with some evidence of an increase in later years (see Figures 6.2 to 6.4).

Banks, savings banks, and credit unions in the southern 12 counties[29] of Mississippi and New Orleans were surveyed by email, snail mail, and with onsite interviews conducted in 2006, 2007, and again in 2015 (see Figure 6.7 for a map of the area considered). Data were collected from online sources and from credit union and bank presidents and staff through interviews and a survey. Altogether, direct contact was made with about 20% of the total population of surviving financial institutions. The original survey consisted of 17 questions about storm damage, volunteer hours, sources of aid, and number of employees, among other things. The survey was e-mailed or hand-delivered to institutions; the credit union leagues of Louisiana and Mississippi helped in its distribution.

Some sample selection bias is likely, given that some of the institutions are small and did not have e-mail addresses, and many very large institutions did not respond. The survey was kept short to encourage responses. A follow up survey was done in 2015 to address similar issues as the first survey, and a shorter open-ended, five-question survey was also used and helped to guide the interviews.

The sample used here includes the total population (based on where their home office was located) of credit unions and banks in New Orleans and in the 12 counties of southern Mississippi that were hit hard by the storm. The total number of credit unions in the area impacted by the storm was 63—41 in New Orleans and 22 in the 12 Mississippi counties hit hardest by the storm. There were also 28 banks in the area— 13 in New Orleans and 15 in southern Mississippi. By May 31, 2006, almost a year after the storm hit, 16 credit unions no longer operated as independent institutions in the same area; typically, they either moved or merged. New Orleans credit unions saw the biggest drop, with a total of 15 fewer credit unions (7 stopped operations or merged, and 8 moved out of New Orleans). Mississippi lost only one credit union during this

---

29   The Katrina micro area used for the financial section here includes 12 counties in South Mississippi (Hancock, Harrison, Jackson, Jones, Wayne, Lamar, Stone, George, Forrest, Greene, Perry and Pearl River) and New Orleans.

period, through a merger, but this was already in the works prior to the storm, as was the case with some of the New Orleans credit unions. These closures are also reflective of the national trend of credit union mergers, with approximately 320 mergers taking place every year at the time that Katrina hit. Banks are usually much larger than credit unions; in fact, in 2005, there were two banks (not in the current sample) with assets of over a trillion dollars, more than all U.S. credit unions combined.

In the immediate aftermath of the storm, credit unions received quite a bit of assistance from other credit unions, nongovernment local organizations, and national credit union associations (Klinedinst 2007). The social network of credit unions, then, seems to be at least partially responsible for their comeback. Support that came from credit union associations, like the Mississippi and Louisiana Credit Union Associations, seems to have been particularly helpful.

New Orleans Total Community Action Credit Union Poster, January 2015

A number of those interviewed at financial institutions spoke of the importance of having cash ready as a key factor in the immediate aftermath of the storm. Unusual efforts were made to get cash on hand, including hiding $1.2 million in a simple cardboard box to drive hundreds of miles back to battered offices. Charles Elliot of the Mississippi Credit Union Association told the story of a credit union manager on the Mississippi coast putting a small vault on the back of his pickup truck, packing a .45 pistol, and handing out money to credit union customers so that they would have some cash on hand to buy whatever few items they could find (Elliot, 2007). After that manager helped his customers, he went and helped another credit union. This manager helped a "competitor," but he also shared the credit union credo of "people helping people." George Schloegel, President of Hancock Bank, became famous on the coast as well for initiating a policy of handing out $200 to people with only an IOU (Schloegel, 2008). In some cases, employees who were further inland slept on the floor where the bank or credit union offices still stood, since their homes were so badly damaged.

The combined assets of the institutions in the sample were more than $42 billion in 2005 and grew 27.6% in one year to almost $54 billion. This infusion was largely made up of insurance money that would hopefully make a dent in the rebuilding of businesses and homes. Some of this "extra cash" made the temptation to buy big-ticket consumer items irresistible. Anecdotal evidence (some by the authors here) pointed to an explosion in demand for large "Katrina TV's." Families unable to have their homes quickly repaired and often times responding to the stress of the storm on their children bought these large TVs as proof that life could go on and even get better. Later loan demand escalated as rebuilding began in earnest in some areas. Hope Credit Union's branch in New Orleans, invited by a church to open in an underserved area in New Orleans right before the storm hit, had a hard time meeting the rapid build up in loan demand following the storm with damaged documents and displacement (King, 2015). This higher loan demand to rebuild came at the same time as speculative home building across the country. As in other parts of the nation, this has been pared back, especially after the "Great Recession" began.

Related to the "Great Recession" was the effort by some to have a "Bank Transfer Day" (BTD). Frustrated and angry over what some considered arrogant monopolistic practices, a number of people switched their resources from banks to credit unions starting in November 2011 (Gelles, 2011; Worth et al., 2012). Often cited as one of the primary individuals behind BTD by her postings on Facebook, Kristen Christian, a small business owner in California said, "With every person I meet at credit union events, my resolve is only strengthened that credit unions offer an opportunity to repair not only our nation's economy but also our morale" (Rubenstein, 2012). This effort to return to financial institutions that could be locally accountable would be one of the few positive macro factors helping the Katrina impacted area.

Figures 6.3 and 6.4 show that there is some evidence that the "Bank Transfer Day" had an impact both nationally and in the Katrina impacted region with growth in membership in credit unions climbing over two percent and six percent respectively in 2012, a growth rate higher than the average over the previous ten years (1.9 and 2 percent).

Table 6.1 below shows that the decline in numbers does not apply for all-sized institutions. Credit unions and commercial banks decline at about the same rate over the whole period (45 and 43 percent respectively), with savings banks declining even more. However, if assets are taken into consideration, we can see that the reduced number of institutions has happened at the same time that the number of "giant" banks, those with assets of over $50 billion dollars, has grown by 164 percent from 1994 to 2013. While other institutions had a rough time during the "Great Recession" (starting date used here is end of 2007), the number of giants stayed the same. This should not be surprising given the close ties of the top banks with oversight agencies (e.g., Barofsky, 2012 and Foster and McChesney, 2012). Credit unions, unlike the large banks, did not take taxpayer bailouts (Gilbert et al., 2012).

The trends that we see in the national data are replicated in the Katrina impacted area, as shown in Figures 6.5 and 6.6. Credit unions, although the most numerous in the area, show a steady decrease, with the hurricane hastening that decline. The only groups to see growth are the large institutions: those institutions with half to one billion in real assets grew 266 percent over the 20-year period.

The asset means in Table 6.2 (Appendix A) show that although credit unions are the most numerous, they tend to be much smaller than their competitors (e.g., commercial bank assets are about 13 times the average credit union's assets). It is interesting to note that the 360 percent growth rate for credit unions over the entire 20-year period is the highest among all institutional forms. This is also the case for the Katrina impacted area with its 388 percent increase. Employment means for the counties in the sample are 318,312 overall.[30] Employment dropped nationally in the sample over the periods 2004-2013 and 1994-2013 by five and one

---

30   There are 3,144 counties in the data set used here. The mean employment of all counties in the country was 45,015 in 2013. The larger mean reported here in 2013 of 303,406 indicates that the headquarters of the institutions were in counties with greater employment than average.

percent respectively. The Katrina area, however, saw a dramatic 29 percent decline over both periods. While the unemployment rate for the Katrina area mirrors the national rate, the Katrina area had a 30 percent decline in the labor force over the whole period, whereas for the nation as a whole in this sample there was zero change. Such a dramatic decline in the labor force means the challenges facing financial institutions are particularly tough in this area. One way to regain employment is to have support for existing businesses and startups through loans. Loan growth for all institutions was 243 percent, while for the Katrina impacted area it was only 206. Notably, for both the national and the Katrina subsample, real lending by credit unions increased by more than the average and greater than all other types of financial institutions, increasing over the 1994 to 2013 period by 340 percent nationally and by 297 percent in the Katrina ravaged area.

Over the whole time period, the mean return on assets (ROA) for credits unions was measured as the same as that of savings banks. All institutional forms showed declines over the period from 1994 to 2013, with the exception of the "giants." In the Katrina zone over the same period, the findings are similar except that the decline in ROA for credit unions and savings banks was larger in both periods. As CUNA's Bill Hampel has stated when he "criticized the practice of assigning credit unions a 'negative hit' when they report an ROA figure that's fallen from the previous year," "In some cases, the credit unions weren't less successful, they were merely returning profits to members per credit union core values" (Anderson, 2009). The relatively large ROA of the giant institutions is not too surprising given the largesse of the Federal Reserve to institutions that were "too big to fail" (Blinder and Zandi, 2010, SIG-TARP, 2012 and Taibbi, 2013). The Return on Equity (ROE) follows a pattern similar to ROA at the national and Katrina area in that credit unions and savings banks are closest to the mean over the whole period and show the largest decline in both periods, with the largest institutions showing the smallest decline.

Instead of just using assets per employee, the amount of real assets per dollar spent on salary is an attempt to make an efficiency measure that might control for variations in human capital. As noted earlier, measures of compensation are often difficult to compare across institutional forms since long-term compensation, incentive payments, executive perks, and more, are often not fully reported or categorized as compensation. In Table 6.2 (Appendix A), when looking at "assets per dollar of salary" (APDOS) for all institutions, it is clear that, relatively speaking, the credit unions perform poorly. Only in the Katrina subsample do credit unions perform better in 2013 and in their growth rates. To try and compare "apples to apples," the numbers were calculated for APDOS with only institutions that have only $50 million or less in assets (which includes 78 percent of the credit unions). Here it is clear that the credit unions have a substantial advantage over banks and savings institutions. The mean APDOS for the whole period is above others at $54.75 and saw growth in the period 2004-2013. The Katrina subsample figures are even more favorable with credit unions at 16.7 percent (i.e., (49.47-42.38)/42.38) above the next closest and also showing positive growth in the 2004-2013 period.

The institutions that survived Katrina's devastation have worked hard to grow in the tough ten years that followed. The number of credit unions in the Katrina impacted area followed the national trend of consolidation, increasing assets, and membership. There is some evidence that Bank Transfer Day had an impact on membership rates both nationally and on the impacted area, leading to higher membership growth rates in 2011 and 2012. This growth has occurred even though the area was beset with both rebuilding after such a huge catastrophe and also during the deepest downturn the U.S. has seen since the Great Depression. The BP oil spill of 2010, which hurt tourism and fishing in the area, a still lower population, and the tornadoes, which have continued to pummel parts of the area, were also a hindrance to growth.

Credit unions in the impacted area had a growth in assets (388 percent) that even surpassed the national average, while commercial banks in the area grew relatively anemically. Credit unions are the most common financial institution and did not receive a taxpayer bailout, yet they continued to offer loans and other services during the economic downturn. Loan growth for the impacted zone, a key to a revitalized business community, was lower than the national rate, but credit unions had higher growth rates nationally, and even in the Katrina area, the credit union loan increase was greater than the national average.

The return on assets and return on equity in the ravaged area was similar to that found at the national level, with the largest institutions (which have the greatest access to the Fed and the Treasury) showing the strongest performance. For credit unions, this metric is problematic since instead of keeping earnings, their lower rate is in fact partly due to their returning money to their owners, the credit union members.

This study used assets per dollar of salary (APDOS) as a metric to try to correct for human capital differences and try to gauge efficiency across institutional forms, which is not easily done because some institutions do not report all labor expenses in their reported salary figures. Commercial banks and "giants" (those with over $50 billion dollars in assets) came out the highest here. Suspicious of the figures supplied by some of these institutions and looking at comparably sized institutions, we then sampled the institutions under $50 million dollars in assets (78 percent of credit unions fall in this category). Credit unions turn out to be the more efficient user of salaries with this measure, nationally and in the Katrina impacted area. With proper attribution of all salary expenses, we suspect that this would be true nationally for all institutions, regardless of size, which is a question that others might soon be able to answer.

A metric introduced in this chapter is the level of employment where the institution is headquartered.[31] Often, for families and communities, jobs in their area are considered one of the highest priorities, if not the highest. By combining employment data on the county level with financial data, we attempted to learn how much credit unions, commercial banks, and savings banks in the area create a climate where employment can grow. Controls for region, year, state, size, and more were used, and the results indicate a strong positive correlation with having a credit union in the area when considering the national data. Loans, as expected, are also positively correlated, but larger institutions seem to have a negative impact. More credit unions are also positively related to job growth in the Katrina area. A number of interviews showed anecdotal evidence that credit unions in the impacted area received help from other credit unions and support organizations, something rarely found with banks. "People helping people" has often been a slogan of the credit union movement, and after Katrina it meant that people had a hand getting their homes and their lives back together.

Ten years after the devastation of Katrina wrecked the lives and communities along the Gulf Coast, the area is growing again. The heroism shown by many, some interviewed for this chapter, and the resiliency of one the most colorful areas of the United States is a testament to the hope we share for a brighter future and the gratefulness for the grace to have survived to help make that future.

---

31   Similar results apply when the sample is restricted to the over 100, 000 observations where the institution has only one office.

Figure 6.1

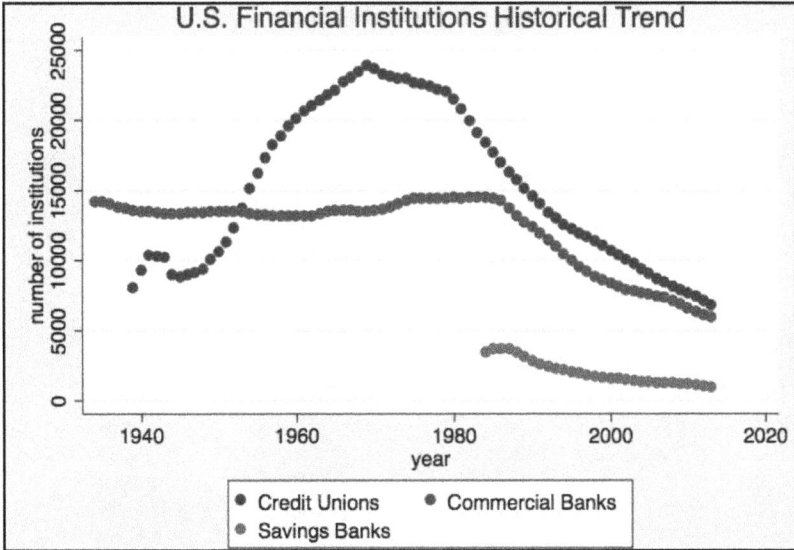

Figure 6.1

Table 6.1
Institutional form over Time for Financial Institutions

INSTITUTION	# IN 1994	# IN 2004	# IN 2013	% CHANGE 2004-13	% CHANGE 1994-2013
Total	24,775	18,106	13,508	-25	-45
Credit Unions	12,199	9,127	6,687	-27	-45
Savings Banks	2,145	1,343	936	-30	-56
Commercial Banks	10,411	7,636	5,885	-23	-43
Giants (Assets over 50 b. $)	14	33	37	12	164
Total in Katrina Micro area	137	110	68	-38	-50
Credit Unions	101	80	42	-48	-58
Savings Banks	11	7	6	-14	-45
Commercial Banks	25	23	20	-13	-20
Giants (Assets over 50 b. $)	0	0	0	NA	NA

Figure 6.2
Total U.S. Credit Union Membership

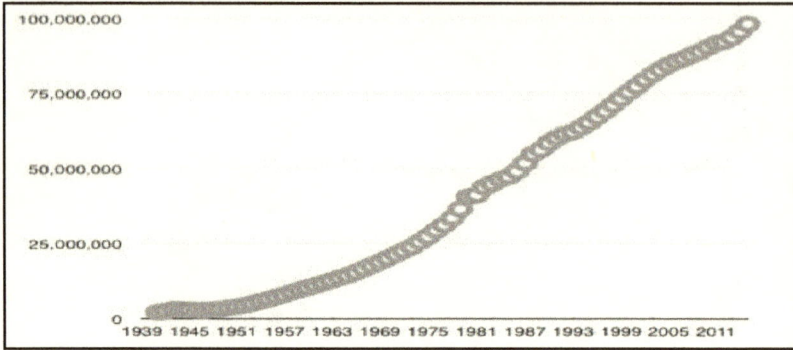

Figure 6.3

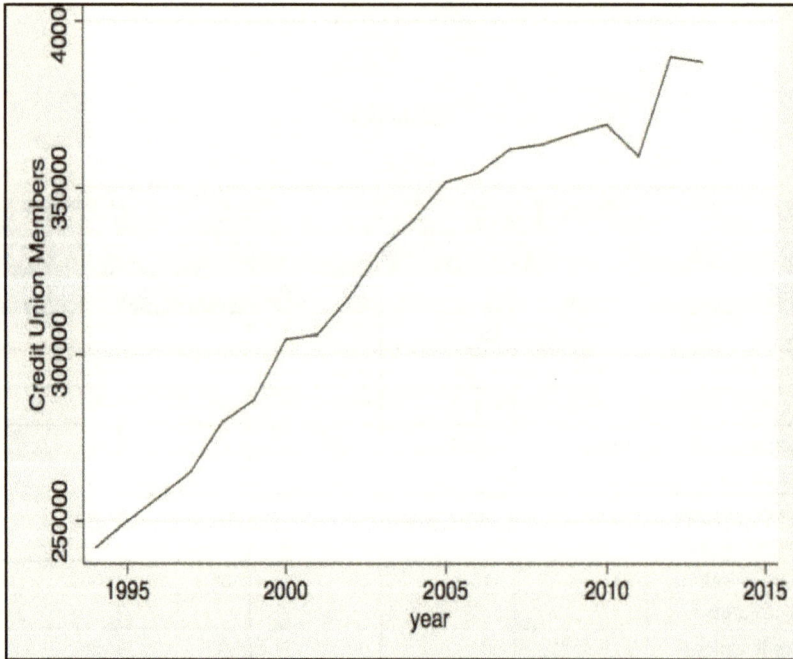

Figure 6.4

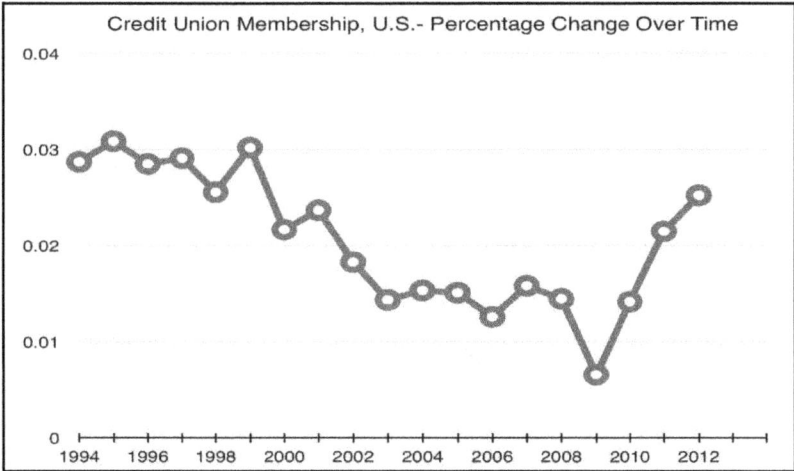

Credit Union Membership, U.S.- Percentage Change Over Time

Figure 6.5

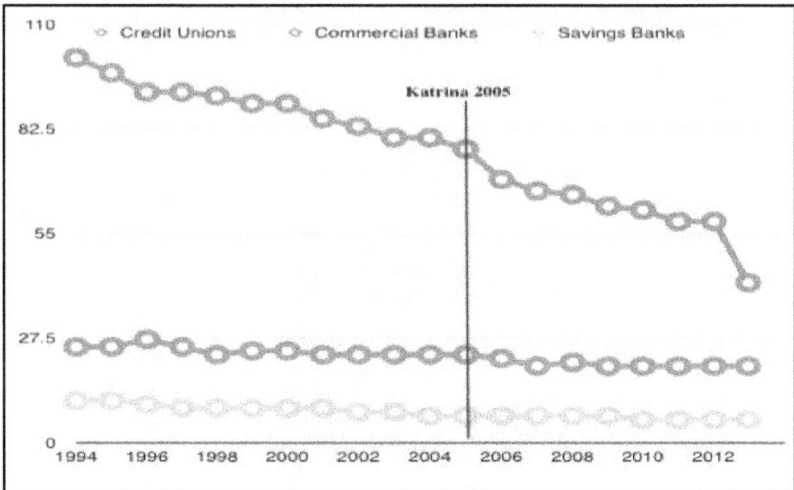

Figure 6.6

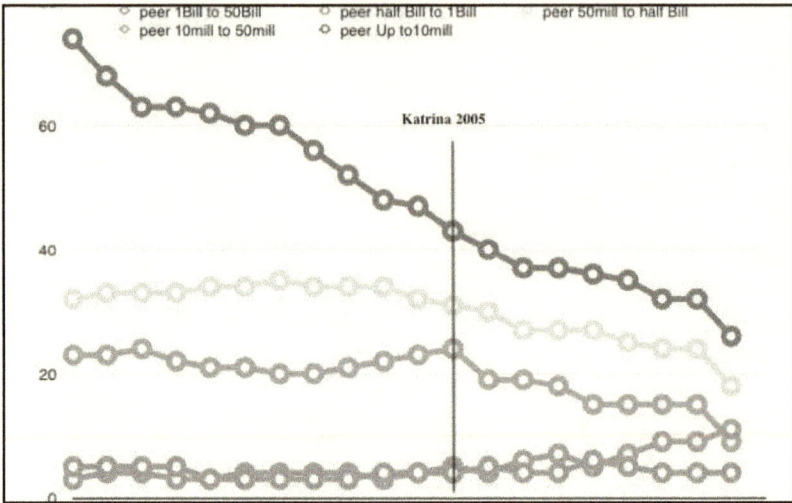

Figure 6.7
Counties in Mississippi and Louisiana in the Financial Micro Study Area

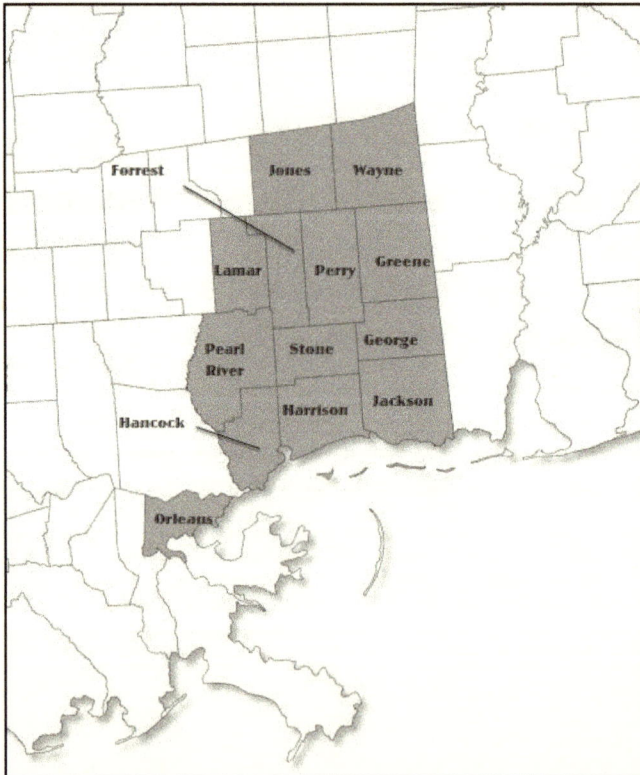

Table 6.2
Means and Changes Over Time for Financial Institutions and Employment
See Appendix A

CHAPTER 7

Corporate Welfare in Progress
The Case of the Southern Company's "Clean Coal" Plant in Mississippi

"…unless you become more watchful in your States and check this spirit of monopoly and thirst for exclusive privileges you will in the end find that the most important powers of Government have been given or bartered away, and the control over your dearest interests has passed into the hands of these corporations."

—President Andrew Jackson (March 4, 1837).

THE PROJECT TO CREATE AN EXPERIMENTAL "CLEAN COAL" PLANT IN MISsissippi is funded by electric utility customers in the poorest state in the United States. The incentives for the project come from the industry capturing the Public Service Commission of Mississippi. The controversial incentives stipulate that the Southern Company can earn a return on money spent to create electrical infrastructure, even if the experimental plant never produces any electricity. The Southern Company's Kemper County Mississippi "Radcliffe" Plant, originally estimated to cost about $1.2 billion, is approaching $6 billion dollars, is still not operational, and may never be a profitable facility. Despite this, over 180,000 of America's poorest citizens are expected to foot the bill. Although this is one of the most intense examples of corporate welfare, the "Radcliffe" Plant is hardly the only current case in the utility industry. The "Public Service Commission" of Mississippi facilitated this large transfer of income from ratepayers to investors in this monopoly. As can be seen in the graphic below, the area of MS Power and customers and the path of Katrina through southern Mississippi are very similar.

Figure 7.1

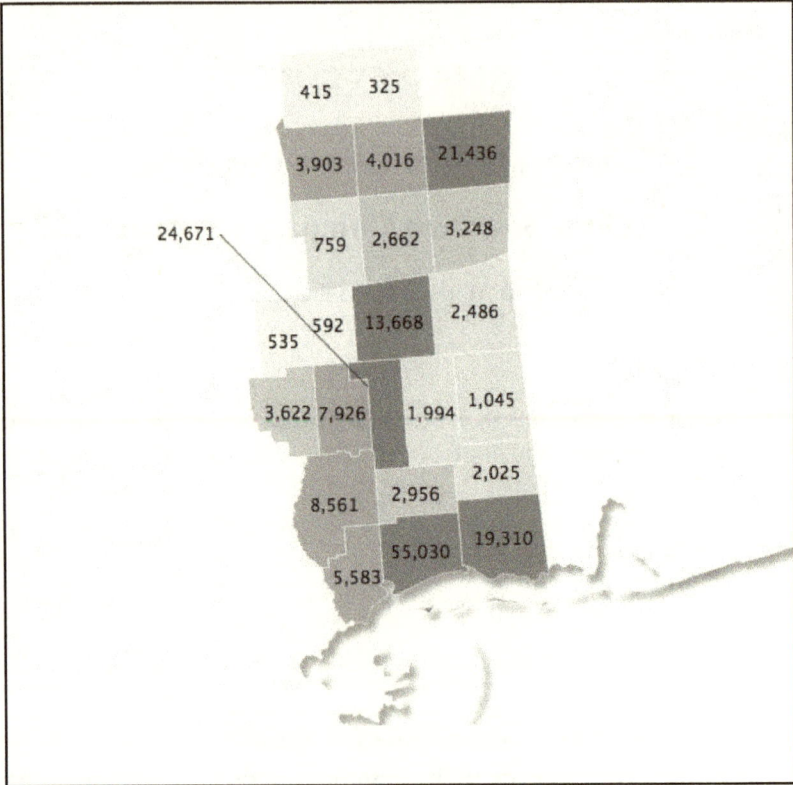

Regulatory Oversight, PSC, and MS Power

REGULATORY OVERSIGHT BEGAN IN EARNEST IN MANY INDUSTRIES AROUND the turn of the last century. Progressive inroads against monopolies and oligopolies resulted in government oversight boards that were theoretically created as a check against the firms' monopoly power.[32] In many instances, the problem that tended to develop was that the agency overseeing an industry—to promote efficiency and keep the general public's interests in mind—became a tool of the industry it was designed to regulate (Stigler, 1971). Hence, this "captured" regulatory institution gives the veneer of public accountability to monopolistic behavior.

---

32   Wisconsin had a railroad commission that in 1907 became the first state oversight board for utilities. Today almost every state has some form of "public service commission" (PSCW, 2014).

Because many of the industries that the commissions oversee are either natural monopolies or have just a few companies, people normally assume that the commissioners' job is to protect industries and consumers from monopoly or oligopolistic over-pricing. Similar to a competitive market, the commissioners will let a utility earn a normal rate of return for services offered. This rate of return can be pushed higher by having little public oversight of the regulatory body, allowing the industries involved to set their own terms. The lobbying power of utilities across a number of states grew to such an extent that they were able to have representatives of their choice on the oversight boards, and they were also able to pass laws that circumvented the regulatory practice of only charging consumers for services rendered. In a competitive marketplace, customers do not normally pay for products that are not sold to them, as may be the case with "Construction Work in Progress" (CWIP) pricing (or, as this chapter contends, as a corporate walkover on the ratepayers and the PSC).

Mississippi (MS) Power, a subsidiary of the Southern Company, gained kudos in the state for its efforts in reinstating electric power after Hurricane Katrina struck in 2005. Hurricane Katrina stands as the single most destructive natural disaster in U.S. history (Insurance Information Institute, 2007 and 2010). A number of MS Power employees deserve our thanks for their hard work on an ongoing basis and especially during the post-Katrina period. A few years later, skilled lobbyists translated this gratefulness into an attack on the basic premises of utility regulation. "Advanced Cost Recovery," or "Baseload" bills, end up having people pay for services that they may never receive (Cooper, 2013). Often, these bills are passed when it is clear that the costs going forward are not well known or that investors may be unlikely to foot the bill (e.g., North Carolina, South Carolina, and Florida's experience). The Kemper Plant is clearly a type of plant where the costs are not well known.[33] A survey conducted at the end of 2013 reported that out of 75 worldwide projects of large-scale carbon capture, five were canceled, one was reduced in size, and seven were postponed (Global CCS Institute, 2013). Mississippi's 2008 Baseload Act allows for this unproven technology, canceled in a number of places, to be paid for by current MS Power customers even

---

33   Even the name for this type of plant is not quite fixed. It is sometimes called the Kemper County "integrated gasification combined-cycle" project (IGCC) and at others "carbon capture and storage" (CCS) or "carbon capture and sequestration."

before they receive any power from this plant. This would be analogous to going to the grocery store and paying for a full cart, and yet the store prevents you from taking the items home. Thomas Blanton, a businessman from South Mississippi in the MS Power serviced area, has argued against the Baseload Act's confiscatory rate increase and the resulting costs from CWIP. In the argument to the Mississippi Supreme Court, Mr. Blanton argues:

At a fundamental level, Mr. Blanton has challenged the 'Baseload Act' because it allows Mississippi Power Company to assess customers such as Mr. Blanton for the construction of a plant that to date has failed to provide Mississippi Power Company customers with any return whatsoever: no electrons per se, no services or activities 'necessary' for the continuous reliable and economic delivery of electrons, no connection to resource planning, customer service, safety, fuel procurement or environmental protection. As of March 5, 2013, and beginning April 1, 2013, customers of Mississippi Power Company are required to pay additional fifteen percent (15%) in 2013 and an additional three percent (3%) in 2014 for the construction of the Kemper County Lignite Gasification Project, which remains untested and non-operational.

This example of paying for services that current customers (in the appendix) may never receive is a radical departure from the regulatory oversight norms. Historically, power companies received permission to raise rates in order to cover their costs of delivering electricity and to make a standard rate of return. The rate of return would be set to allow a "fair" rate that encouraged investors in the company to continue investing but not so high that customers (residential and commercial) were forced to pay exorbitant prices. Although not without problems (e.g., need for on-going prudent review, influence peddling, Averch-Johnson effect, etc.), the rate of return method, inflation adjusted, and other methods have set standards that help rein in arbitrary regulatory burdens and, at the same time, attempt to bring some of the discipline of a competitive market to monopolistic industries.

Flattening Demand

A NUMBER OF FACTORS HAVE CONVERGED TO MAKE THE DEMAND FOR centralized electricity grow at a relatively slow pace, especially in the MS Power service area of Mississippi. Hurricane Katrina and the Great Recession are only partly to blame. Clearly, the trend for real production in the state surpasses that for power supplied by MS Power, as seen in Figure 7.2. From 2000 to 2013, Mississippi's overall state product increased by 13.8% while MS Power's electric production only increased by 6% during the same period.[34]

Figure 7.2

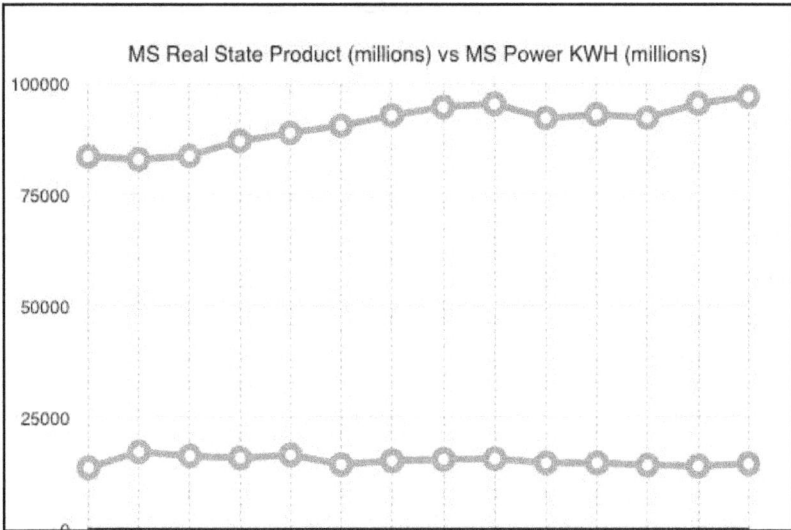

MS Real State Product (millions) vs MS Power KWH (millions)

Figure 7.3, which separates out the power demanded on a larger scale, shows signs of an even negative trend.[35]

---

34   Figures for real total gross domestic product for Mississippi in chained 2005 dollars are from the U.S. Department of Commerce: Bureau of Economic Analysis. The KWH figures come from Mississippi Power's Financial Annual Reports 2000-2013. The actual figures for Mississippi GDP are (96979-83563)/96979= 0.138 and for KWH are (14592-13714)/14592=0.060.

35   The fitted line on the year coefficient (x in the equation) has a t-value of -1.93.

Figure 7.3

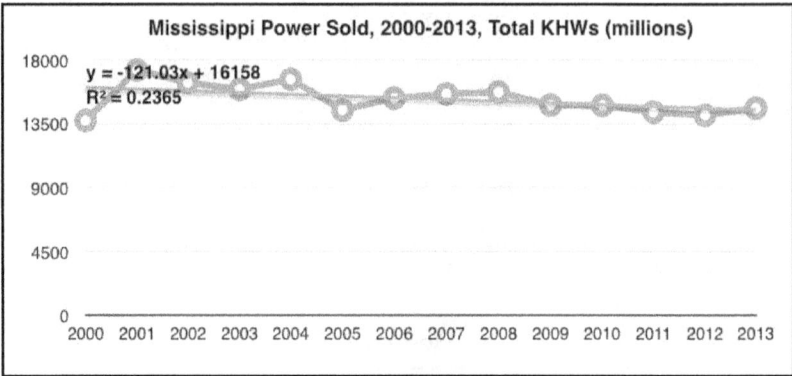

Mississippi Power Sold, 2000-2013, Total KHWs (millions)

$y = -121.03x + 16158$
$R^2 = 0.2365$

This trend in Mississippi is similar to the demand pattern seen for the country as a whole, as Figure 7.4 shows a negative trend in later years. As other technologies become more cost effective, the elasticity in demand for centrally produced electricity may grow over time. This tendency for slower growth in electric demand will only be strengthened by the rate increases from the Kemper plant that MS Power is trying to levy on ratepayers.

Figure 7.4

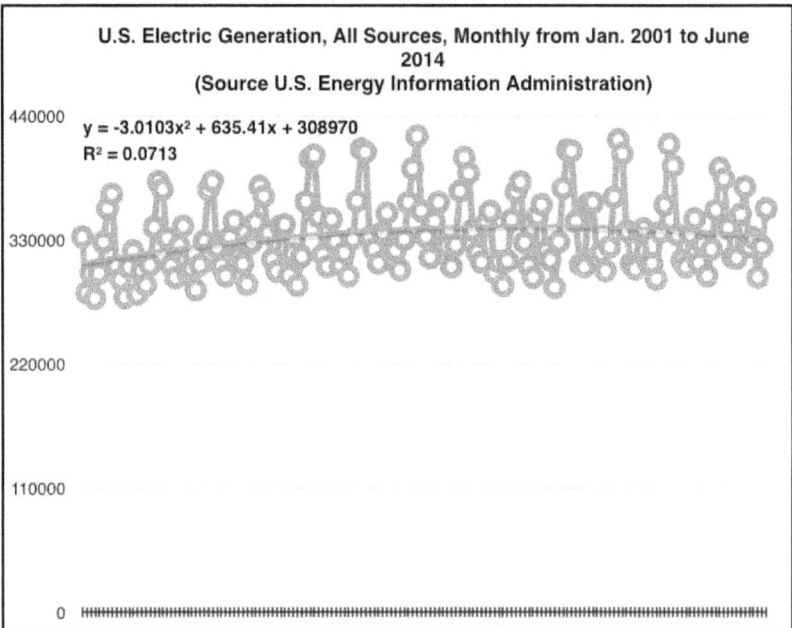

U.S. Electric Generation, All Sources, Monthly from Jan. 2001 to June 2014
(Source U.S. Energy Information Administration)

$y = -3.0103x^2 + 635.41x + 308970$
$R^2 = 0.0713$

Rate Hike Impacts

THE KEMPER COUNTY PLANT'S RATE INCREASES HAVE CREATED A SUBSTAN-
tial impact on Mississippi citizens, especially considering Mississippians'
lack of means. To gauge the effect the rate increases would have on the
region, we will explore the commonly accepted parameter ranges for
expenditure multipliers and the number of jobs lost in the 23 county
service area of MS Power predicted by these ratios, as well as the actual
number. The impact is not likely to affect everyone equally across income
levels and demographic groups. Commercial entities are also negatively
impacted by the rate increases because of the consequent loss of income
and reduced employment opportunities.

In March 2013, the total employment in the 23 counties of the MS
Power service area was 399,232.[36] By August 2014, after the rate hikes
began in April 2013, the total employment was only 394,392, a drop of
4,840 jobs (see Figure 7.5 and Figure 7.6). Over this same period, our
state increased its non-farm payroll by 7,000. If we add back in the 4,840
jobs lost in the MS Power area to get the employment growth for the 59
remaining counties, we get 11,840 (7,000 plus 4,840). This is an average
of about 200 added jobs in those 59 counties (11,840 divided by 59). If
the MS Power service area had the average job growth of the rest of the
state, we should have added 4,600 jobs instead of losing 4,840. That is a
difference of 9,440 jobs, which is a huge loss to this area.

The Congressional Budget Office (CBO), often thought to be "middle of the road" in its economic analysis, estimates that the impact of government spending on goods and services ranges from 0.5 to 2.5 (CBO,
2012)[37]. Given that other factors are held constant (e.g., Federal Reserve
policies, natural disasters, etc.), if we take the mean estimate from the
CBO of 1.5, we can see that the cost of a rate increase could have a crip-
pling impact on Mississippi consumers and businesses. What the bond
markets and rating agencies, such as Moody's and Fitch (Williams, 2012

---

36   U.S. Bureau of Labor Statistics.

37   Other studies estimate that the impact is over one, especially during periods of
high unemployment; some studies have estimated that the impact is as high as 3.42
(Auerbach and Gorodnichenko, 2012, Moretti, 2010, Neal, 2007 and Swenson, 2010).
Further, Mississippi has a higher unemployment rate than the rest of the country. In
fact, as of August 2014, Mississippi had the highest state unemployment rate in the
nation (WDAM, 2014).

and MS Business Journal, 2014), see as too risky, Mississippi customers will have to pay (Liu, 2013).

Figure 7.5

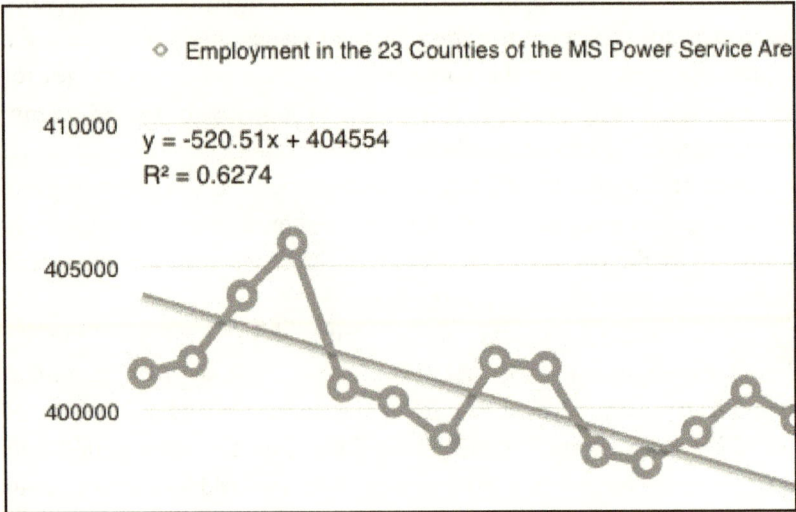

$$y = -520.51x + 404554$$
$$R^2 = 0.6274$$

Figure 7.6
Employment in the 23 counties of the MS Power Service Area
(October, 2009 to December 2014)

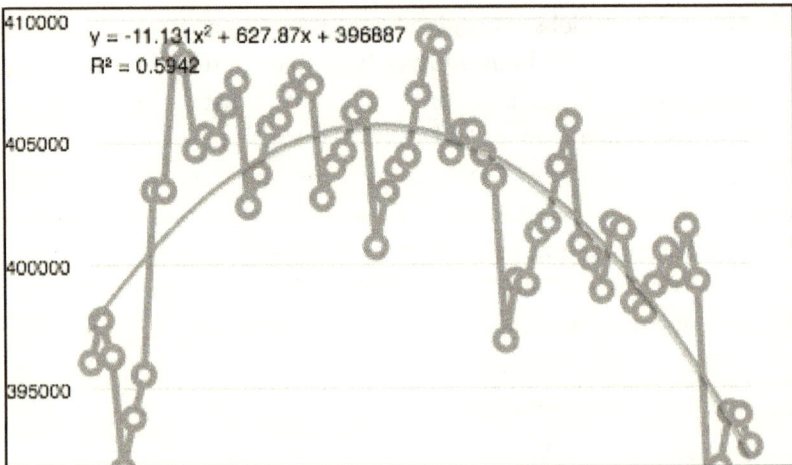

$$y = -11.131x^2 + 627.87x + 396887$$
$$R^2 = 0.5942$$

Taking a $100 million rate increase as a simple metric and applying the middle of the road estimate from the CBO of 1.5, we can expect that a $100 million rate increase will have approximately a $150 million long-term negative impact on the MS Power service area. What this means for jobs in the area can be roughly extrapolated from a number of different angles. Taking the 2013 median wage in Mississippi for all occupations of $13.57, and multiplying that as if the person worked full time (2000 hours a year, or 40 hours a week for 50 weeks), amounts to $27,140 for a yearly income. Taking $150 million out of the area with a rate hike means a yearly income for 5,526 people. Since some of the rate hikes could be multiplied to recover Kemper's costs—possibly $500 million a year with the use of the multiplier—the equivalent loss in each year of income can potentially amount to 27,630 individuals (5,526 times 5). The impact of this job loss on communities large and small in South Mississippi could be devastating.

Another way to consider an estimate of the number of jobs that could be lost is to take the number of jobs in the MS Power service area and compare that with the total income in that area. The ratio of dollars per job in the area would give an alternative idea of how many jobs may be lost with the higher fees that MS Power will charge. Running these numbers, as outlined in Table 7.1, shows 5,930 jobs potentially lost a year; over a seven-year period, this would total about 41,510 jobs in just the 23 counties MS Power services.

Table 7.1

1	2	3	4
TOTAL INCOME IN 23 COUNTIES OF MS POWER IN 2012	TOTAL EMPLOY-MENT IN 23 COUNTIES OF MS POWER	INCOME PER EMPLOYED PERSON IN 23 COUNTIES OF MS POWER (COLUMN 1 DIVIDED BY COLUMN 2)	POSSIBLE $500 MILLION RATE INCREASE PER YEAR/INCOME=JOBS LOST PER YEAR
$33,800,000,000	400,937	$84,303	5.930

These rate hikes are hitting homeowners and businesses hard. Even with extra efforts at conservation, an 18% increase in electricity costs will typically mean cut backs. The University of Southern Mississippi is budgeting an extra million dollars for utilities for the 2015 fiscal year (Kemp, 2014). Businesses that would have cut prices or hired more workers may now have to scale back. The loss of 4,840 jobs already in the area (over 9,000 if the area had the rate of increase of the rest of the state) is hard on companies and residents. Figure 7.6 shows that the decline in the number of jobs in the area was already on a downward trend after the Great Recession hit. The extra costs that residents and businesses experienced when the electric rates went up to pay for a plant that may never actually be fully turned on seems to have added to the burden of the recession. Individuals faced with these increased electric rates have tough choices to make as well. For those already on the edge (and as a state we have quite a few), the choice may come down to buying food or being warm. How many increased fatalities will this area suffer due to illnesses that will be exacerbated from inadequate heating or cooling (Breitner et al, 2014)? Our elderly will probably endure some of the greatest problems from these causes.

The increase in rates charged by MS Power are especially curious given the growth of energy supplies and recent technological advances (U.S. Energy Information Administration, 2014). With low demand growth and lower costs for fuels, the decision to embark on an experimental lignite plant (that has seen delays and cost overruns) seems to be quite risky, unless you have the support of the MS Public Service Commission. This is not a chapter meant to disparage the hard working professionals at MS Power that we saw in action after Hurricane Katrina. We should focus our attention on individuals and corporations in higher levels of power and ask them to be more accountable to Mississippians. South Mississippi businesses and individuals should not have to pay for an expensive and experimental plant that costs billions more than alternative power sources and has yet to even operate. The MS PSC needs to make sure that electric rates are "just and reasonable" for South Mississippians and not just cover poor decisions designed to enrich a few.

Recently, after the Mississippi Supreme Court ruled in favor of Mr. Blanton (who is currently running as a candidate for the November 2015 election to serve as a commissioner on the PSC), the Public Service Commission voted 3-0 to follow the directions of the court and begin refunds of the Kemper plant extra costs on businesses and consumers (Amy, 2015). The company will probably try to recoup these losses by some other method, but the hard work of concerned citizens and groups like the Sierra Club have prevented, at least temporarily, a costly increase on some of the poorest citizens of our country who are still in the process of putting their lives back together ten years after Katrina.

CHAPTER 8

The Green Project

David Reynolds

"Charitable and government organizations and programs, as well as volunteers contributing materials and labor, were essential. New Orleans and The Green Project cultures remained intact, reemerged, and evolved. Recognizing and husbanding local culture, knowledge, relationships, and energies after a disaster, then proffering resources in their support promises economy and mitigates risk during recovery."

—David Reynolds

New Orleans—A Small NGO Manages

FIFTY-FIVE MILES WEST FROM BAY Saint Louis—a very long way when this stretch was the Katrina frontier for a few years after 2005—takes us to a New Orleans neighborhood close to the stylized one of Tennessee Williams' *A Streetcar Named Desire*. "I have always depended on the kindness of strangers," Blanche DuBois reflects in the 1947 play. Something like that, gratitude and lament, characterized the experience of many in the Katrina zone. What follows anchors on a spirited, community oriented business. The story takes a somewhat economic bent but is just as importantly a story, this being New Orleans, one of those places where stories are served along with food and music.

The Green Project (www.thegreenproject.org) was, and still is, a New Orleans not-for-profit, non governmental organization (NGO) that subsists on earnings from retail and service operations to recover, condition, and market salvaged and surplus building materials and components, paints, and certain furniture and keepsakes. Those primary activities wholly or partially support other educational, social, retail, and innovative enterprises and activities dedicated to the nearby community, the City of New Orleans, and the Greater New Orleans Metro region. The Green Project applies for and receives grants sometimes, for forward looking projects, but revenue from day to day operations pays the staff, operates the building, and puts away a little for a rainy day.

The Green Project was an incidental name. The originators, a few of whom are still involved, were distressed over the amount of paint going into landfills, especially near wetlands (in the Greater New Orleans Metro, all elevations are low). Discarded paint was often still liquid when it reached the landfill as ordinary, non-hazardous waste. The Green Project began as a weekly collection of paints in a convenient public location where it also resold paint at low prices, just sufficient enough to meet expenses. Paint that could not be recycled stayed around to dry, then, with containers compacted to reduce volume, went to the landfill. Word (and paint) spread. Business days and hours became more and longer. Eventually, perhaps inevitably, surplus building materials and building components came into the picture, and remained.

By the time of Katrina in late August of 2005, The Green Project owned and occupied an approximately 20,000 square foot former beverage plant a few miles from its original site. The facility included a store, office spaces, loading docks, a dumpster dugout, and finished, drained, indoor and outdoor areas for cleanup, storage, and display of lumber, boards, millwork, fencing, doors and windows, tools, small appliances and household or shop equipment, masonry, and even gardening and landscaping items and materials, including live plants.

A tenant and staff member brought art, theater clothes, and sets. Individual volunteers and groups helped the staff with daily operations: cleaning, repairing, painting, grooming, and improving the grounds.

They created art from discarded items—some of it practically useful as furniture, made music and performed theater, prepared impromptu meals, and held community meetings and educational gatherings, mostly around "green" knowledge and practices to promote and enable economical, comfortable, healthy, secure, and sufficient housing, small businesses, and communities.

By the time that I joined The Green Project in 2002 as a volunteer (eventually assistant director and director), full time staff numbered between eight and 16 at intervals. There were dedicated grants, including a photovoltaic electrical generating system that sharply reduced peak electrical demand and associated charges. There was an active Board of Directors and extensive relationships with builders, contractors, artisans, businesses, organizations, officials, and residents. I used to say to staff colleagues, partially in jest and partially to acknowledge how far The Green Project had come, "We are 13 years old and we act our age." The Green Project was strong, energetic, in need of maturing in many ways, but clearly an enduring and growing part of the business and community landscape in the old, mixed use, New Marigny neighborhood, a block from where St. Claude Avenue crosses the railroad into the Ninth Ward, six blocks from the Mississippi River, and a mile from the edge of the French Quarter. Sales volume was gaining steadily, and along with it, staff pay, benefits, and retention. Ongoing repairs, cleanup, and improved financial capacity brought opportunities to plan and experiment with green methods and equipment. These were regular activities at The Green Project before Katrina.

The neighborhood was doing better too, as commercial buildings became occupied again and people fixed up residences. Commercial and residential renovations, repairs, and painting brought progressively more drop-offs and sales. Among renovation contractors, both economy and aesthetics enlarged and shaped The Green Project's niche. Staff responded with improvements in their knowledge of the building process, receiving and loading, material and equipment conditioning, display, familiarity with inventory, product knowledge, pricing and negotiation, and the practical, hands-on understanding of contractor work and the needs and desires of residents, especially in older neighborhoods.

Katrina flooded the facility hip deep with muddy water that drained away only gradually, removed much of the roof covering, burst doors, took down fences and gates, soaked and randomly redistributed inventory and office contents, disrupted utilities for months, and scattered staff, board members, volunteers, contractors, and artisans who were both regular customers and donors. At the same time, a great volume of old and new millwork, boards and lumber, and decorative elements became available for deconstruction and salvage. In company with the rest of the New Orleans, the Metro area, and the Mississippi Coast, The Green Project began recovering slowly and painfully.

Where'd Everybody Go?

IN DISASTER INCIDENT RESPONSE, SAFETY OF LIFE IS THE EARLIEST CON-cern. Security and well being of people and property follow at once. Easy enough to say, given suitable plans and resources, but Katrina disabled emergency services on at least a hundred mile stretch of well populated coast and a considerable way inland. Jackson, Mississippi, the state capi-tol, almost 200 miles north of the coast, took sufficient damage to limit normal business operations for weeks. Half way to the coast, Hatties-burg, Mississippi was much more extensively damaged than Jackson and set back proportionally; similarly, the parishes (counties) along and north of Lakes Ponchartrain and Maurepas were significantly affected by the storm. Law enforcement, fire protection, health care, water and food dis-tribution, roadway, bridge, and signal maintenance all curtailed, some completely and for a long time. Military responded in proportion to the mobility and mission of each command, but, if not part of an established disaster response plan already, then not until the decision to deploy came down from civilian authority.

The Coast Guard was present quickly and continuously with search and rescue. Other armed services joined soon, providing security, drink-ing water, and managing the complex logistics of evacuation. As time went on, the National Guard became the chief branch present, with forces coming from various states. An Ohio deployment, for example, arrived in a few days. Eventually, civilian fire and police, with their vehicles and equipment, came and stayed. Shipments of food, personal care items, household supplies (many donated, along with transportation, by indi-viduals and an impressive variety of small organizations) were dispatched.

Still, the first days and weeks after the storm brought horrible sit-uations and incidents in New Orleans: masses of people sheltering in hellish conditions in the Superdome and Convention Center, shootings of pedestrians on the Danziger Bridge, the ordeals of hospital medical staff and patients without electricity or ventilation, and many, many more incidents. People helped one another, shared food, supplies, kindnesses, and comforts. They located bodies, salvaged personal belongings, protected their buildings, and slept on porches in the moist heat, comforted once in a while by an indolent breeze. They challenged and drove off looters and robbers. A great number scattered across the U.S. Families, relatives, and colleagues sometimes didn't know each other's whereabouts, conditions, or circumstances for long intervals. In most areas, quiet prevailed by day in what had been a busy, noisy city like most others. Nighttime deepened the quiet to silence and darkness in most of New Orleans, including the neighborhood of The Green Project.

Within a few weeks, one of the Board members, a contractor and property manager, had been to The Green Project and made a gross assessment. Roofing was mostly torn loose. Fences, gates, and doors were broken or stuck. Sales, processing, warehouse, and office spaces were ruined or covered in mud, with contents scattered by water, wind, and, apparently, intruders. Utilities were off and would remain so for months. The same scene repeated all over Orleans and adjacent parishes. While the hurricane winds were powerful everywhere, especially in eastern sections, water level and energy varied widely. Homes and businesses in New Orleans neighborhoods below levee breaches were swept away and piled in heaps, while in others, close to the Mississippi River and along Esplanade Avenue, slight elevations kept flood levels low or even dry. Flooding inside The Green Project, six blocks from the Mississippi River and still slightly elevated by the natural levee across from the sharp bend in the river at Algiers Point, was a few feet deep. This was less than in many locations, but the water was muddy and contaminated. With drainages blocked and replenishment from every rain, water and mud stayed around.

The National Guard patrolled, Red Cross brought calories, and people fed scraggly pets. Interior demolition commenced in scattered locations nearby The Green Project. Reusable material, much of it antique, piled up on sidewalks and streets in older neighborhoods. Collapsed, leaning, and wobbly buildings everywhere invited deconstruction (methodical disassembly) that would yield old wood and components to gather, sort, protect, and reuse—a core objective of The Green Project. New Orleans carpenters would want these later. Boards and lumber of old growth timber, hidden since original construction, could be reworked as finishes in repaired homes, "something old, something new" to warm the heart and please the eye. Where to begin? Staff and finances were our first considerations. And please, Red Cross, more seasoning in the food handouts, OK? We love you, but we're still New Orleans.

Anyone Awake?

FOR A FEW MONTHS, LIFE IN NEW ORLEANS WAS SURREAL. DRIVING IN Baton Rouge, the North Shore (above Lake Ponchartrain), and other inland locations in a crescent extending from Louisiana to Alabama, was stressful and dangerous due to heavy traffic. Damaged cities and towns near the coast were eerily quiet. Moving about New Orleans proceeded gently to conserve fuel (if you'd managed to locate any), with a careful look around at intersections, where traffic signals were inoperative and where muddy water, silt, and piled debris blocked the view and took up parking places. Cell phone operation and charging followed a soon familiar protocol: weak or busy signal, if any, and constant disconnection. Finding a place with a generator running when your batteries were drained out took planning. At the same time, almost everyone greeted one another warmly, yielded at intersections, helped out with work, found and returned pets, and shared water, food, drink, ice, portable toilets, tools, equipment, and whatever else there was to share.

Opening The Green Project, even perfunctorily, would be an important gesture and boost for everyone with a stake because the word would spread. Paradoxically, communication among key personnel, and with The Green Project insurance carriers and banks, was an obstacle that diminished slowly and unpredictably. We—senior staff and the Board— knew that The Green Project had a long, complicated journey ahead, no matter the obstacles, opportunities, directions and destinations, but we could speak only infrequently and quickly, due to difficulty in placing a call at all hours, dropped calls, and low batteries. Meeting in person was mostly impractical. We were scattered, often in makeshift or temporary living and working circumstances, with the same factors affecting our private lives as those holding back The Green Project, and all costing time, energy, and good will.

On behalf of The Green Project, we needed to join together to:

- Arrange to reopen as soon as possible, even on a minimal schedule, then increase operations as staff trickled back, volunteers offered to work, and we could provide safe, sanitary, and minimally serviceable spaces, facilities, and equipment.

- Plan, finance, initiate, and carry through facility repair and restoration.

- Discover, evaluate, and make effective use of help from organizations and individuals focused on the Katrina zone, of market and community opportunities, and of special requirements imposed by authorities.

- Reconsider and adapt our strategic plans and objectives in light of evolving circumstances, then reformulate and try out suitable tactics.

In November, we met as a group in one board member's street level office downtown in the Central Business District. Traffic was still almost non-existent and parking casual, sharing the curb with sand and debris. Electrical power had come back just a few days before. We cried, not for the first time, rejoiced, rediscovered real coffee, and got to work.

We're Open

THE FIRST REOPENING, IN MID FALL OF 2005, WAS MOSTLY A GESTURE. A few staff and executive committee members had begun to show up at intervals to clear and secure space for minimal operations. They posted a small OPEN sign, giving limited days and hours. Neighbors, contractors, and artisans noticed and stopped in. Opening for a few hours a few times per week was the best that The Green Project could do. Revenue the first day was under $50. Material donations were modest—all that could be handled in any case. Expenses were zero. Book keeping ledgers that survived reopened.

The Green Project realized an early advantage in recovering the facility: inventory. Salvaged for a second time since its donation, the inventory served for initial repairs. At a time when sources of new building supplies, materials, equipment, and tools were few, mostly distant, often in short supply, slow and clumsy to buy and load, and crowded at any hour, we had plenty.

"Where is everybody?" resolved only gradually. Each week, a few more residents returned to the neighborhood. Everyone who returned had repairs to make and items to donate. Staff called in from distant or near locations or just showed up. At the same time, the whole Katrina zone experienced an influx of people and organizations of great variety, number, purpose, and affiliations, bringing aid, resources, knowledge, connections, needs, and requirements. A number of these figured in the early course of The Green Project.

A board member, who had long performed critical facility management functions for The Green Project, began insurance claims and received initial, partial payments. A few bank offices reopened, but none nearby. Customer experiences there were similar to buying groceries and supplies: few vendors, inconveniently located, crowded, with few and slow services—but making an effort.

After a while, cell phones worked relatively often. Gasoline and diesel were reliably available here and there. We were thankful to the National Guard and the Red Cross for security, water, calories, friendly faces and voices, and breaks from work in the dirt and heat. Nutrition went from sustenance to dining with the arrival of food trucks that followed Mexican and Central American workers. We fed wandering pets until their owners returned or someone adopted them. Water and electricity connections were still months away. Potable water, portable toilets, and batteries showed up, stayed available, and supplies were renewed. Darkness was in oversupply almost everywhere as the days shortened. A dozen or so young men and women, Bedouin, seemingly, slept on the second floor of The Green Project. Gulf Coast Fall tends to be dry so they were mostly untroubled by rain showers—or the absence of showers for bathing. They were affiliated with an organization and movement that helps out in impoverished and wrecked neighborhoods. They worked every day in the surrounding area, returned at night, and moved on after a few months.

The Recovery Stretch—Winter 2005-2006 and After

WITH OUR MISSISSIPPI COAST HOME GONE AND OUR NEW ORLEANS apartment still officially subleased (and not ready for occupancy in any case), my family relocated to Jackson, MS. The home office of my wife's employer was there and welcomed her. We purchased a home and moved in with just backpacks. As soon as I could arrange transportation, I sought disaster recovery work that included lodging in the Katrina zone. I hoped to aid The Green Project and other homegrown organizations serving communities in the New Orleans Metro area, directly or indirectly. Gasoline became more available each week, but at high prices. I purchased a used compact pickup and accepted a job offer from an NGO specializing in recovering sustainable community economic life after catastrophes and war throughout the globe—which had established an office in Baton Rouge and begun recruiting a team that included several local members to help with contacts, resources, and culture. By good fortune, another hire was a renovator, woodworker, and advocate of The Green Project, who was also a customer, donor, advisor, and neighbor. We knew one another from regular contact and mutual interests. My colleague was personally familiar with people and organizations working along the same lines as The Green Project and located near to the U.S. headquarters of our employer.

Our assignments soon included envisioning, outlining, and planning how The Green Project could regroup and recover, enabled and accelerated by financial help, expert personnel, and material aid. The team leaders and their headquarter executives followed through judiciously in evaluating whether The Green Project could serve as one of their featured projects to help New Orleans communities strengthen, endure, and grow after Katrina. At the previously mentioned meeting in downtown New Orleans in November of 2005, that process was largely completed. The relationship would go forward. I would leave the NGO and return to The Green Project full time to manage operations. Circumstances at The Green Project, already dynamic, became even more so. The large block of assistance, with its set objectives and targets, depended heavily on how well recycling buildings in New Orleans could follow the model established in the headquarter city of the NGO. Doing so would require forming, training, equipping, and insuring additional field teams, expanding warehouse capabilities, and improving processes to discover and contract jobs. Meeting goals and objectives depended as well on marketing of deconstruction as an alternative to fast demolition and removal using heavy equipment. Local government policies supporting deconstruction would be needed after the bulk of buildings made unserviceable by Katrina were no longer in play.

I frequently drove three hours from Jackson in the early morning, arriving before 8:00 to briefly inspect the empty homes of a few The Green Project volunteers and friends, and to check on a dog hanging around, hopeful for the return of her owner. (Dog and owner were eventually reunited.) I slept at the homes of friends and colleagues, sometimes going to our home site in Bay Saint Louis to pick through personal possessions strewn around the property and the blocks nearby. Traffic was so bad with the loss of the Interstate 10 Bridge over the eastern end of Lake Ponchartrain that I could almost have driven to Jackson in the same time. I worked on my laptop for long periods while stalled in traffic, engine stopped and windows open. At The Green Project, water, sewer, electricity, and a roof were still a long ways off.

Traffic everywhere in what I called the corona (for that intensely turbulent and fiery zone around the Sun) was constant, varying from fast, close, and aggressive, to slow, stopped, and even more aggressive. From Baton Rouge, east across the Interstate 12 corridor to Slidell, Louisiana, and into the inland southern Mississippi, traffic delays were constant. Closer to the coast, things were still eerily quiet. The National Guard patrolled. Flat tires, due to scattered nails formerly holding together people's homes, were the norm. If you went there, you fueled up inland first. I kept two spare wheels and a jack handy in the back of the pickup.

Continuity and Discontinuity—The Green Project Recovers

BY EARLY 2006 AT THE GREEN PROJECT, OUR CONCERNS WERE THE return of staff, volunteers, and neighbors, first aid to the facility, and financial management. The New Orleans business milieu called for more and more attention as recovery strengthened and opportunities, complications, contingencies, and risks grew rapidly.

On a Saturday afternoon around Christmas, 2005, the board president, a volunteer from the Seattle area, and I worked in the rapidly darkening second floor of The Green Project, filling two dumpsters from ten feet above with ruined items and materials formerly stored and now heaped, along with demolition debris, near the jammed open cargo loading door, facing Press Street and the railroad. Unwieldy pieces to handle and trip over were scattered on the loose floor tiles, nails sticking out to snag or step on. Useless wiring and fixtures hung from overhead, with dangling ceiling sections. Volunteers, with limited guidance from staff (who were mainly occupied with customers and material donors on the first floor and grounds), had demolished damaged ceilings, walls, attachments, and furniture leftover from the era when the building served as a beverage plant. Their work was energetic, but, with little experience and short intervals on the job, often incomplete. Managing volunteers to work safely proved a constant challenge.

Dumpsters were scarce and expensive for a long time after Katrina. That The Green Project usually had one or two at the same price as for years previously from the character of the local provider, a small business, and a reliable friend. This late afternoon we had *two*, each of 40 cubic yards (8 feet deep, 8 feet wide, and 20 feet long)! It was worth my staying around, climbing in and out of each to arrange things as they came down in order to fill all available space. In the failing light, we didn't always get our communications right about which dumpster I occupied and where to throw, or possibly my colleagues found my light colored hard hat a sporting target. Anyway, over several hours we crammed both dumpsters, exchanged high fives, and parted pleased and satisfied. Our provider picked up the next day, at half the then going price, and serviced his more temporary (and higher paying) customers when the official workweek began on Monday. He never failed us. He tipped the dumpsters and we tipped the drivers. We filled containers promptly and completely when they arrived, but never so much as to be at hazard for falling off onto the road. Our ingenuity and efficiency in packing, never under or over loading, were points of challenge, pride, economy, necessity, and maintaining of enduring business relationships.

Water, electricity, staff, and more volunteers arrived in the winter and spring of 2006. Managing people, space, and materials safely were constant concerns. Incoming donations of materials multiplied, varying widely in quality. Some amounted to little more than rubbish, brought to get around finding and paying for a dumpster. These the staff turned away, but dumping at our facility off-hours or out of sight of staff while open were constant problems. A mission of The Green Project was and still is to serve the natural environment and reduce costs to the public by diverting into local reuse items and materials that would otherwise enter the solid waste stream to landfills. Ironically, the more that we recognized, extracted, processed, handled, stored, displayed, then sold or donated, the more we filled scarce dumpsters with the leftovers. Filled dumpsters picked up from our dugout meant better performance of our mission, so long as we sorted well. Incoming materials became the second flood of Katrina. Processing and display areas, loading docks for pickup and drop off, yards, offices, toilets, break and conference rooms, even around the checkout counter—every space barely kept up with demand, and only then with inventive in-store uses and promotions. Donors occasionally brought keepsakes, or stashes of shop and cleaning supplies, gadgets, parts, wire, fastenings, bits of metal and wood, paints, solvents, insecticides and fertilizers, repairable lamps and furniture, fuel cans, and a few tools, in batches salvaged from a collapsed shed not touched since a grandfather or an uncle passed away years before. While our policies were not to accept poisons and most solvents, containers would arrive in cartons among other items and be accepted. Sorting personal lots felt like a duty and required unreasonable amounts of time and consultation among staff. Sometimes the donor would stay a while, telling family stories. The shelves and cabinets around the checkout counter began to look like a museum.

Making Deconstruction Sustainable

BY EARLY 2006, OFFERS OF ARCHITECTURAL COMPONENTS AND CHOICE materials, providing that The Green Project deconstruct (take apart systematically and remove cleanly) the donation, multiplied quickly as demolition and gutting of buildings took place for miles around. Full deconstruction, ending in a bare and groomed site for redevelopment, was a principal feature of the agreement reached a few months previously with the NGO benefactor. I traveled with a board member of The Green

Project to view deconstruction in Portland, Oregon. In return, a deconstruction crew from The Rebuilding Center (http://rebuildingcenter.org/deconstruction-services/about/) came to New Orleans to join with our field staff in taking down, removing, transporting, and processing a partially collapsed old New Orleans home donated for the purpose.

Deconstruction—first day of a demonstration project with The Rebuilding Center. The collapsed house in the Treme yielded multiple large loads of vintage lumber, boards, and millwork (treehugger.com)

This project, and others that followed, yielded valuable material in quantities large enough to suggest architectural and decorative possibilities to designers and renovators of homes and commercial spaces. In addition to millwork, such as hearths, rails, moldings, and antique wood widows and doors, we obtained unfinished boards and lumber, logged and sawn from old growth forests more than a century before. The wood showed intriguing grain patterns and colors, and bore distinctive tool marks and sometimes hand written scripts, which had been hidden behind finished walls, in attics as roof decking, under floors as sub flooring, or in structural (frame) members such as rafters, joists, studs, posts, sills, and girders. These components often contained complex joints common in those times.

The Green Project promoted highly visible, essentially decorative use of such wood, employing the phrase "inside-out" to bring to mind long hidden parts of old New Orleans buildings to be newly seen and prized. This development was particularly important because modern building codes and methods would not normally accommodate the same wood for conventional construction purposes. That was just as well. We would have disliked having any of it hidden again. Modern lumber is well suited for framing purposes, but much less interesting and varied in visual character than what deconstruction can make available. Wood comes from trees, a perfectly obvious thought, but modern silviculture, though economically efficient, produces wood of quite a different quality than contained in saw logs when forests were unmanaged. Another advantage of "inside out" was that the wood was unpainted, so dealing with lead based paint was not a consideration as it was with painted siding and millwork, which often turned up often in donations brought to The Green Project.

The Green Project also deconstructed or assisted with the whole or partial demolition of buildings dating from after WWII. These jobs yielded framing lumber of modern dimensions for use in repairs and minor renovations but less suitable for structural applications in large renovations due to engineering, code, and quantity requirements. During the same interval, progressively more new building materials became available at good prices in New Orleans. In deconstruction, crews and staff tracked materials, expenses, and revenues from sales and services. The agreement with our NGO benefactor included budgets for material handling and storage equipment (forklift, carts, warehouse grade racks, trucks and trailers, tools.) We located such things, mostly in used condition, then purchased, transported, set up, and adjusted. We conducted safety training, insured equipment and operations, and planned equipment maintenance.

Further considerations with growth of operations were security against theft of equipment and stock, both on job sites and in the facility. We rearranged facility spaces, repaired fences and locks, and added security cameras and recorders. Lawlessness came back strongly as New Orleans revived. Crew safety against criminals became a consideration. A returning crew told of taking shelter from gunfire at a job site. I inspected the truck and found fresh scars from bullets along the frame near the back, where one of the gunmen took shelter to exchange fire with his adversaries.

We received a progressively decreasing allowance for operations, but at the same time, earned revenues gained. We were able to pay staff well, offer steady employment, meet increased liability and workman's compensation insurance expenses, and improve employee benefits. Still, our deconstruction volume lagged projections. Various factors contributed, from equipping, hiring, training, and managing crews, to the complicated physical conditions of damaged buildings in partial collapse, to obtaining and scheduling jobs at a time when people were in a hurry and heavy equipment plentiful, to processing, storing, and selling recycled wood and building components in the large quantities obtained.

Looking forward to the time when general deconstruction should be entirely self-supporting, financial projections did not promise that The Green Project would hold a market niche in deconstruction in the New Orleans of a few years in the future. The materials gleaned were much the same as what we obtained from delivered donations, so net revenue was much less. At the same time, and for a variety of reasons, removing and putting aside useful but not especially valuable materials during "gutting" or taking down a building became a more common practice among contractors. For a while after the storm, when debris blocked streets, removal was often subsidized, but free pickup gradually stopped. Several New Orleans commercial companies and contractors existed in the wood recycling business space before Katrina, and new commercial and not-for-profit organizations started up. Two, long established, dealt only in old lumber, boards, and millwork, and added value by resawing and milling large dimension lumber into paneling and flooring, then storing in lots, out of the rain and sun, for sale to specialized renovators with high end customers. This wasn't a niche well aligned with the vision and mission of The Green Project, nor, in the near future, would as many old buildings be demolished as after Katrina. They and we gratefully referred business to one another though, and visited when nearby for coffee and conversation. Everyone benefitted, and less went to the landfill.

Another factor limiting the sustainability of deconstruction was that local officials and politicians did not seem ready to support ordinances requiring that deconstruction be pursued as an alternative to conventional removal when obtaining a demolition permit. The mindset across the Katrina Zone strongly favored knockdown by heavy equipment and bulk transport to landfills. Deconstruction could match the cost of conventional demolition but not the speed—a weeks versus a few days. Nor could the slowly growing deconstruction segment meet the near term capacity required. This left The Green Project with specialized deconstruction instances, such as removing a damaged two or three-story building leaning on or very close to one next-door, where heavy equipment could not maneuver effectively. These jobs took careful and ongoing evaluation, planning, and close supervision. In others, the owner wished to retain valuable materials. The Green Project performed these as a paid service, but such opportunities would become fewer as time passed.

All in all, ongoing, full deconstruction, keeping multiple crews busy in the field and in processing of materials was not economically sustainable by The Green Project. We tried variations—selling from site, drop shipping, being more selective about jobs, subcontracting—all without improving financial results and prospects. We also learned that the deconstruction organization example that we followed, which had been operating for some time and benefitted from local policies favoring deconstruction, did not yet itself break even and relied on subsidies from other parts of the business from time to time.

In the same interval, The Green Project derived good economic, community, and environmentally sustainable performance from cooperation with demolition and general contractors. The Green Project crews, suitably insured and trained, were called to job sites after or in between demolition activities to remove and transport salvageable materials and items. We came to picture our role not so much as the shark (the main demolition provider), but the pilot fish, which accompanies the shark and lives from what the shark tears off but doesn't eat. What were scraps to the shark became sustenance for the pilot fish. Less than full-scale deconstruction to bare ground was proving sustainable, but our benefactor didn't find this niche compliant with the agreement for support entered into the previous year, which envisioned full deconstruction on a scale greater than The Green Project had achieved. On this basis, the benefactor withdrew funding short of the full period and amount arranged but left The Green Project a grateful, viable, and productive organization, reliably and sustainably serving community and environment, while meeting expenses and growing as a desirable place to work.

The Green Project staff loading pine flooring on a customer truck. Installed and refinished, these boards will show impressive figure, color, and endurance. (Twitter, @TheGreenProject)

The main facility steadily became more accommodating and inviting as a place to work, donate, and shop. Each neatening, streamlining, rearrangement, and repair led the staff to initiate more. One board member and a suitably experienced staff member worked steadily on insurance claims and contracted repairs. We qualified for and obtained commitments of a few months each from six AmeriCorps teams, spaced over nearly a year, and one longer term administrative appointment from AmeriCorps. We were obligated to set, track, and adjust tasks and objectives for each team of a dozen or so AmeriCorps workers, with a staff member participating full time or quickly available. On several occasions, AmeriCorps teams slept, bathed, cooked, and ate on the now much improved second floor. AmeriCorps teams completed a good deal of facility repair and refurbishment, but staff attention to all volunteers, working with or without their own management and leadership, took a toll. Staff members were already pulled in several directions. Simultaneously, insurance settlements brought outside subcontractors for tasks like roofing, installing sheetrock in the stairwells, and floor repair and refinishing. The subs did high quality work quickly, but required orientation in personal protection against air born dust and fumes, fall prevention, and electrical shock—mostly in Spanish.

Donated paint that we consolidated and remixed was in good supply. AmeriCorps workers were enthusiastic painters, though not so proficient in minor repairs and surface preparation. They were mostly apartment dwellers just out of college, and viewed these important steps as concepts, perhaps, more than as processes and techniques applicable in the present. They were good humored about taking guidance though. All in all, AmeriCorps, and a steady stream of other volunteers, made possible levels of work and undertaking of projects that the staff could not have undertaken.

Making Paint Recycling Sustainable

KEEPING PAINT FROM GOING TO LANDFILLS, WHILE FURNISHING PEOPLE on tight budgets with opportunities to spruce up their surroundings and protect against sun and rain, were central to the mission of The Green Project from its beginning, more than a decade before Katrina. During 2004, the year before Katrina, amounts of paint received and space devoted to holding, processing, and retailing paint were larger than at any time in the past, but the labor intensive methods and inconsistent quality of product for sale to customers were basically unchanged. New volunteers were invariably assigned to paint (or to removing nails from donated wood, another labor intensive task that could be difficult and tedious). Staff made improvements in paint intake and processing efficiency and consistency. One staff member, who worked with paint at The Green Project for years, demonstrated and taught safe, quick, efficient, thorough, and clean practices, the best obtainable by the methods and equipment in use. We adapted demonstration and sales practices to deliver better and more consistent quality but without basic changes in method or approach. Paint contributed relatively small revenue proportionate to resources expended but was a core component of the mission and goals of The Green Project. In the summer before Katrina, reexamining and possibly reengineering the paint endeavor was nearing the top of my list of needs and opportunities. A strong consideration was that, surely, another organization of comparable scale was consolidating and recycling paint more effectively than The Green Project. With support from our benefactor, we soon met two.

At the end of our time in Oregon, we visited a paint recycling facility that produced a strong triple bottom line—financial, social, and environmental. Metro Paint (www.oregonmetro.gov/tools-living/healthy-home/metropaint) processed paint volumes many times those of The Green Project, collecting from and mostly distributing back into the Portland metro area, a market roughly the size of the New Orleans metro area. Metro Paint worked with incoming stock of comparable quality and variety as The Green Project. Highlights included:

- Quality, uniformity, consistent palette, and availability of product—sufficient to meet demand and specifications of government and civilian construction and retail markets.

- Partnering with rehabilitation programs to obtain full time paid staff, who stayed or moved on to work in the coatings industry.

- Gleaning a substantially larger portion of unwanted paint in their geographic area than The Green Project did in New Orleans.

The principal matters favoring a Metro Paint-like approach at The Green Project were (in no particular order): low and incremental startup and growth costs; scalable size and capacity; obtaining, training, and retaining staff; space in a suitable facility already available; low technology; commercially available equipment; improved product quality; reduced waste and very low environmental risk; marketable product using a well known brand; and safety of workers and the environment. We began planning for transition while keeping up with the demanding and still growing processing of paint and other material donations and with deconstruction. Not long after, a board member and I attended a conference on paint recycling programs hosted by Okaloosa County in northwest Florida. The program drew on practices and experiences in several U.S. locations. Okaloosa County officials saw recycling as a method of compliance with waste disposal regulations that would cost less than alternatives, meet and reinforce expectations for care of the environment, and provide employment and a product for local consumption. We also learned that numerous paint sellers and the coatings industry accepted and accommodated paint consolidation, as consistent with environmental responsibility. In New Orleans, an established paint retailer and friend of The Green Project assured us that stocking and selling recycled paints, as long as they were consistently available and certified as to quality and color, would not diminish new paint sales, and would bring more traffic into the store.

Our NGO benefactor, while acknowledging the community service and environmental benefits, did not share our concept of the role of paint in The Green Project as instrumental to economic stability or aligned with agreed upon goals centering around deconstruction. Nonetheless, processing paint would continue to be a sustainable business area for The Green Project.

Alongside The Green Project

It is spring of 2006. Leave The Green Project at 2831 Marais Street and walk a few blocks toward the River then turn on St. Claude in either direction. Take any side street toward or away from the River and walk another few blocks. Occasional food trucks are still around, but neighborhood restaurants, coffee shops, and bars (often one in the same) are opening. There is less debris, especially on the street. Most of the cars and trucks look like they run. There's more going on.

From Twelfth Night to the Mardi Gras in 2006, things were not exactly celebratory, but they sure brightened up. Most of us cleaned up a little. It was a pleasure to be able to do so. Water and sewer, electricity, even retail, gradually showed up and stayed. "Business casual" replaced overalls and work jeans in banks and offices, now that there *were* more banks and offices. You would see repaired roofs, along with new paint on the front porches, doors, windows, and siding of houses here and there— sometimes even on the sides and back.

"Clean up" might be thought of in another sense as well: money coming in from all over, especially "government" money, enough to swim in, now that the water had receded—that is, if you could find room in the pool, given the number of officials and consultants who would in due time be replaced or depart. The collective view of the post Katrina public sector largesse, made popular by politics and sensationalized by news and social media, might be justifiable in some instances but was not strongly evident in The Green Project neighborhood. Clearly, major public infrastructure projects would be funded. Since Katrina, capital projects of all sizes have taken place one after the other—a number of them concerned with flood protection and transportation, but even more involve business, health care, education, housing—funded by mixed and diverse sources and agreements.

New Orleans and the metro area have come back strongly, for the most part. My focus here will remain small and local, however, summarily comparing and contrasting two early, worthy efforts intended to directly serve households, neighborhoods, and communities damaged, displaced, or hanging on with great difficulty after Katrina. The two represent different philosophical, economic and planning, or design approaches that contrast decidedly.

Turn Key

One of a number of original designs built in New Orleans by Make It Right
(makeitright.org)

THE FIRST PROMISED AS GIFTS HOMES, PERHAPS 150, IN THE LOWER Ninth Ward, an area in almost complete disarray and destruction after the Industrial Canal levee burst near the St. Claude Avenue Bridge. Actor Brad Pitt became interested in the situations of stable, long established New Orleans communities with mostly low household incomes and correspondingly low expenses before Katrina. Large numbers of residents of these areas did not return due to complications and expenses of rebuilding. He chose the Lower Ninth Ward (so called because it is down river, "lower" relative to the upper ninth ward, on the upriver bank of the Industrial Canal). He formed an NGO that initiated a project to bring back the community, concentrating first on residences.

The ambitious project, begun in 2007 under the auspices of Make It Right, a foundation with projects in other, distant cities as well, coalesced relatively early in recovery. Associated with a famous actor and raising the image of a modern, redesigned community with the old culture rising from wreckage, the project attracted a great deal of attention: media, celebrity, official, political, professional, commercial, and local. Much has been written and filmed about it, some complimentary, some less so. Approximately one hundred complete homes existed by 2013, built at a relatively high cost per dwelling. Over time, materials and features vulnerable to New Orleans rain, moisture, and sun have had to be removed or replaced with modified designs. The hoped for community with residences and small retail stores, reflecting circumstances before Katrina, has not reemerged strongly. Lydia DePillis, in a 2013 article on the subject of urbanism in New Republic writes of the project intentions, circumstances, and history. All in all, the project has not been as strong a success as first envisioned, despite the comfortable quarters, appreciable funding, and exclusive preference given to as many of pre-storm established residents as could be found and interested. From economic efficiency, social, and cultural points of view, other initiatives toward neighborhood and community recovery, with a variety of sponsors, have experienced lower costs and increased involvement of residents working with closely guided volunteers. An example is lowernine.org.

Keep the Keys and Stay

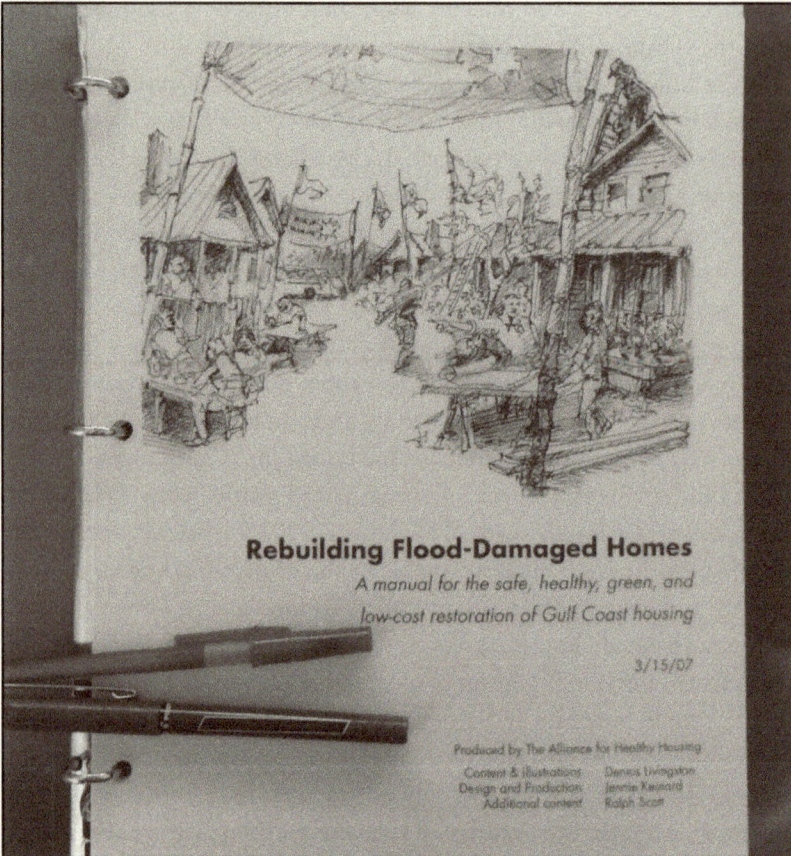

Rebuilding Flood Damaged Homes, A manual for the safe, healthy, green, and low-cost restoration of Gulf Coast housing, still maturing in 2007 (The Alliance for Healthy Housing, March 2007, with subsequent editions appear under the auspices of the National Center for Healthy Housing, nchh.org)

A CONTRASTING APPROACH RESTS ON THE PREMISE THAT THE PEOPLE who can stay in or soon reoccupy their own damaged homes and/or businesses in relatively safe and secure conditions can recover in place. Moreover, their presence will bring others to do so. This idea underlies a research and educational project, Rebuilding Flood-Damaged

Homes, completed in early 2007 under a small grant from the Alliance for Healthy Homes.

Rebuilding Flood-Damaged Homes teaches and coaches restoration work that is feasible while occupying the building or living nearby, and it is designed to produce less vulnerable buildings that recover more quickly after the next hurricane or flood. Of course, a standing building is prerequisite, one that can be occupied provisionally or visited conveniently until occupation is feasible. The project addresses old buildings, and was as a consequence applicable in New Orleans neighborhoods such as the Marigny, Bywater, St. Roch, and others not far from The Green Project where buildings remained standing.

To begin and continue the recovery, community workshops took place to gather local knowledge and identify existing capabilities and resources. The leaders of Rebuilding Flood-Damaged Homes were themselves personally experienced with community organization and with practical problems and techniques. They understood the nuances and tradeoffs to be encountered. Interested parties from the community, who would carry out the approach in their own properties, supplied particular understandings of local buildings, availability of materials and supplies, and what could be repaired and reused or discarded. In older buildings, a great deal of the foundation, frame, roof, floors, outer walls, windows and doors, and plumbing could stay and be repaired, tuned up, or renewed. Much of the wood of earlier times was not much affected by wetting and drying out and retained its strength and dimensions. Understandably, there was a great deal of such material to use whenever it could be obtained ahead of the heavy equipment and dump trucks that seemed to be everywhere.

With a secure and adequately clean and comfortable living space established, performing work, or standing by to assist and make decisions during rebuilding or repair became possible in terms of time, energy, and funds. The results, obtained with economy and owner/occupant knowledge and presence, would decidedly reduce risk of future flood damage and enable quicker and less expensive reoccupation after the next flood and/or wind. In the present, the approach can produce a safe and secure building and site that is comfortable and economical to manage and maintain. Just as important is that this approach strongly serves community and warrants interest and support for that reason alone.

In contrast to the creators of the Make It Right project, which created new designs to adopt and brought in materials to adapt, the organizers of Rebuilding Flood-Damaged Homes did not shy from identifying and employing updated materials and components where these would be of practical good. Making use of original, still in place, or locally salvaged components and materials was paramount. These had endured as originals in the same locale and could give long service life when repaired or reconditioned correctly. At the same time, newer components and technologies fit into the scheme when these promised utility and resistance to future damage. Easily obtainable tools, new or used materials, work skills and habits that could be mastered, and small to moderate amounts of money were the total resources needed, and not all at once. Domicile on or near the work site, even if in temporarily austere lodging, could bring reliable rest, visiting, encouragement, sharing, and cooperation.

While at The Green Project, I contributed details of New Orleans and Gulf Coast construction, materials, techniques, and associated safe work practices to those published and taught in Rebuilding Flood-Damaged Homes. The project was not in itself a community reconstruction from bare ground, as was the case in the worst of the Lower Ninth Ward or in the western end of the Mississippi Coast and parts of several coastal parishes, but it promoted and enabled remaining in place, close to the work, in community, beginning with the end in mind. Of course, what would be in mind would be shared labor, food, drink, music, talk—just as before.

The Green Project in 2015

THE GREEN PROJECT IN 2015 IS REMARKABLY TRUE TO THE VISION AND mission before Katrina but enhanced and elaborated throughout in objectives, strategies, and implementations. Several members of the Board of Directors, productive before Katrina, are involved and active now. Others have joined, widening popular interest through events and programs serving the City and metro region. My (and everyone's) friend, Butch: neighbor, volunteer, quiet (mostly), capable and good humored (always), retired from maintaining a printing plant (his wardrobe is always black shirts, black slacks, black shoes, black socks) is there still. Community service projects arise, evolve, and give rise to others. The bills are paid. Staff members are cared for and about. The Green Project diverts from the landfill several hundred tons of usable wood, building products, paints, metals, and masonry yearly. The facility is attractive, well cared for, and largely utilized. Work proceeds constantly, with adjustments and improvements. The Green Project of 2015 minds the triple bottom line: economic, environmental, and social—minds it well.

The niche of The Green Project, with its donors, customers, and community members, reflects participants related economically, ecologically, and socially to one another and to their place. Deconstruction as a primary program could not be made to support itself but is practiced in New Orleans by building and demolition contractors who donate some of the materials gleaned and purchase from The Green Project as well. Today in New Orleans, recycling household electronics, a multi-year project that required appreciable space and handling at The Green Project, is executed efficiently elsewhere by a big box electronics retailer. Alkyd (oil based) paints proved problematic also, but specialists in reclamation or incineration now divert these from the landfill. The Green Project faced difficult strategic choices after Katrina, but has kept a consistent vision, mission, and culture, only adjusting strategies and objectives to be part of the ecology, economy, and community of New Orleans.

Processing lumber and paint at The Green Project (thegreenproject.org)

How Do We Solve a Problem Like Katrina?

WHETHER THE VIEW IS ECONOMIC, ECOLOGICAL, OR SOCIETAL, IT IS PLAIN that The Green Project was able to obtain sufficient resources after Katrina and utilize them to stabilize, grow, and serve. Charitable and government organizations and programs, as well as volunteers contributing materials and labor, were essential. New Orleans and The Green Project culture remained intact, reemerged, and evolved. Recognizing and husbanding local culture, knowledge, relationships, and energies after a disaster, then proffering resources in their support, promises economy and mitigates risk during recovery.

Recovery follows after emergency or incident response. Incident response is mostly a functional, logistic, material undertaking that leads to recovery and rebuilding. Recovery incorporates progressively more social, cultural, and economic considerations. A strong, long established pre-disaster culture bodes well for recovery. New Orleans, robust and productive ten years after Katrina, is worth understanding by all entities intending to offer assistance toward continuity of organizations and communities. The same will likely be said of older communities and locales within the Hurricane Sandy zone. While large losses and changes are inevitable, continuity of community and culture is a strong strategic consideration.

Katrina wrecked the built environment. The rest was consequent: huge, awful in many instances, then grinding, enormously expensive in terms of fortune, time, energy, and spirit. My Bay Saint Louis neighbors of decades, in their 70s by 2005, were prosperous, helpful, and community minded. They brought humor, projects, ideas, and good company into our daily life. They sheltered from Katrina nearby and then evacuated. Several years of relocations, all-day trips coming back to salvage and store a few belongings, dealing with insurance and authorities, building a small, inexpensive home nothing like their previous one overpowered and drained them. Eventually, they could not overcome. First one, then the other, passed away, years before what might have been the case otherwise. Everyone in the Katrina zone was wearied, with prospects dimmed or scrambled. Being castaways, or emigrants, or left without neighbors was hugely consequential after Katrina. The least capable, for reasons of money, age, health, employment, or family circumstances, did not come back, or did not survive long if they remained. Some live close to former neighbors in cities like Houston, but New Orleans lost many who would not have wanted to leave the world so soon or live anywhere else.

A Framework for Recovery

THE WORST DISASTERS AND WARS CAN OBLITERATE A CULTURE. LARGE hurricanes wreck the built environment but leave pieces and seeds to continue in the ways that people felt, thought, and related to one another: their language, personal lives, work, friendships, symbols, foods, recreation, entertainment, and so on. I bring a facility management point of view to this final section. Facility management is about people, places, and processes *considered together* around the built environment. The facility manager's viewpoint is that catastrophe, incident response, and recovery constitute a cycle to recognize, prepare for, and carry through. Facility management emphasizes conferring continuity of businesses, organizations, and communities who are stakeholders of the built environment.

Facilities have a life cycle. Conceiving, financing, designing, constructing or renovating, commissioning, occupying, operating, maintaining, and eventually transferring or retiring buildings and other infrastructure—all to best effect—span the life of a facility and derive its value to organizations, business, and communities. Consequential interruptions by emergency incident or disaster at any life cycle stage occur frequently enough to warrant attention by executive leadership to obtain effective incident response and recovery. Facility managers expect—and may have to propose and persuade—executives to set high level objectives for response and recovery. Organizations, institutions, businesses, and communities all have their own tolerances for risk, critical processes and capabilities to retain, and stakeholder interests to protect and recover.

Facility managers routinely work with practitioners in real estate, business, finance, architecture, engineering, design, construction, human factors and health, building systems operation, technology, property and space management, cleaning, safety and security, compliance officers, public officials, and the community. Readiness to respond and recover from emergency incident or disaster integrates the input of all of these under the high level objectives. Doing so brings understandings in advance with business and community leaders as to what is critical to protect and revive and when, leading in turn to mitigating risks before an incident. Some, mostly large, organizations in the Katrina zone, with plans and provisions made and rehearsed around people, places, critical processes, and technology, recovered by degrees in planned sequences, but others, especially smaller, less formally organized and governed communities and their members lacked specific plans and resources. With members scattered and resources few, they recovered slowly and irregularly. Response and recovery do not have to be that way. In that light, we will briefly revisit emergency response before considering recovery.

Response

DURING AND RIGHT AFTER A STORM, SAFETY OF LIFE IS THE FIRST CON-
cern. Katrina overran organized life protecting and saving capabilities. Warning the entire central Gulf Coast area frequently and intensively, starting almost a week earlier, diminished the numbers of people directly in harm's way when the storm arrived. Unfortunately, some who remained were the most vulnerable. Examples include those of limited means, in medical and elderly care facilities, and in prisons and jails. Some who stayed died or suffered severely. Others bravely gave help or received help.

Largely, police, fire, health care, and civil authorities either fell back or were disabled by conditions, ruined equipment, and failed communications, with no available means of repair or replacement. Many stayed on the job, acting in steadily worsening conditions during and after, without support. Local government officials had not much to work with and spoke without a unified voice. Chain of command in the core Katrina zone sundered. In the periphery, it overloaded.

The geographic extent of Katrina was so large that mustering adequate forces for incident response took days and weeks, even for emergency management agencies at the state and federal levels. Military, hundreds of non-government civilian groups and individuals, and local governments from far off performed search and rescue, combed systematically and exhaustively for bodies, or sent and brought aid expeditiously for survival and comfort. But performance and effectiveness of civilian government agencies, especially the Federal Emergency Management Agency (FEMA), which possessed major statutory responsibilities, varied widely and irregularly. Integration, coordination, and communication to the public and nation were absent or fragmented during the early response.

Incident response is nonetheless a well developed discipline, defined under statute, policy, process, and procedure, with permanent staffs, bodies of knowledge and practice, and ties with agencies and organizations like businesses, institutions, local governments, civic associations, and clubs. It can work well by repeating a cycle of planning, hypothetical exercises and simulations, drills, evaluations, and revisions. Why wasn't the Katrina incident response better? Why didn't public facilities perform much better? The answers can be found and understood with reference to the cycle just described.

We move on to recovery, remaining mindful that, when funded, led, staffed, and managed well, incident response can be predictably effective in mitigating what is mostly a functional, material, and logistical situation. Hurricanes present a big challenge for incident response. Large hurricanes inflict more damage and loss directly on the built environment than other natural and man made disasters, short of acts of war. Response planning, training, practice, and execution are prerequisites for the recovery and continuity of community and business life.

Recovery

CONTINUITY OF PEOPLE, PLACES, AND PROCESSES IN A QUICKLY EVOLVING environment is the valid and challenging focus of recovery, no matter the degree, amount, and extent of loss. After a hurricane, resources in large quantity may have to come from afar, first to save life and property, then for recovery, calling for financial and managerial capabilities and capacities that are themselves disrupted locally. People present before a storm, who wish to remain afterward, not only have legitimate interest in their homes, communities, and businesses, but they hold the culture of a community or organization. Cities and communities evolve, of course, but the built environment speaks from and to culture. Where culture is strong, keeping people together or at least in contact is a top priority so that their decisions can be central to recovery of the built environment and life therein. The sooner that people return in stable and supportive arrangements, the faster and more economical the rest of recovery. But many will be scattered, dispossessed, shocked, tired, and unsure of how and what to do. Just when recovery aid and involvement from outside are ramping up, capabilities inside are absent, or just waking up and taking stock.

People present before the storm, who wish to remain afterward, can and should be looked to in setting the pace and flavor of recovery as they themselves recover. Too much of outside intervention and assistance after the emergency response phase can feel like an invasion and occupation, requiring inordinate amounts of time, energy, communication, and good will to sort, understand, and manage the outsiders, to the extent that they will permit themselves to be managed. To many in the Katrina zone, recovery became the storm after the storm. People who remain or return are truly the customers of agencies, organizations and interests furnishing aid and administering claims. They will want to take stock, salvage for reuse, regroup, and talk about the future. Patience, listening, sharing information, and furnishing resources from set asides are their due. Their initiative, wellbeing, stability, and economy will improve and progress, rewarding themselves and every organization and individual giving help. The relationship sought in the recovery and continuity phase, the one that will confer success, is realized after those in the disaster zone join the recovery team. A relationship of saviors and victims, essential at first during incident response, cannot be allowed to dominate the recovery and continuity phase, even as resources pour in.

Conclusion

READINESS TO RECOVER DEPENDS GREATLY ON PREPARATION. THE CHALlenge in zones subject to hurricanes is not only to husband buildings and infrastructure to resist damage or loss, but to work with organizations and communities ahead of time to identify people and processes critical for economic and social continuity and to prepare and provide for these. In the recovery and continuity phase, outside organizations share a stake in recovery, serving best as providers of funds, technical and logistical capabilities, perspective, knowledge, and information, but only specialized and temporary leadership. Facility managers are trained to work among stakeholders to bring continuity of business and community, recognizing the prominent and decisive role of the people most affected to set the pace. This way brings resilience.

Ten years after Katrina, the case for doing better before and after large scale destructive weather events and discovering sustainable ways of going about it is evident. Humans are about 7 ½ billion in 2015, up from 5 ½ billion just 25 years ago. The Earth is experiencing climate and weather born of an energized, kinetic atmosphere and circulation. Weather events will almost certainly increase in frequency and severity. Must losses be as great in the future as experienced with Katrina? Disasters are specific in both agency and place, but similar enough so that the previous can inform the response to and recovery from the next. Katrina and Sandy were both large, powerful, tropical hurricanes in the coastal U.S. that came seven years apart, on different coasts. Both areas suffered losses due in part to avoidable vulnerabilities and in part to assistance too often not well conceived, defined, planned, communicated, checked in practice, coordinated, committed, delivered, and received. To a remarkable extent, in my awareness shaped by Katrina, communications and media reports after Sandy, and two brief visits, people in the Sandy zone fared during recovery roughly as did their Katrina counterparts. Sandy did not do damage as far inland, and much of the Sandy zone is richer in people, capabilities, and resources than the regions struck by Katrina. Why haven't things gone much better for small businesses, organizations, communities, and individuals after major hurricanes? What may be missing? Competent and regular planning, preparation, and local prerogatives in managing recovery of the built environment can bring more satisfying outcomes more economically. We can do much better and with less expense by being ready to respond initially and retuning the conduct of recovery to emphasize community based leadership and decisions. The latter calls for a new learning and effort by government, organizations, and communities, but promises improved resilience.

CHAPTER 9

The Lower Ninth

Coral Pogue

"Forty years after the passage of the federal Fair Housing Act, residential segregation still permeates New Orleans," said James Perry, executive director of the Greater New Orleans Fair Housing Action Center. "Homes in communities of color still have lower values than those in white communities even when the condition, style and quality of the homes are comparable. Louisiana's program builds on this history of discrimination. Only when housing opportunities are created for all residents of New Orleans will our recovery truly be successful."

—(GNOFHAC Press Release, 2008)

THE LOWER NINTH WARD BECAME THE SPOTLIGHT OF THE MEDIA'S attention following Hurricane Katrina with images of residents stranded atop their flooded homes airing on news stations across the globe. It is the area in New Orleans that sustained some of the worst flooding due to the federal levee failures, and it is where many of the deaths in the city occurred (Brunkard, 2008). The struggle for the residents of this community to rebuild and return home continues even ten years later as its recovery has trailed far behind the rest New Orleans.

What is the Lower Ninth Ward?

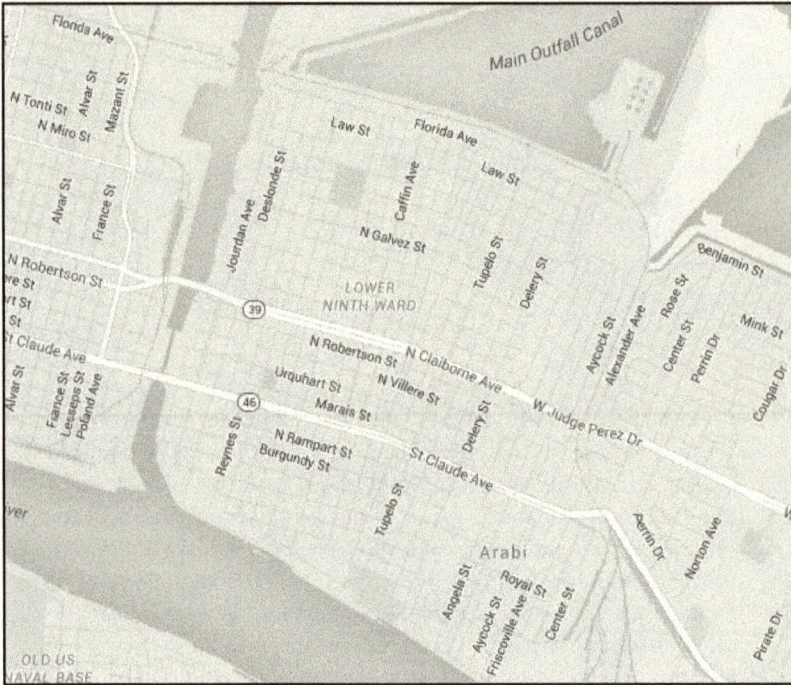

Map data 2015 Google

THE LOWER NINTH WARD IS A PLANNING DISTRICT IN NEW ORLEANS. Its official parameters span just over two square miles. The boundaries include the Industrial Canal to the east, St. Bernard Parish to the west, Bayou Bienvenue to the north, and the Mississippi River to the south. There are two neighborhoods within the Lower Ninth Ward District: one retains the Lower Ninth Ward's name, and the other is called Holy Cross. Holy Cross obtained its name by the area's association with Holy Cross Catholic School, a well-known, historical all-boys school that had resided in the area since 1895. St. Claude Avenue, the lower of the area's two main roads, separates the neighborhoods, and it serves as the northern border of Holy Cross, which extends to the Mississippi River, and the southern border for the Lower Ninth Ward, which continues north to Bayou Bienvenue.

Before Katrina

PRIOR TO HURRICANE KATRINA, THE LOWER NINTH WARD WAS A HEAV-
ily populated African American community. There were many small shops
and businesses found along its streets, from daycares to eateries, churches
to corner stores. In 2000, African Americans accounted for ninety-five
percent of the area's population. The community was also abundantly
poor, with over a third of residents (34 percent) living below the federal
poverty line (compared to 28 percent in Orleans Parish and 12 percent
nationwide)(GNODC). Despite the level of poverty, the Lower Ninth
Ward had an impressive 54 percent homeownership rate (GNODC),
higher than the city's average and, for African Americans, higher than
even the state and country overall (U.S. Census Bureau). The area has
historically been composed of working class, low to middle income families that have been deeply rooted within the community—with many
residing here for generations. As a result, homes here were often passed
down within families, leading to over half of all homeowners owning
their homes outright before Katrina.

The concentration of African Americans in the Lower Ninth Ward
is due in part to white opposition to school desegregation during the
1960s. New Orleans was one of the first cities in the Deep South to
take on school integration and one of the first schools to be integrated
in New Orleans, McDonogh #19 (later renamed Louis D. Armstrong
Elementary), was located in the Lower Ninth Ward. Three of the first
four African American school girls selected to attend New Orleans' all-
white schools were also from the Lower Ninth Ward, and the fourth girl
was from the Upper Ninth. The three Lower Ninth Ward girls, Leona
Tate, Tessie Prevost, and Gail Etienne, integrated McDonogh #19. The
fourth, Ruby Bridges, integrated William Frantz Elementary located in
the Upper Ninth. The opposition to school integration led to white residents leaving the area for more suburban parishes, predominantly neighboring St. Bernard. The flooding brought on by Hurricane Betsy in 1965
further strengthened white emigration (Landphair, 2007). In 2000, St.
Bernard Parish had a white population that accounted for 84.3 percent
of its total population with only 13.1 percent living below the poverty
line (GNODC).

Historical activism and disaster is not all that the Lower Ninth Ward
was known for. Rock and roll legend Fats Domino was born and raised
in the Lower Ninth. World-renowned musician and co-founder of the

Rebirth Brass Band, Kermit Ruffins, spent his childhood here. It is also home to Jackson Barracks, the headquarters of the Louisiana National Guard, which is located along the St. Bernard Parish line. The neighborhood of Holy Cross is even recognized locally and nationally as a historic district.

The Storm

ON AUGUST 29, 2005, HURRICANE KATRINA WREAKED HAVOC ON THE city of New Orleans and the neighboring Gulf Coast region. The storm brought a scale of devastation not ever seen before on U.S. soil in terms of economic loss. An estimated total of $135 billion was accumulated in damages as a result of Hurricane Katrina (Plyer, 2014). In New Orleans, flooding from the levee breaches throughout the city caused most of the damage. By morning on August 29th, Katrina's storm surge had made its way to the city of New Orleans. The first of the levee failures occurred on the eastern side of the Inner Harbor Navigational Canal (Industrial Canal). A wall of water had overtaken the concrete levee wall and eroded the soil on the other side, ultimately causing it to collapse. Just a few hours later, a second breach occurred blocks down from the initial failure. Together, the levee breaches reached 1000 ft. in length—releasing floodwaters into the Lower Ninth Ward with such a force that homes were pushed completely off their foundations and carried several blocks from where they once stood (Levees.org).

Industrial Canal Levee Breach, "Katrina NOLA levee break FEMA." Licensed under Public Domain via Wikimedia Commons 38

THERE WERE STILL PEOPLE IN THEIR HOMES WHEN THIS BREACH occurred. In an attempt to escape the floodwaters, many had climbed into their attics thinking the height would keep them safe from the rising water. Unfortunately, as seen on news reports in the days following the storm, floodwaters surpassed the height of attic spaces, completely sub-merging homes. Some families and individuals were able to escape the rising waters either by breaking through the rooftops or seeking refuge on top of nearby homes. In the days that followed, those who had not per-ished in the flooding had to endure prolonged exposure to the extreme Louisiana summer heat as well as a lack of food and fresh drinking water. Livelihoods, as well as many lives, were lost.

While there were individuals who decided to ride out Katrina as they had probably done through storms many times before, there were very real constraints on people's ability to evacuate. For far too many, the deci-sion to stay or leave was largely made for them. These were mostly disad-vantaged people, such as the elderly, the sick, and the poor. In the Lower Ninth Ward, the elderly accounted for 13 percent of the population, with

---

38   Retrieved from https://commons.wikimedia.org/wiki/File:Katrina_NOLA_levee_break_FEMA.jpg#/media/File:Katrina_NOLA_levee_break_FEMA.jpg

31 percent living alone. Thirty-three percent of the population did not even have access to a vehicle (GNODC). Without a city-assisted evacuation plan in place, these people were left with few options. Katrina also arrived at a time of the month when many were left with very little cash to spare. Since many large expenses, such as rent, had already been paid, groceries had been bought, and other bills due had already reached their due dates, the end of the month leaves little room for extra expenses. Having enough savings to cover an impromptu evacuation for a few days, let alone an indefinite amount of time, can be nearly impossible, especially for those with low or on fixed incomes.

How it Happened

IT IS WIDELY KNOWN THAT THE LEVEE BREACHES IN NEW ORLEANS EXACerbated the Katrina catastrophe. The communities closest to the poorly maintained floodwalls and levees bore the brunt of this devastation. The Lower Ninth Ward knew this truth all too well as it had suffered Hurricane Betsy's wrath forty years earlier. And yet again, it experienced the greatest devastation as a result of its proximity to the Industrial Canal.

Katrina's storm surge was funneled through several manmade waterways before it reached the Lower Ninth Ward- the Inner Harbor Navigational Canal (Industrial Canal), the Gulf Intracoastal Waterway (GIWW), and the Mississippi River Gulf Outlet (MRGO). Created in 1923, the Industrial Canal was the first of these waterways to be built. The five and a half mile long canal system, designed to allow large ships access to wharves on the Mississippi, connected Lake Pontchartrain to the Mississippi River by severing the Ninth Ward in two. In fact, it wasn't until its construction did people start making the distinction between the Upper and Lower Ninth Ward. Next was the GIWW, completed in 1946 as a section of the larger Intracoastal Waterway that runs from the Florida panhandle to the southern tip of Texas. MRGO is a shipping canal shortcut between New Orleans and the Gulf of Mexico, completed in 1965 with the arrival of Hurricane Betsy. With the creation of MRGO, saltwater from the Gulf began feeding into the Bayou Bienvenue Wetland Triangle—the only remaining cypress swamp of a former grand Mississippi River Delta swamp that borders the top of the Lower Ninth Ward. The salt-water contamination effectively killed all of the freshwater wildlife in addition to the densely populated cypress forest, which had served as a buffer for the surrounding communities during storms over the years.

Together, these three manmade waterways functioned as shipping routes to allow easier access to the New Orleans port industry. Unfortunately, at the time of Katrina, they funneled the storm surge to the city's most vulnerable areas. Katrina's waters first entered MRGO leading into the GIWW and then, with the convergence of water from Lake Pontchartrain, into the much narrower Industrial Canal before overwhelming the levees and releasing the water into the Lower Ninth Ward. MRGO has since been closed off by a rock dam, which has dramatically reduced the amount of Gulf water able to enter the bayou, lessening the chance of a future storm following the same path.

Aftermath

A REPORT RELEASED BY THE U.S DEPARTMENT OF HOUSING AND URBAN Development estimating the damage to areas affected by Hurricanes Katrina, Rita, and Wilma in terms of housing unit damage illustrates the ruin Lower Ninth Ward residents would find once the floodwaters receded. The report ranked damage levels into three categories: Minor Damage, Major Damage, and Severe/Destroyed. Of the 6,138 occupied homes counted in the 2000 census in the Lower Ninth Ward, 82% percent of them were deemed "Severe/Destroyed" in this analysis, meaning that either 50 percent of the home was damaged or the damage estimates totaled at least $30,000.[39] Not only homes, but also schools, churches, and local businesses, were all but physically washed away. Jackson Barracks, where nearly 400 residual personnel rode out the storm, was also mostly destroyed. The facility, which is the last structure before the parish line, took on as much as 20 feet of water in some places as a result of the levee breach and flooding from St. Bernard Parish (NY Times, 2005).

39 Current Housing Unit Damage Estimates Hurricanes Katrina, Rita, and Wilma. February 12, 2006. Data from FEMA Individual Assistance Registrants and Small Business Administration Disaster Loan Applications. Analysis by the U.S. Department of Housing and Urban Development's Office of Policy Development and Research.

Critics will argue that New Orleans is doomed by its geography even though half of the city sits at or above sea level. The Lower Ninth Ward is also not entirely below sea level, and its elevation is not the reason it laid in ruins on August 29th (nor is its name an indicator of its elevation but rather telling of its location down the Mississippi River). Regardless, almost immediately, talks about whether or not to rebuild the Lower Ninth Ward began. It had been so badly flooded that officials questioned if it were not a safer option to allow most of the area to return to nature. These conversations infuriated residents who argued that neighborhoods with similar damage were not brought into the conversation. New Orleans and its Lower Ninth Ward are similar to many cities in the U.S. built in close relationship with the water around it. Over half of the U.S. population lives in counties protected by levees (FEMA, 2009). Many residents felt that politicians were using this as an opportunity to rid New Orleans of this predominantly poor, black community.

Recovery

NEARING A DECADE SINCE HURRICANE KATRINA TOOK ITS TOLL, THE Lower Ninth Ward looks as if it is only in the primary stages of recovery. There have been efforts made in the neighborhood. Actor and philanthropist Brad Pitt dedicated 150 green homes through his Make It Right Foundation in the area of the Lower Ninth Ward nearest to the levee breaches where homes were completely inundated or washed away. Today, 100 of them stand. Global Green USA, an environmental nonprofit, also built five energy-efficient homes in Holy Cross- four are residential and the fifth operates as a visitors' center. Despite these and the efforts of many other groups and organizations over the years, much of the area remains quite desolate, especially above Claiborne Avenue.

The most recent population estimates gauge return to the Lower Ninth Ward at just 48 percent of its June 2005 population, far behind the city's 89.3 percent (GNODC). Even areas that experienced similar damage to the Lower Ninth Ward, such as New Orleans East, Gentilly, and Lakeview, have come back much stronger.

Table 9.1
Comparing the New Orleans Most Damaged Communities

PLAN-NING DISTRICT	% BLACK (2000)	% WHITE (2000)	% ASIAN (2000)	% HIS-PANIC (2000)	LIVING BELOW THE POV-ERTY LINE (2000)	HOUS-ING UNITS: 2000 CENSUS	MAJOR DAMAGE	SEVERE / DESTROYED	POPU-LATION RECOV-ERY SINCE JUNE 2005
Orleans Parish	66.6%	Asian (2000)	% His-panic (2000)	3.1%	27.9%	188,251	26,345	78,810	89.3%
New Orleans East	86%	10%	1%	2%	19%	26,437	5,084	19,692	83%
Village de L'est	55.4%	3.6%	37.1%	2.4%	29.9%	3,290	697	2,559	72%
Gentilly	69%	25%	1%	3%	15%	16,096	1,690	11,356	84%
Lakeview	2%	91%	1%	4%	6%	10,978	1,334	7,214	86%
Lower Ninth Ward	95%	3%	0.06%	1%	34%	6,138	858	4,679	48%

Of those who have begun repopulating the Lower Ninth Ward, more people are found to be settling in the neighborhood of Holy Cross. Because it is located near the Mississippi River, its higher elevation and overall distance from the breach site helped the homes in this neighborhood since they were not as severely damaged. The low priced historic New Orleans-style shotgun and bungalow homes also make it appealing for real estate investors and individuals who can restore the properties and either sell them or avoid the high costs of homes elsewhere in the city. However, you can easily still find remnants of Katrina down every block with overgrown and abandoned homes that still bear the infamous Xs left by search and rescue teams.

As you near the section of the neighborhood that was most heavily impacted by the flooding, homes become very scarce. Apart from the Make It right Houses, which sit in a cluster near the base of the Claiborne Avenue Bridge, the surrounding blocks remain mostly desolate. Weeds and brush have overtaken many homes and even entire streets. Concrete steps and slabs that mark where homes once stood can still be found scattered throughout the area.

The Lower Ninth Ward has not only recovered at a dramatically slow pace in terms of population but also regarding access to services and basic amenities. Martin Luther King Jr. Charter was the first school to be reopened in the Lower Ninth Ward in June 2007- nearly three years after the storm. The school currently teaches pre-kindergarten through the 12th grade. The only other active school in the area today is St. David Catholic School, which opened in June 2014 and operates as a Total Community Action Head Start for children aged three to five. There is a new school under construction on the former site of Alfred Lawless High School, which was destroyed in the storm. This school will be Dr. Martin Luther King Jr. High School and is planned to house the 9th through 12th graders of the current Dr. King Charter. The school is anticipated to be complete before the end of 2015.

In November of 2010, the headquarters of the Louisiana National Guard finally returned to their post at Jackson Barracks, which totaled $325 million to restore. And taking over nine years, it was in the last quarter of 2014 that the Lower Ninth Ward had a fire station return to the area. Also recently opened, as of May 29th, 2015, was the $20.5 million Andrew P. Sanchez & Copelin-Byrd Multi-Service Center. The Multi-Service Center brings back more amenities than the area has seen in almost ten years, equipped with valuable services such as a NOPD substation, health clinic, and senior center.

"Historically, the Andrew Pete Sanchez Center served as an anchor for the community, and provided a one-stop shop offering a variety of services to the residents of the Lower Ninth Ward -- senior activities, healthcare, and daycare for preschoolers. This new center will be all that and more, providing a state-of-the-art building with state-of-the-art amenities."- District E City Councilmember James A. Gray II

Only as the ten year mark of Hurricane Katrina approaches is the Lower Ninth Ward seeing the return of these vital services. And the area continues to lack many other important features that stifle the growth of the community, such as banks, grocery stores, and business services. The Lower Ninth Ward is cut off from the rest of New Orleans by the Industrial Canal, which means that in order to reach these other services the residents must cross one of three drawbridges or travel into St. Bernard Parish.

Impediments

IN LOUISIANA, THE FEDERAL ASSISTANCE PROGRAM, ROAD HOME, created to put money in the hands of homeowners, became infamous for its inability to provide fair assistance. "State-wide, it was reported that the average Road Home applicant fell about $35,000 short of the money needed to rebuild their home, with highly flooded, historically African-American communities particularly impacted. The result has been a complete lack of redevelopment of specific communities and neighborhoods like the Lower Ninth Ward"(Un-Natural Disaster: Human Rights in the Gulf Coast, Amnesty International). It is estimated that the funding gap for Lower Ninth Ward residents averaged $75,400 (GNOCDC).

The Louisiana Road Home Program

IN AUGUST 2006, THE LARGEST SINGLE U.S. HOUSING RECOVERY PROGRAM ever created opened in Louisiana. A product of the Louisiana Recovery Authority (LRA) and the Office of Community Development, the Louisiana Road Home Program was created to provide financial assistance to Louisiana homeowners whose properties had sustained damage during Hurricanes Katrina or Rita. The program's "goal" was to return as many displaced Louisiana residents home "as quickly and fairly as possible" (Road Home FAQ, 2007).

There were two major Road Home housing programs: a program for Homeowner Assistance and a Small Rental Property program. The Homeowner Assistance program was designed to grant up to $150,000 to homeowners who wished to rebuild their storm-damaged properties. It would also provide compensation for those who wished to sell their properties and move elsewhere. If homeowners elected to move out of Louisiana, they would receive 40 percent less than if they were moving elsewhere within the state (Finger, 2008).

The Small Rental Property program was created to encourage landlords of small-scale rental units to repair their buildings so that they could add to the low to middle-income rental market. The idea was that forgivable loans would be made to these landlords if they agreed to provide affordable housing for low- to middle-income families and individuals. These grants were competitive and awarded based on a landowner's ability to meet certain criteria that would make them a viable candidate to supply affordable housing.

Road Home was created specifically for and by the state of Louisiana for its residents. In June 2006, the program was contracted out to a private Virginia based consulting and technology services firm, ICF International. With LRA oversight, ICF's job was to administer Road Home—a task that no other had ever come close to in ICF's history. For 37 years, ICF International operated as a private entity. Once the company secured the $756 million contract from the State of Louisiana, it stepped into the public market by issuing its first IPO—resulting in soaring revenues as well as profits. Within the first two years, gross profits nearly tripled, and, furthermore, a large bonus of $1.5 million was awarded to ICF's CEO. ICF's contract was subsequently granted an additional $156 million in December of the same year notwithstanding its poor performance during Road Home's first year.

The initial scope of the program, while mammoth in comparison to any other undertaking of its kind, was ill-equipped to meet the needs of Louisiana residents. Program funding was vastly underwhelming since it intended to fund only 123,000 applications throughout the state with $7.5 billion allocated to the program. By July 27, 2007, just one week before the initial application due date of July 31st, 167,934 applications were received; this further demonstrated the shortsightedness as well as insufficiencies in estimating grants to only 123,000 applicants.

In all, Road Home received 229,432 applications of which 148,493 were eligible to receive Road Home funds. The 80,939 that were ineligible included those that had occupancy/ownership disputes, no first appointment, were made ineligible by FEMA assessment, sold their home, or were tangled in title/heirship issues (and nearly half, 39,670, were duplicate applications). As of April 2015, 130,038 homeowners had received their Road Home payments with disbursements totaling just over $9 billion. Excluding grant amounts of zero, which accounted for 14,507 eligible applicants, payments averaged $69,210 (Louisiana Office of Community Development, 2015).

There were innumerable failings in the program: fast deadlines, continual changes of the rules and regulations, errors in insurance deductions, lack of transparency, and many others, but perhaps the biggest of all was its method of valuing grant awards. Instead of simply assessing the cost of rebuilding and distributing funds that would cover that amount (less insurance and other assistance payouts), the program compared the pre-storm value of homes to the actual cost of rebuilding and chose the lower of the two estimations. Not surprisingly, this method significantly disadvantaged people that lived in low-income neighborhoods since home values were depreciated much lower than in wealthier neighborhoods, even if the size and condition of the home were very similar. This meant that in higher income neighborhoods, the cost to rebuild would often times be lower than a home's pre-storm value, meaning that the payout would be sufficient for homeowners to rebuild because it would guarantee the actual cost of rebuilding. In lower income neighborhoods pre storm, in contrast, value was many times much lower, due to the home's location, than the cost to rebuild, resulting in payments that were insufficient.

The discriminatory nature of the Road Home program's grant evaluation process eventually led to a class action lawsuit. On November 12, 2008, the Greater New Orleans Fair Housing Action Center and the National Fair Housing Alliance (NFHA), along with five African American homeowners representing more than 20,000 African American homeowners in New Orleans, filed a lawsuit against the LRA and the U.S. Department of Housing and Urban Development. They argued that the formula Louisiana's Road Home program used to determine grant amounts racially discriminated against New Orleans African American homeowners.

"Forty years after the passage of the federal Fair Housing Act, residential segregation still permeates New Orleans," said James Perry, executive director of the Greater New Orleans Fair Housing Action Center. "Homes in communities of color still have lower values than those in white communities even when the condition, style and quality of the homes are comparable. Louisiana's program builds on this history of discrimination. Only when housing opportunities are created for all residents of New Orleans will our recovery truly be successful." (GNOF-HAC Press Release, 2008)

On June 6, 2011, a settlement was finally reached in which the LRA and Department of Housing and Urban Development agreed to pay up to $62 million in supplemental rebuilding grants.

"Finally, we have a decision to make more people whole. The settlement represents progress on this issue, but more must be done to assist homeowners impacted by Hurricane Katrina. Unfortunately, for some storm survivors, this decision is too little too late."- Congressman Cedric L. Richmond (LA-02) (Press Release, 2011)

There were countless difficulties residents of the entire Katrina affected area faced in their recovery. Some of these obstacles included insurance agencies, mortgage lenders, and contractors who saw desperate storm victims as easy prey. In New Orleans, for example, there were 1,159 complaints of contractor fraud filed with the Better Business Bureau between September 2005 and August 2007. During the same period, more than 6,000 were filed with the Attorney General's office compared to 150 the office had averaged annually before Katrina. Unfortunately, "Louisiana's Attorney General only handled as criminal matters cases in which money was received but no work was done. Such cases accounted for about 700 of the 6,000 complaints it received from consumers (Jurgens, 2008)." The remaining cases in which contractors failed to finish a project, did shoddy work, or likely both, could not be charged criminally. Too many also encountered insurance agencies that were unwilling to pay claims. Mortgage lenders further took advantage of homeowners by forcing them to pay their balances off with funds they received from insurance and/or other assistance programs. Many disadvantaged neighborhoods, such as the Lower Ninth Ward, lacked the resources to combat these wrongdoings, resulting in detrimental effects for the community's recovery.

Continuing Efforts

As evident in the case of the Lower Ninth Ward, New Orleans' recovery has not affected communities proportionately. In Katrina's aftermath, the Lower Ninth Ward became the focus of the media frenzy, but that attention did little to help the victims once the floodwaters disappeared. Today, the Lower Ninth Ward continues to be painted as a community that has been mostly forgotten. While the neighborhoods here may only be a fraction of what they once were, and many people have been forced to rebuild their lives elsewhere, those who have fought their way back over the last ten years remain determined in reviving their beloved community.

CHAPTER 10

Hell and High Water

Michael Marks

"Our nation was stunned by the events that unfolded post-Katrina in Mississippi and Louisiana. The destruction of entire towns in Mississippi and the flooding of New Orleans was almost biblical in scope. While people from around the country were quick to open their homes, hearts and wallets to give emotional, physical and financial support, we were all shocked by the dysfunction of our own government and a president who seemed almost oblivious to the epic proportions of this disaster."

—Michael Marks and Mackenzie Westmoreland.

I REMEMBER LANDING AT THE JACKSON, MS AIRPORT ON THE LAST FLIGHT into Mississippi before the facility was ordered to shut down. I flew in from Washington, D.C., where as a national officer for the National Education Association I was attending a meeting with our national board of directors. Everyone kept asking, "You say you have to leave because it is raining?" Folks from above the Mason-Dixie Line couldn't possibly understand. Snow and ice, yes. Hurricanes, no. Even folks who knew how to deal with hurricanes didn't know what to expect with this one.

As far as the eye could see, thousands of cars, bumper to bumper, lined Highway 49, headed towards the state capital, Jackson. In the lanes headed south, just me. I stopped at a store in Magee, half way to Hattiesburg. Not a battery, loaf of bread, water... nothing. The cupboards were bare. I finally made it home and inspected my new laundry room. I called to thank Billy for building it while I was in DC. I could still smell the paint drying on the new addition to 2003 Adeline Street. All was calm on "The Avenues," as they call this beautiful oak tree-lined section of The Hub City.

Since my car was in the shop (I loaned it to my best friend Mackenzie, and he hit a deer going down Bloody 98 toward Perry County), my garage was empty. The Finlow Family across the street had relatives that evacuated from Metairie, Louisiana, and they asked if they could park their brand new SUVs under my garage. Friends of mine dropped by to plan a hurricane party. After all, the local weather was always wrong about hurricanes in Hattiesburg. They never amounted to anything but a good party. We knew it would be bad for the Mississippi coast, but we were 60 miles inland, right?

I called my mom in Magnolia and begged her to leave with Cousin Rolfe as he headed to Jackson. I tried to explain to her that this was going to be really bad and that she need to leave. Her reply to me was, "The Good Lord will determine how bad it will be and when I need to leave." So at 4 am the next morning, my cousins had to drive back from Jackson to Magnolia to pick Mom up who was finally convinced that the weather might be "a little rough." Now, what could have been an hour and a half trip of 86 miles from Pike County to Hinds County had become a 14 hour journey of bumper to bumper traffic, complete with looters, robbers, and vandals preying on stranded cars along the way. Did I mention that my mother had $40,000 in cash in her purse? Finally, she made it to my cousin's three-bedroom home in Jackson where she would spend the next five days with eighteen people.

That morning, you could feel the stillness in the air. As the rain bands moved in, there was the feeling that something was not quite right. Then all hell broke loose. I opened my side door to assess the situation, and all I could see was the air swirling. I was looking dead into the middle of a tornado spawned by the hurricane. That's when the first of four trees crashed through my living room, missing Keith, who had come over for the hurricane party, by four inches as he jumped to safety. We ran to the opposite end of the house only to hear that awful cracking sound again. Tree number two took out the newly built laundry room. Tree number three settled to demolish the two new SUV's in the garage. Tree number four decorated the back corner of the house and backyard.

The last telephone call that I remember was from a neighbor, Sidney, a retired professor from Kansas who had absolutely no experience with hurricanes. He was pinned in by a tree in his kitchen so we went to help him. He would end up spending a couple of days in my house. I thought he was going to have a heart attack. Finally, I calmed him down enough to make a plan for when the storm passed, if we survived.

Katrina made Adeline Street in Hattiesburg, MS resemble a war zone.

When Katrina had passed, we went outside. I felt like Sidney was not the only one not in Kansas anymore. We all knew the world had changed forever. Adeline Street looked like a war zone. It was the worst hit area in Hattiesburg. Slowly but surely we had to check on neighbors to make sure that there were no medical needs. It would be awhile before cars could get in and out or before the Finlow crew arrived with chain saws to cut the first tree in half. Once we knew everyone was ok and there were no casualties or immediate medical needs that we could tell, it was exciting … in the sense that you were experiencing something that you have never felt before. That's when the real hurricane party started. There were cookouts. I felt like Hoke Colburn, a character I played many times in the Alfred Uhry stage play *Driving Miss Daisy*. During the ice storm, Daisy would always say to Hoke, "Eat all you want. It's all going to ruin anyway." Daisy was right. You had to cook everything in your freezer in the next couple of days because it was all going to spoil. For a time, cooking out with friends, no meetings to attend, no school … it was a made-to-order vacation!

We hiked as far as we could to see what the rest of the city looked like. It was awful. You felt like a passerby looking at a wreck. You want to look away but you just can't. I hiked a mile to get to the only known working phone to call the folks back at NEA and let them know that I was alright. When I spoke to the operator, she told me that President Weaver was in a conference but if I left my number he would call me back immediately. Little did she know. Cell phones lasted for a little while but then batteries faded. We began that ritual of asking our neighbors, "Who have you heard from and are they alright?"

Then reality set in. It was over a hundred degrees in The Pine Belt, and there was no air conditioning. I lost most of my windows and a couple of doors. Flies and mosquitoes loomed large. Tempers rose. I laid a country cussing on Keith when he gave his dog my last bottle of water. Another friend, Chamberlan, came by to check on me and brought his dog to what was left of my house. He, too, was cussed severely. Everybody knows I don't like dogs. I told him, "I may not have much left in this world, but I'll be damned if I'm going to share it with a dog." He apologized. So did I. We calmed down. How many candles do I own? How many matches? Thank goodness Sidney has a pool next door. We can't get in his house, but we can at least get water to flush toilets. My buddy Scott rode his bicycle all the way from neighboring Petal, MS and brought barbecue chicken, the first real food I had since the cookouts. This is friendship.

Life was not easy. No electricity for three weeks. No water for three weeks. Finally, after cell service returned, I was able to call my insurance agent, who gave me instructions on what to do before the adjuster came to write up the damage claim. Imagine my surprise when she finally arrived. A sophomore at the University of Iowa. Blonde. Blue-eyed. She fit the description: Nice house. Nobody home. Storm Trooper Barbie wrote my house damage up, and the sum total she recommended that I receive from State Farm was $22,000. I went from a $130,000, ten-room house to having two bedrooms and a kitchen left and she recommends $22,000? I paid $5,000 for the new laundry room alone. I knew then I was in for a rough haul. Over the next year things would get worse. Thanks to educator liability insurance, I had a team of the best attorneys who could plead my case. My case fell on deaf ears. There was an industry decision made. Insurance companies were not going to pay. I guess if Mississippi Senator Trent Lott couldn't save his house, I had little reason to believe that I could help mine.

State Farm sent me a check for $22,000. I had instructions to sign it and send it to the mortgage company for a co-signature and then I could cash it and try to put my house and life back together. I kept personal logs. I made over 152 calls to my mortgage company, who refused to send the check back. Each time their operative would say, "I'm going to forward you to your own personal claims agent to better assist you."

I would respond by saying, "You are lying. You and I both know that I will go to a recording and no one will ever reach out to me from your company. May I have your name and title to document this call, please?" Teachers always keep good records.

Finally, I was able to break through to a company vice-president in California. I told her my story (for the umpteenth time). I told her that I had negotiated with the insurance company in good faith and believed that her company would reciprocate by sending me the check that was rightfully mine. Then I got a little more inventive. Teachers always have a backup lesson plan. I told her that I had written a stage play about my hurricane experience; that my theatre students at Hattiesburg High School, in the days after the Category 5 storm, had gone to the coast, Mobile, and their own neighborhoods and recorded the experiences of those who suffered mental and physical losses during Hurricane Katrina.

I told her that my debaters had been trained by The Center for Oral History and Cultural Heritage at The University of Southern Mississippi and that the script of the play, in tectonic theatre fashion, was born from those interviews. I told her that I was expecting an on-air interview with CNN the next day to promote the docudrama that would be staged in Orlando, Florida the next week. I hinted that I would expose her company for fraud on national television. Ok, so I lied about the CNN part … but we did open in Orlando, Philadelphia, Boston, and Dallas. In fact, Senator Lott's office, thanks to a former debater turned Chief of Staff, arranged for a command performance for Congress in Washington, D.C. And I got my check, Federal Express, the next day.

The play that I co-wrote with Mackenzie Westmoreland traveled the nation and to date has generated over $300,000 in relief monies to disaster victims. This August, ten years after Katrina, with the help of Just Over the Rainbow Theatre (how appropriate is that title?!) and Hattiesburg Public School District, I have staged a revival production. According to the rights and royalties agreement that I negotiated with Playscripts, Inc., every performance of the play generates dollars for disaster victims. I have networked with theatre educators in Australia, Canada, Scotland, Great Britain… all performing The Katrina Project: Hell and High Water. And, of course, the show continues to be performed here in the U.S. as well. Yesterday, I spoke with a gentleman who is going up with the show at The University of Kentucky.

X Factor Finalist Greg Spencer of Collins, MS plays the role of Kanye West in the revival of The Katrina Project. Here he sings "Wade in the Water."

Life is not always easy. I spent all of my savings as a 30-year educator to rebuild my house. I got passed to the fourth mortgage company after Katrina when I was informed that my new mortgage rate would be $3,000 a month. $3,000 a month? In Hattiesburg, MS? On The Avenues? I got a plain white envelope from my desk drawer, enclosed the house key, and mailed it to them. My next call was to Chamberlan—remember the dog? He said of course he had a great apartment that was ready for his old debate coach. Things were looking better. A fresh start might not be so bad.

I was lucky. No one in the family hurt. Nothing that was irreplaceable was lost. My favorite upright piano was a casualty, but I found a great deal on a baby grand that was being replaced by a local church. Life goes on. Ten years later, I have come full circle. Once again, life lessons are taught by the play.

The tragic aftermath of Hurricane Katrina has profoundly challenged our nation. But in the face of adversity, the people of the Gulf Coast—and all Americans—are coming together as we have so many times before. The American spirit is at work—and despite unimaginable losses, amazing progress is being made. Community by community. Block by block. Neighbor by neighbor.

Indeed, in these days following Katrina, our community spirit shines its brightest. The determined, roll-up-your-sleeves commitment of so many sustains our hope. And hope is central to rebuilding this special place we call home.

Once everyone realized that I was quite serious about writing a production about life on the Gulf Coast during the Category 5 Hurricane, Hattiesburg High School's (HHS) Forensics Department became immersed in the play of a docudrama that would prove to be both educational and therapeutic. In addition, our hope was to generate dollars for the hurricane relief effort.

The first step in the project, the collection of stories, began immediately after the storm. While schools were struggling to reopen, HHS thespians interviewed evacuees and those whose lives had been impacted by the storm. With the cooperation of The University of Southern Mississippi's Department of Oral History and Cultural Heritage, our students were trained on interview techniques for oral history. The collected data, both scientific and anecdotal, is currently housed in a permanent collection at Southern Miss.

Ultimately, Hurricane Katrina will make us stronger as a region—bringing us together as neighbors to respond, restore, and rebuild. Bob Jones High School's Technical Theatre Department exemplifies the generosity that was extended to our region from all across the country. When we were challenged for materials and labor as a result of Katrina's impact on the local economy, Dwayne Craft and his technical theatre students offered their assistance during the 2005 run of the play. For that, and other random acts of kindness, we are grateful.

I've always said that theatre should entertain but that it has a deeper obligation to educate as well. This was a teachable moment that I could not pass up. For my students—many who suffered tragic personal losses—it was an opportunity to develop courage, grit, and determination as we became a lighthouse for schools south of Hattiesburg. We delivered food, consumable supplies, and provided cleanup services. For our community, it was a chance to heal.

Tectonic theater's mission is twofold: (1) to examine the subject at hand, and (2) to explore theatrical language and form. Hearing the stories of the people who survived Katrina has been a real lesson in sadness and revelation. Transferring those emotions to the stage, we have learned even more about ourselves, our ideas, and about our nation. In the play, there is a character who describes the power of the storm. I agree with her words: "It was both terrifying and beautiful at the same time."

Life has been hard since Hurricane Katrina. Imagine functioning with no house, no credit, no nothing and trying to remain optimistic. Did I mention that I was unemployed for three years? I went from being national teacher of the year to not being able to get a job at the local Head Start Program. We remain optimistic because we know that life is not about houses and cars and all the other things that you can buy with sufficient cash. Rather, it is about that indomitable spirit of humanity, that optimism that makes us believe that we "can do." And it is about friends who come to see about you. Even if they insist that you must love dogs. Ugh, nobody deserves hell and high water.

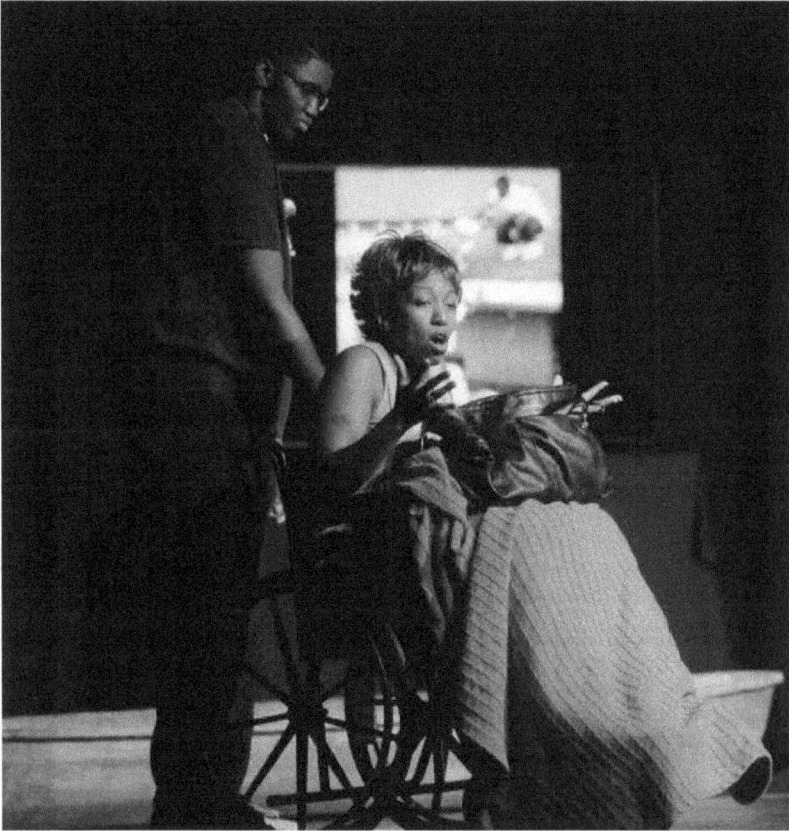

Hattiesburg High School Debater Ben Parker and Bay Springs High School Principal Kesia Pope play a delivery room physician and a woman who swam through raw sewage in order to deliver her child in a hospital in the docudrama.

CHAPTER 11

Spirit

"They spent their money, and the time to come do this. They didn't have to do this. They didn't have to do that. But that's so indicative of so many people. ...I guess what really stands out is the spirit. ...there was no bickering. There was no fighting. Everybody was pulling the same direction. Everyone was trying to get to the place where we used to be. ..."

—Hattiesburg Mayor Johnny DuPree (August 1, 2006)

THE PEOPLE AND COMMUNITIES IMPACTED BY SUCH A LARGE DISASTER have made uneven but tremendous progress in rebuilding their shattered cities. Ten years after the devastation of Katrina wrecked the lives and communities along the Gulf Coast, the area is growing again. The heroism shown by many, some interviewed for this book, and the resiliency of one the most colorful areas of the United States is a testament to the hope we share for a brighter future and the gratefulness for the grace to have survived to help make that future.

Many factors came together to make Hurricane Katrina a killer storm: the reorganization and budget reductions of FEMA; the reorganization and budget reductions of the Army Corp of Engineers who helped maintain the levees of the New Orleans area; the lack of coordinated command, control, and pre-positioning of needed aid; complacency about hurricanes from years of close calls and "we did just fine"; and warmer waters in the Gulf of Mexico.

The large size of Katrina meant that an area greater than the United Kingdom would ultimately be devastated, causing the largest diaspora in modern American history. The fact that human institutions and their preparation or lack of preparation meant that this was also a not just a "natural disaster" but one partly made by us. The tens of thousands of businesses and the hundreds of thousands of homes destroyed made this the most expensive disaster to hit the U.S., not including the costs of war. Over one million people were evacuated before the storm. As Lieutenant General Russell Honoré, the commander of military relief in New Orleans and Mississippi stated, "we had over 85 percent of people actually evacuated before the storm, so that was a very good evacuation in terms of the number of people and percentage. The problem is that 20 percent that stayed back was from the vulnerable population" (Honoré, 2010). Although we will probably never have a precise estimate of the number of deaths related to Katrina, the death toll often cited is 1,836, but others have criticized this number as being probably a low ball figure, especially when deaths related to the loss of medicine, proper medical care, water, food, and more in the weeks following landfall are taken into account.

Although the evacuation was relatively successful in getting many people out of harm's way, the large number who stayed behind, often due to not having a clear way out, shows a lack of clear planning and decision-making at the highest levels of government. The Department of Homeland Security, which is the department where FEMA is located, did not effectively preposition assets to ensure that those who needed transportation out of the city beforehand and those who needed to be rescued once the levees had been breeched could be brought to safer ground. Neighbors helped neighbors, strangers offered assistance, and the Coast Guard and numerous pubic officers at the local level risked their lives to save others. Those most able to rely on their own resources often fared the best, not waiting for "official" or federal help that was slow to appear. FEMA and the federal government often became the talk of derision due to their seemingly glacial move to help. This was not a good omen for future disasters that will inevitably strike the U.S.

The truly heartening development in the wake of the storm was the way people helped people, often with those in official positions and those with useful skills (chain-sawing, barbecuing, rescuing, boating, etc.) spending long hours to help bring back their communities. The area was flooded with volunteers from around the country, and aid was offered from all over the globe. Faith-based and all manner of service and volunteer organizations showed up to lend a hand at this crucial time. Betty Press's piercing photo essay shows the devastation and the signs of hope and thankfulness that showed along the coast.

Linda VanZandt's compassion and energy are evident in the way she describes the Vietnamese communities in Biloxi and New Orleans. The hardships the people have overcome have given them a strength not only to weather traumatic events but also a strong community that has time and again been their bulwark. Not only did many of them escape from North Vietnam as a result of war and persecution, they then fled South Vietnam in overcrowded boats to ultimately land on the Gulf Coast where they could ply their fishing skills in a climate similar to their homeland. Many of these people gained employment in the seafood industry as shuckers, laborers, and ultimately as shrimpers with their own boats, and this employment helped the gulf area to grow its reputation for quality seafood. Many of these Vietnamese residents built restaurants and other small businesses anchored in their neighborhoods, relying heavily on clientele from their communities. They then survived another disaster with Hurricane Katrina devastating their homes and livelihoods, followed by the Great Recession and finally, maybe most damaging, the BP Deepwater Horizon oil disaster. Strong religious, family, and community ties helped sustain them during the post-Katrina rebuilding, and they were tested even further when the oil spill ruined the fisheries. Thanks to the vision and perseverance of the younger generation who teamed up with older members in the community, they have created community development agencies and other advocacy groups to wade through the red tape, provide language and legal support, work for their just reparations from BP, and create new employment opportunities. Their efforts to fight for their rights in the oil spill settlement continue to this day, but many felt pressured to accept a meager settlement early on, forfeiting their right to fully recover their losses or pursue any further legal action later. Now they see the BP oil reparation money being used for projects other than directly helping to restore their livelihoods in the seafood industry— projects like a minor league baseball stadium with a view of casino row in Biloxi. Thao Vu, director of the Mississippi Coalition for Vietnamese American Fisherfolk and Families, says, "We should not use funds from a disaster that disproportionately affected fishing communities for a stadium. Neither the governor nor the state agencies made meaningful attempts to reach out to us to ask for our input" (Weldon, 2015). For many Vietnamese Americans on the Gulf Coast, it is the fifth anniversary of the BP oil disaster and the final settlement news that overshadows the tenth anniversary of Hurricane Katrina, but they have learned that votes matter and their bonds of community will probably once again land them on solid ground.

There was looting and other crime that happened after Katrina, but often what actually happened was much less than the rumors portrayed. People secured food, water, and other necessities from damaged stores unlikely in many cases to actually be useable once the crisis was over. The perception of crime was probably much higher because people were thrown together with others they did not normally know, and people who survived the storm were tired, hungry, and scared, susceptible to rumor and panic.

After the storm, many people had moved out of the direct path of the storm to all 50 states. Orleans Parish saw the greatest drop in population, and the majority of the displaced were African-Americans. New Orleans has seen a growth in population since 2006 of over 80 percent, but the population is still not back to pre-storm levels. The Mississippi coast, which saw a smaller displacement after the storm, has a higher population than it had in 2004. Settlement, especially along the Mississippi coast, has tended away from areas that are prone to flooding. The Hispanic population has seen strong double-digit growth in all areas on the coast and in New Orleans, and often they came to help in the reconstruction.

The growth in the area's income after 2006 has been impressive. Even when comparing the latest figures to 2004, a year before the storm, the coastal areas are ahead and New Orleans is close to where it was in 2004. Real median household income, which has trended down for the nation as a whole over the years 2004 to 2014 due to the aftermath of the Great Recession, shows up with a negative trend for Mississippi and one of its coastal counties, but New Orleans showed a strong 11 percent gain. New Orleans, with a one percent decrease in the poverty rate, also bucked the trend in the nation, Mississippi, and Louisiana, with many of those areas seeing a double-digit increase. These areas typically have greater poverty rates than the nation as a whole, and the recession led many to substantially increase their use of the Supplemental Nutrition Assistance Program. The unemployment rate of the Katrina impacted area mimics that of the U.S. as a whole, except for 2005 and 2006. Employment, however, is a tough hurdle to increase given the blows that were sustained with all the coastal counties of Mississippi and New Orleans showing negative growth from 2004 to April 2015. From 2006 to April 2015, though, all these same areas show positive employment growth.

The economies of Louisiana and Mississippi grew at a much slower rate than the U.S. as a whole from 2004 to 2014 (6, 7, and 17 percent respectively). From 2010 to the present, this lower growth may come in part from policies that a number of people believe, including some of the governors' Republican friends, may tend to have slowed the states' economies, such as turning down federal money related to the Affordable Care Act.

Teachers in both states have been trying deal with the storm's effects and the slow growth in state budgets. With the aid of numerous volunteers and committed staff, schools reopened after the storm. Along the Mississippi coast, enrollment numbers and test scores are up, while in New Orleans the number of students is still below past figures and the city has implemented controversial reorganization.

Not unlike other parts of the country, corruption in both Mississippi and Louisiana has had a long history in channeling money into the pockets of politicians, oligopolistic interests, and the friends of politicians, but corruption is probably more endemic in these two states. Numerous questions have arisen given the large amount of money poured into the region. There are signs of "smoke" that are often unseen in sweet heart deals made at the federal, state, and local levels. At the federal level, the amount of money poured into Mississippi compared to Louisiana seemed to have a bias toward the Republican governor at the time, Haley Barbour.

Looking at the banking sector in detail, we found that credit unions (the most common financial institution in the country) and banks mostly survived the storm and have done well. Heroism was found in many cases of employees and managers trying to get their institutions up and running, even to the extreme of handing out cash from the back of a pickup truck, sleeping on floors, and transporting large amounts of cash in their own personal vehicles. A number of smaller credit unions ceased to exist right after the storm in New Orleans. Financial institutions in the area were buffeted not only by the storm, but also by the tribulations brought on by the Great Recession and the concomitant collapse of real estate, and the BP oil spill on fishing and leisure related industries. Consolidation and concentration have continued among institutions, both nationally and in the Katrina impacted area. Credit unions in the area seemed to be impacted by the efforts to gain members through the "Bank Transfer Day" campaign, reflecting gains made nationally as well. Loans, key to getting businesses and individuals back to pre-Katrina functioning, grew at a greater rate for credit unions nationally and in the impacted area. Credit unions, although more numerous, typically smaller, and with less political clout as banks, did not benefit directly from the large bailouts from the federal government given to banks, but they could rely on the assistance of other credit unions and associations that volunteered enormous amounts of time and resources to help the area get back on its feet.

Chapter 7 looked at an industry that is key to survival and regrowth: the electric power industry. This case study of the Mississippi Power Company, like we showed in an earlier chapter about the oligopolistic hold that the insurance companies have in the area, is an example of how concentrated industry control can choke off job growth and recovery. After Katrina, Mississippi Power's workers went the "extra mile" and helped the area get back on its feet. After the storm, however, the status quo power brokers in the state, with the help of expertise from the parent company, the Southern Company, managed to put together an unusual scheme whereby the approximately 186,000 customers in the southern part of the state, which coincidently coincides with where the brunt of Katrina's wrath was felt, were obligated to pay for a new "experimental" lignite coal gasification plant that may never actually become fully operative. The billions of dollars of burden this plant represented may have been perceived by the power brokers in the state and company as way to create construction jobs and increase shareholder value, but many individuals, groups, and businesses have stood up to fight what they perceive as an unfair gouging and constraint of regrowth. The fight over this plant and costs is not over, but the state supreme court of Mississippi has, at the time of this writing, sided with the customers wanting reasonable utility oversight and supports rebating money collected to fund this costly experiment.

David Reynolds recalls the final days of his much loved 1880s home in Bay St. Louis. He details the coming of the storm, with his perception informed by his experience gained in the Coast Guard. Glimpses of the years that followed Katrina lead up to a mostly recovered coastal community, lovely in its renewal. He and his family recently rebuilt there—just a weekend retreat, but they entertain friends once again.

His story soon moves to The Green Project, a sustainable practice business and community nexus between the Marigny and Bywater neighborhoods of New Orleans, at the edge of the Ninth Ward. His humor and compassion for people and community there shine in his prose.

The Green Project started out of concern over leftover paint contaminating landfills intended for solid waste in low lying southeastern Louisiana. What started out from volunteers working to make a sustainable future was a going concern—for over ten years by the time that Katrina struck. The prolonged and strongly successful effort to repair and recover The Green Project illustrates that recognizing community and culture in exceptional times can give the best chance to rejoin people and places in ways that will endure and thrive. Volunteers and NGOs from all over were essential, alongside experienced management at The Green Project, but not always aligned. David adds two initiatives by outside organizations to illustrate some key ingredients in bringing back The Green Project and this area of New Orleans.

This is a story framed around a highly visible and valuable community asset that today provides good jobs, diverse products, and services, functions as a gathering place, and diverts several hundred tons of useful goods and materials away from landfills and into hands that will use and enjoy them.

Even today, as some communities, such as the Lower Ninth Ward outlined in Chapter 9, are still very much on the road to recovery, individuals and service organizations are picking up where the government has failed. One organization in particular is lowernine.org, a volunteer organization that rebuilds homes for pre-storm Lower Ninth Ward residents. The organization was founded in response to the government's inadequate support for residents wanting to rebuild and continues to bring residents back to the community with no sign of quitting. If this is telling of anything, it is that the spirit of the people and their determination is not waning. Despite the slow return of services, overgrown blocks, and pothole-lined streets, which make some roads entirely inaccessible, the residents still seek to reestablish the community they knew before Katrina.

After years of scoffing at hurricanes that came through inland Hattiesburg, Mississippi, Michael Marks met his match in Hurricane Katrina, a storm that was no laughing matter. Catching the last flight back to the Magnolia State from his office in Washington, DC., he arrived in time to ride out the former Category 5 storm in his house. During tornadoes spawned from the storm, four oak trees demolished most of his home, leaving only two bedrooms and the kitchen from his ten-room house. Having been looted twice in this house that now had no windows or doors, he used his life savings to secure his home when insurance refused to pay for the damage. As if life for three weeks without water, electricity, or a car was not hard enough, he was passed from one mortgage company to another until the last one finally announced that his new monthly rate would be almost $3,000. He mailed them the key and never looked back.

His experience and the stories of others worse off than he was are chronicled in his play, *The Katrina Project: Hell and High Water*, a stage production and documentary of what actually happened during and after the storm. Born from actual survivor interviews, Katrina's story was told by his theatre students, cast from Hattiesburg High School. The docudrama traveled the country and even enjoyed a command performance for Congress. The real work, however, was the service mission that accompanied the play—providing goods and help to others. To date, the benefit performances have generated over $300K via worldwide performances. Katrina changed Michael's life forever. He learned that we should never depend wholly on the government. Our real strength lies in the hope and optimism inherent when we work together to fend for ourselves in times of need.

Some places where the storm hit will never be the same. Lives, homes, businesses, and neighborhoods were lost that will never return to exactly the way they were before. The Mississippi coast and New Orleans have a rich tradition to create a future that will hopefully be even more resilient when the next "big one" comes.

APPENDIX A

Tables

Table 4.1

Demographic Profile—Comparing the U.S., Louisiana, Orleans Parish and Mississippi Coastal Counties[40]

VARIABLE	2004	2006	2014	% CHANGE 2004-06	% CHANGE 2004-14	% CHANGE 2006-14
POPULATION						
U.S.	293,389,000	298,930,000	318,857,056	0.02	0.09	0.07
Louisiana	4,552,238	4,302,665	4,649,676	-0.05	0.02	0.08
Orleans Parish	461,702	208,653	384,320	-0.55	-0.17	0.84
Mississippi	2,889,010	2,904,978	2,994,079	0.01	0.04	0.03
Hancock Co.	45,406	38,407	45,949	-0.15	0.01	0.20
Harrison Co.	193,420	171,070	199,058	-0.12	0.03	0.16
Jackson Co.	133,840	127,890	141,137	-0.04	0.05	0.10
ORLEANS PARISH						
White alone	143,223	83,933	135,491	-0.41	-0.05	0.61
Black or African American alone	332,738	135,245	229,813	-0.59	-0.31	0.70
American Indian and Alaska Native alone	1,289	879	1,357	-0.32	0.05	0.54

---

40   Source is the U.S. Census Bureau.

VARIABLE	2004	2006	2014	% CHANGE 2004-06	% CHANGE 2004-14	% CHANGE 2006-14
POPULATION						
Asian alone	11,885	6,842	11,646	-0.42	-0.02	0.70
Native Hawaiian and Other Pacific Islander alone	187	191	305	0.02	0.63	0.60
Two or More Races	4,443	3,082	5,708	-0.31	0.28	0.85
Hispanic	16,825	11,146	21,300	-0.34	0.27	0.91
HANCOCK CO.						
White alone	42,180	35,936	40,331	-0.15		
Black or African American alone	3,259	2,814	3,855	-0.14	0.18	0.37
American Indian and Alaska Native alone	244	241	271	-0.01	0.11	0.12
Asian alone	415	396	526	-0.05	0.27	0.33
Native Hawaiian and Other Pacific Islander alone	18	21	32	0.17	0.78	0.52
Two or More Races	601	679	934	0.13	0.55	0.38
Hispanic	1,163	1,169	1,665	0.01	0.43	0.42
HARRISON CO.						
White alone	143,401	126,952	138,988	-0.11	-0.03	0.09

VARIABLE	2004	2006	2014	% CHANGE 2004-06	% CHANGE 2004-14	% CHANGE 2006-14
POPULATION						
Black or African American alone	42,510	37,975	47,793	-0.11	0.12	0.26
American Indian and Alaska Native alone	1,084	1,051	1,057	-0.03	-0.02	0.01
Asian alone	5,448	4,871	5,941	-0.11	0.09	0.22
Native Hawaiian and Other Pacific Islander alone	232	224	226	-0.03	-0.03	0.01
Two or More Races	3,296	3,376	5,053	0.02	0.53	0.50
Hispanic	7,048	6,959	10,726	-0.01	0.52	0.54
JACKSON CO.						
White alone	101,382	99,263	103,412	-0.02	0.02	0.04
Black or African American alone	28,340	28,435	31,131	0.00	0.10	0.09
American Indian and Alaska Native alone	532	537	635	0.01	0.19	0.18
Asian alone	2,311	2,602	3,239	0.13	0.40	0.24
Native Hawaiian and Other Pacific Islander alone	80	89	132	0.11	0.65	0.48

VARIABLE	2004	2006	2014	% CHANGE 2004-06	% CHANGE 2004-14	% CHANGE 2006-14
POPULATION						
Two or More Races	1,589	1,791	2,588	0.13	0.63	0.45
Hispanic	3,895	4,213	7,793	0.08	1.00	0.85

Table 5.1

Economic Performance—Comparing the U.S., Louisiana, Orleans
Parish and Mississippi Coastal Counties[41]

VARIABLE	2004	2006	2014	% CHANGE 2004-06	% CHANGE 2004-14	% CHANGE 2006-14
REAL TOTAL GROSS PRODUCT (2009 DOLLARS)						
U.S. (billions)	13,950.4	14,716.9	16,294.7	0.05	0.17	0.11
Louisiana (millions)	204,293	211,389	215,968	0.03	0.06	0.02
Orleans Parish	15,941,256	12,956,018	15,421,522	-0.19	-0.03	0.19
Mississippi (millions)	88,614	92,645	94,466	0.05	0.07	0.02
Hancock Co.	1,318,327	1,295,277	1,454,743	-0.02	0.10	0.12
Harrison Co.	6,036,000	6,020,814	6,579,192	-0.00	0.09	0.09
Jackson Co.	3,962,347	4,085,533	4,731,300	0.03	0.19	0.16
REAL MEDIAN HOUSEHOLD INCOME (2009 DOLLARS)						
U.S. (billions)	49,740	51,099	49,021	0.03	-0.01	-0.04
Louisiana (millions)	39,510	41,260	41,500	0.04	0.05	0.01
Orleans Parish	30,690	35,197	34,000	0.15	0.11	-0.03
Mississippi (millions)	38,458	36,507	35,830	-0.05	-0.07	-0.02
Hancock Co.	40,709	42,608	41,158	0.05	0.01	-0.03
Harrison Co.	39,914	44,227	39,082	0.11	-0.02	-0.12
Jackson Co.	45,346	44,962	44,858	-0.01	-0.01	-0.00

41 For "Real Total Gross Product," source is the U.S. Bureau of Economic Analysis.
For the income data in this section, the parish and county figures only run to 2013.
For "Real Medium Household Income," source is the U.S. Census Bureau and figures
only run to 2013.

VARIABLE	2004	2006	2014	% CHANGE 2004-06	% CHANGE 2004-14	% CHANGE 2006-14
ALL AGES IN POVERTY PERCENT						
U.S.	12.7	13.3	15.8	0.05	0.24	0.19
Louisiana	19.2	19.4	20.0	0.01	0.04	0.03
Orleans Parish	27.0	23.7	26.6	-0.12	-0.01	0.12
Mississippi	19.3	20.9	23.9	0.08	0.24	0.14
Hancock Co.	16.6	18.5	20.2	0.11	0.22	0.09
Harrison Co.	16.9	16.0	22.7	-0.05	0.34	0.42
Jackson Co.	15.0	15.8	16.4	0.05	0.09	0.04
SNAP RECIPIENTS (SUPPLEMENTAL NUTRITION ASSISTANCE PROGRAM)						
U.S. (millions)	23.811	26.549	46.536	0.11	0.95	0.75
Louisiana	731,916	644,661	877,340	-0.12	0.20	0.36
Orleans Parish	116,978	32,743.0	78,591	-0.72	-0.33	1.40
Mississippi	379,239	411,647	656,871	0.09	0.73	0.60
Hancock Co.	4,518	3,205	9,322	-0.29	1.06	1.91
Harrison Co.	18,828	17,262	42,350	-0.08	1.25	1.45
Jackson Co.	12,318	10,931	23,984	-0.11	0.95	1.19
ESTABLISHMENTS						
U.S.	8,364,795	8,784,027	9,370,095	0.05	0.12	0.07
Louisiana	115,944	121,568	125,332	0.05	0.08	0.03
Orleans Parish	12,496	11,639	11,332	-0.07	-0.09	-0.03
Mississippi	66,199	68,456	71,233	0.03	0.08	0.04
Hancock Co.	823	736	844	-0.11	0.03	0.15
Harrison Co.	4,537	4,316	4,451	-0.05	-0.02	0.03
Jackson Co.	2,299	2,388	2,384	0.04	0.04	-0.00

VARIABLE	2004	2006	2014	% CHANGE 2004-06	% CHANGE 2004-14	% CHANGE 2006-14
EMPLOYMENT:						
U.S.	129,278,176	133,833,834	136,603,124	0.04	0.06	0.02
Louisiana	1,865,164	1,807,563	1,922,747	-0.03	0.03	0.06
Orleans Parish	247,260	151,931	187,462	-0.39	-0.24	0.23
Mississippi	1,105,915	1,122,474	1,102,294	0.01	0.00	-0.02
Hancock Co.	13,470	11,693	13,021	-0.13	-0.03	0.11
Harrison Co.	89,631	79,241	82,740	-0.12	-0.08	0.04
Jackson Co.	46,995	48,381	49,221	0.03	0.05	0.02
EMPLOYMENT: (RESIDENCE BASED)						
Orleans Parish	185,607	0	167,922	-1.00	-0.10	
Hancock Co.	18,565	18,914	16,926	0.02	-0.09	-0.11
Harrison Co.	87,667	73,988	78,292	-0.16	-0.11	0.06
Jackson Co.	56,625	53,620	54,412	-0.05	-0.04	0.01

Table 5.2

Industry Employment Growth[42]

VARIABLE	2004	2006	2013	% CHANGE 2004-13	% CHANGE 2004-13	% CHANGE 2006-13
UNITED STATES						
Total employment	169,036,700	176,123,600	182,278,200	0.04	0.08	0.03
Wage and salary employment	137,601,000	141,915,000	142,173,000	0.03	0.03	0.00
Proprietors employment	31,435,700	34,208,600	40,105,200	0.09	0.28	0.17
Farm proprietors employment	1,894,000	1,827,000	1,839,000	-0.04	-0.03	0.01
Nonfarm proprietors employment 2/	29,541,700	32,381,600	38,266,200	0.10	0.30	0.18
Farm employment	2,719,000	2,579,000	2,629,000	-0.05	-0.03	0.02
Nonfarm employment	166,317,700	173,544,600	179,649,200	0.04	0.08	0.04
Private nonfarm employment	142,576,700	149,537,600	155,604,200	0.05	0.09	0.04
Forestry, fishing, and related activities	802,500	817,500	902,800	0.02	0.12	0.10
Mining	779,400	930,200	1,607,000	0.19	1.06	0.73
Utilities	575,400	570,700	577,600	-0.01	0.00	0.01
Construction	10,367,600	11,460,900	9,267,400	0.11	-0.11	-0.19
Manufacturing	14,800,900	14,685,200	12,747,100	-0.01	-0.14	-0.13
Wholesale trade	6,188,500	6,489,800	6,343,500	0.05	0.03	-0.02

42   Data from U.S. Bureau of Economic Analysis, total full-time and part-time employment by North American Industry Classification System (NAICS) industry.

VARIABLE	2004	2006	2013	% CHANGE 2004-13	% CHANGE 2004-13	% CHANGE 2006-13
Retail trade	18,385,500	18,845,800	18,371,300	0.03	-0.00	-0.03
Transportation and warehousing	5,427,800	5,761,900	5,998,600	0.06	0.11	0.04
Information	3,553,100	3,546,500	3,254,300	-0.00	-0.08	-0.08
Finance and insurance	8,027,000	8,366,800	9,873,900	0.04	0.23	0.18
Real estate and rental and leasing	6,515,300	7,465,500	7,985,300	0.15	0.23	0.07
Professional, scientific, and technical services	10,688,900	11,331,800	12,453,000	0.06	0.17	0.10
Management of companies and enterprises	1,801,400	1,915,700	2,265,400	0.06	0.26	0.18
Administrative and waste management services	10,182,000	10,805,500	11,325,100	0.06	0.11	0.05
Educational services	3,413,300	3,668,500	4,221,300	0.07	0.24	0.15
Health care and social assistance	16,504,600	17,360,900	20,585,600	0.05	0.25	0.19
Arts, entertainment, and recreation	3,388,700	3,548,400	4,114,500	0.05	0.21	0.16
Accommodation and food services	11,438,800	12,003,200	13,093,400	0.05	0.14	0.09
Other services, except public administration	9,736,000	9,962,800	10,617,100	0.02	0.09	0.07

VARIABLE	2004	2006	2013	% CHANGE 2004-13	% CHANGE 2004-13	% CHANGE 2006-13
Government and government enterprises	23,741,000	24,007,000	24,045,000	0.01	0.01	0.00
Federal, civilian	2,798,000	2,785,000	2,826,000	-0.00	0.01	0.01
Military	2,082,000	2,040,000	2,032,000	-0.02	-0.02	-0.00
State and local	18,861,000	19,182,000	19,187,000	0.02	0.02	0.00
State government	5,092,000	5,148,000	5,260,000	0.01	0.03	0.02
Local government	13,769,000	14,034,000	13,927,000	0.02	0.01	-0.01
LOUISIANA						
Total employment	2,430,744	2,409,153	2,632,302	-0.01	0.08	0.09
Wage and salary employment	2,014,739	1,951,365	2,042,221	-0.03	0.01	0.05
Proprietors employment	416,005	457,788	590,081	0.10	0.42	0.29
Farm proprietors employment	22,945	22,254	22,539	-0.03	-0.02	0.01
Nonfarm proprietors employment 2/	393,060	435,534	567,542	0.11	0.44	0.30
Farm employment	30,638	31,121	28,824	0.02	-0.06	-0.07
Nonfarm employment	2,400,106	2,378,032	2,603,478	-0.01	0.08	0.09
Private nonfarm employment	1,983,342	1,995,272	2,225,438	0.01	0.12	0.12
Forestry, fishing, and related activities	19,289	17,870	18,758	-0.07	-0.03	0.05

VARIABLE	2004	2006	2013	% CHANGE 2004-13	% CHANGE 2004-13	% CHANGE 2006-13
Mining	50,654	57,860	83,177	0.14	0.64	0.44
Utilities	9,961	9,790	9,498	-0.02	-0.05	-0.03
Construction	168,643	195,140	188,175	0.16	0.12	-0.04
Manufacturing	158,611	158,385	153,294	-0.00	-0.03	-0.03
Wholesale trade	81,435	79,318	80,100	-0.03	-0.02	0.01
Retail trade	266,222	263,851	269,567	-0.01	0.01	0.02
Transportation and warehousing	89,449	90,760	99,205	0.01	0.11	0.09
Information	34,746	32,112	31,851	-0.08	-0.08	-0.01
Finance and insurance	87,743	84,976	107,044	-0.03	0.22	0.26
Real estate and rental and leasing	79,151	86,335	105,053	0.09	0.33	0.22
Professional, scientific, and technical services	116,699	123,065	138,540	0.05	0.19	0.13
Management of companies and enterprises	23,084	23,007	28,755	-0.00	0.25	0.25
Administrative and waste management services	129,096	139,518	151,442	0.08	0.17	0.09
Educational services	43,156	40,252	50,808	-0.07	0.18	0.26
Health care and social assistance	243,701	236,627	291,285	-0.03	0.20	0.23
Arts, entertainment, and recreation	53,036	45,944	53,417	-0.13	0.01	0.16

VARIABLE	2004	2006	2013	% CHANGE 2004-13	% CHANGE 2004-13	% CHANGE 2006-13
Accommodation and food services	179,062	166,639	201,215	-0.07	0.12	0.21
Other services, except public administration	149,604	143,823	164,254	-0.04	0.10	0.14
Government and government enterprises	416,764	382,760	378,040	-0.08	-0.09	-0.01
Federal, civilian	34,736	32,422	30,602	-0.07	-0.12	-0.06
Military	41,333	36,303	39,737	-0.12	-0.04	0.09
State and local	340,695	314,035	307,701	-0.08	-0.10	-0.02
State government	116,295	107,225	91,922	-0.08	-0.21	-0.14
Local government	224,400	206,810	215,779	-0.08	-0.04	0.04
ORLEANS PARISH						
Total Employment	312,904	207,976	259,864	-0.34	-0.17	0.25
Wage and salary employment	271,835	169,881	204,853	-0.38	-0.25	0.21
Proprietors employment	41,069	38,095	55,011	-0.07	0.34	0.44
Farm proprietors employment	0	0	0			
Nonfarm proprietors employment 2/	41,069	38,095	55,011	-0.07	0.34	0.44
Farm employment	0	0	0			
Nonfarm employment	312,904	207,976	259,864	-0.34	-0.17	0.25

VARIABLE	2004	2006	2013	% CHANGE 2004-13	% CHANGE 2004-13	% CHANGE 2006-13
Private nonfarm employment	249,902	171,323	217,970	-0.31	-0.13	0.27
Forestry, fishing, and related activities	456	361	492	-0.21	0.08	0.36
Mining	4,757	4,342	3,612	-0.09	-0.24	-0.17
Utilities	1,020	621	291	-0.39	-0.71	-0.53
Construction	8,964	9,323	8,921	0.04	-0.00	-0.04
Manufacturing	8,165	7,305	4,700	-0.11	-0.42	-0.36
Wholesale trade	6,821	4,971	4,199	-0.27	-0.38	-0.16
Retail trade	21,990	12,526	16,188	-0.43	-0.26	0.29
Transportation and warehousing	12,765	9,222	9,674	-0.28	-0.24	0.05
Information	5,930	4,181	5,411	-0.29	-0.09	0.29
Finance and insurance	11,801	8,034	9,503	-0.32	-0.19	0.18
Real estate and rental and leasing	8,889	7,315	10,456	-0.18	0.18	0.43
Professional, scientific, and technical services	20,642	18,699	23,022	-0.09	0.12	0.23
Management of companies and enterprises	4,742	3,152	3,331	-0.34	-0.30	0.06
Administrative and waste management services	20,213	14,387	14,786	-0.29	-0.27	0.03
Educational services	17,155	14,505	19,190	-0.15	0.12	0.32

VARIABLE	2004	2006	2013	% CHANGE 2004-13	% CHANGE 2004-13	% CHANGE 2006-13
Health care and social assistance	30,524	14,359	21,793	-0.53	-0.29	0.52
Arts, entertainment, and recreation	10,936	7,328	9,481	-0.33	-0.13	0.29
Accommodation and food services	37,313	20,772	36,824	-0.44	-0.01	0.77
Other services, except public administration	16,819	9,920	16,096	-0.41	-0.04	0.62
Government and government enterprises	63,002	36,653	41,894	-0.42	-0.34	0.14
Federal, civilian	12,724	9,544	9,137	-0.25	-0.28	-0.04
Military	5,912	3,856	4,051	-0.35	-0.31	0.05
State and local	44,366	23,253	28,706	-0.48	-0.35	0.23
State government	22,118	13,926	13,348	-0.37	-0.40	-0.04
Local government	22,248	9,327	15,358	-0.58	-0.31	0.65
MISSISSIPPI						
Total employment	1,473,046	1,510,572	1,535,589	0.03	0.04	0.02
Wage and salary employment	1,204,364	1,219,001	1,182,655	0.01	-0.02	-0.03
Proprietors employment	268,682	291,571	352,934	0.09	0.31	0.21
Farm proprietors employment	36,637	35,636	33,876	-0.03	-0.08	-0.05

VARIABLE	2004	2006	2013	% CHANGE 2004-13	% CHANGE 2004-13	% CHANGE 2006-13
Nonfarm proprietors employment 2/	232,045	255,935	319,058	0.10	0.37	0.25
Farm employ-ment	44,733	45,329	40,879	0.01	-0.09	-0.10
Nonfarm employment	1,428,313	1,465,243	1,494,710	0.03	0.05	0.02
Private nonfarm em-ployment	1,146,515	1,189,820	1,217,475	0.04	0.06	0.02
Forestry, fishing, and related activ-ities	14,963	14,597	14,505	-0.02	-0.03	-0.01
Mining	8,095	9,548	16,774	0.18	1.07	0.76
Utilities	8,141	8,102	8,182	-0.00	0.01	0.01
Construction	87,515	103,559	90,194	0.18	0.03	-0.13
Manufactur-ing	183,395	179,683	141,999	-0.02	-0.23	-0.21
Wholesale trade	38,797	40,676	38,548	0.05	-0.01	-0.05
Retail trade	168,157	172,596	164,566	0.03	-0.02	-0.05
Transpor-tation and warehousing	50,805	52,778	54,184	0.04	0.07	0.03
Information	17,037	16,306	15,697	-0.04	-0.08	-0.04
Finance and insurance	46,815	48,435	56,870	0.03	0.21	0.17
Real estate and rental and leasing	35,285	40,009	45,744	0.13	0.30	0.14
Professional, scientific, and technical services	51,472	54,449	54,692	0.06	0.06	0.00

VARIABLE	2004	2006	2013	% CHANGE 2004-13	% CHANGE 2004-13	% CHANGE 2006-13
Management of companies and enter-prises	10,400	10,086	11,995	-0.03	0.15	0.19
Administrative and waste management services	64,760	74,615	91,618	0.15	0.41	0.23
Educational services	19,361	21,511	25,512	0.11	0.32	0.19
Health care and social assistance	120,430	126,960	150,975	0.05	0.25	0.19
Arts, enter-tainment, and recreation	19,745	17,955	21,354	-0.09	0.08	0.19
Accommoda-tion and food services	118,854	115,422	121,488	-0.03	0.02	0.05
Other ser-vices, except public admin-istration	82,488	82,533	92,578	0.00	0.12	0.12
Govern-ment and government enterprises	281,798	275,423	277,235	-0.02	-0.02	0.01
Federal, civilian	25,562	26,277	25,524	0.03	-0.00	-0.03
Military	34,466	30,197	29,259	-0.12	-0.15	-0.03
State and local	221,770	218,949	222,452	-0.01	0.00	0.02
State govern-ment	67,930	65,779	66,565	-0.03	-0.02	0.01
Local govern-ment	153,840	153,170	155,887	-0.00	0.01	0.02
HANCOCK COUNTY						
Total employ-ment	22,535	20,764	22,679	-0.08	0.01	0.09

VARIABLE	2004	2006	2013	% CHANGE 2004-13	% CHANGE 2004-13	% CHANGE 2006-13
Wage and salary employment	15,327	13,424	15,324	-0.12	-0.00	0.14
Proprietors employment	7,208	7,340	7,355	0.02	0.02	0.00
Farm proprietors employment	253	244	230	-0.04	-0.09	-0.06
Nonfarm proprietors employment 2/	6,955	7,096	7,125	0.02	0.02	0.00
Farm employment	269	267	248	-0.01	-0.08	-0.07
Nonfarm employment	22,266	20,497	22,431	-0.08	0.01	0.09
Private nonfarm employment	17,912	16,398	17,695	-0.08	-0.01	0.08
Forestry, fishing, and related activities	278	(D)	277		-0.00	
Mining	96	(D)	168		0.75	
Utilities	110	120	202	0.09	0.84	0.68
Construction	2,124	2,704	1,892	0.27	-0.11	-0.30
Manufacturing	1,080	1,133	943	0.05	-0.13	-0.17
Wholesale trade	209	199	235	-0.05	0.12	0.18
Retail trade	2,292	1,975	2,077	-0.14	-0.09	0.05
Transportation and warehousing	501	508	380	0.01	-0.24	-0.25
Information	148	109	94	-0.26	-0.36	-0.14
Finance and insurance	561	507	586	-0.10	0.04	0.16

VARIABLE	2004	2006	2013	% CHANGE 2004-13	% CHANGE 2004-13	% CHANGE 2006-13
Real estate and rental and leasing	1,057	1,061	1,103	0.00	0.04	0.04
Professional, scientific, and technical services	2,133	2,005	2,126	-0.06	-0.00	0.06
Management of companies and enter-prises	(D)	(D)	(D)			
Administrative and waste management services	(D)	(D)	(D)			
Educational services	219	(D)	(D)			
Health care and social assistance	1,100	(D)	(D)			
Arts, enter-tainment, and recreation	528	556	974	0.05	0.84	0.75
Accommoda-tion and food services	2,265	1,129	1,852	-0.50	-0.18	0.64
Other ser-vices, except public admin-istration	1,352	1,196	1,314	-0.12	-0.03	0.10
Govern-ment and government enterprises	4,354	4,099	4,736	-0.06	0.09	0.16
Federal, civilian	1,576	1,795	2,038	0.14	0.29	0.14
Military	567	574	718	0.01	0.27	0.25
State and local	2,211	1,730	1,980	-0.22	-0.10	0.14

VARIABLE	2004	2006	2013	% CHANGE 2004-13	% CHANGE 2004-13	% CHANGE 2006-13
State government	62	59	61	-0.05	-0.02	0.03
Local government	2,149	1,671	1,919	-0.22	-0.11	0.15
HARRISON COUNTY						
Total employment	125,326	112,718	119,662	-0.10	-0.05	0.06
Wage and salary employment	109,304	95,586	98,586	-0.13	-0.10	0.03
Proprietors employment	16,022	17,132	21,076	0.07	0.32	0.23
Farm proprietors employment	342	322	299	-0.06	-0.13	-0.07
Nonfarm proprietors employment 2/	15,680	16,810	20,777	0.07	0.33	0.24
Farm employment	362	358	330	-0.01	-0.09	-0.08
Nonfarm employment	124,964	112,360	119,332	-0.10	-0.05	0.06
Private nonfarm employment	93,935	84,696	91,355	-0.10	-0.03	0.08
Forestry, fishing, and related activities	(D)	(D)	(D)			
Mining	(D)	(D)	(D)			
Utilities	1,293	1,231	884	-0.05	-0.32	-0.28
Construction	6,748	9,648	6,675	0.43	-0.01	-0.31
Manufacturing	4,497	4,433	4,483	-0.01	-0.00	0.01
Wholesale trade	1,987	1,950	1,853	-0.02	-0.07	-0.05
Retail trade	13,906	13,229	12,833	-0.05	-0.08	-0.03

VARIABLE	2004	2006	2013	% CHANGE 2004-13	% CHANGE 2004-13	% CHANGE 2006-13
Transportation and warehousing	3,118	2,829	2,940	-0.09	-0.06	0.04
Information	1,407	1,393	1,098	-0.01	-0.22	-0.21
Finance and insurance	3,088	2,883	3,380	-0.07	0.09	0.17
Real estate and rental and leasing	3,581	3,682	4,243	0.03	0.18	0.15
Professional, scientific, and technical services	3,722	3,933	3,879	0.06	0.04	-0.01
Management of companies and enterprises	1,043	931	744	-0.11	-0.29	-0.20
Administrative and waste management services	5,561	6,689	8,328	0.20	0.50	0.25
Educational services	700	741	1,318	0.06	0.88	0.78
Health care and social assistance	8,235	7,553	9,237	-0.08	0.12	0.22
Arts, entertainment, and recreation	4,720	2,158	3,797	-0.54	-0.20	0.76
Accommodation and food services	23,615	15,496	18,435	-0.34	-0.22	0.19
Other services, except public administration	6,125	5,380	6,515	-0.12	0.06	0.21
Government and government enterprises	31,029	27,664	27,977	-0.11	-0.10	0.01

VARIABLE	2004	2006	2013	% CHANGE 2004-13	% CHANGE 2004-13	% CHANGE 2006-13
Federal, civilian	6,465	6,493	5,994	0.00	-0.07	-0.08
Military	12,166	9,749	9,173	-0.20	-0.25	-0.06
State and local	12,398	11,422	12,810	-0.08	0.03	0.12
State government	2,043	1,843	2,097	-0.10	0.03	0.14
Local government	10,355	9,579	10,713	-0.07	0.03	0.12
JACKSON COUNTY						
Total employment	62,287	62,934	64,742	0.01	0.04	0.03
Wage and salary employment	53,598	53,387	53,971	-0.00	0.01	0.01
Proprietors employment	8,689	9,547	10,771	0.10	0.24	0.13
Farm proprietors employment	449	415	381	-0.08	-0.15	-0.08
Nonfarm proprietors employment 2/	8,240	9,132	10,390	0.11	0.26	0.14
Farm employment	475	451	410	-0.05	-0.14	-0.09
Nonfarm employment	61,812	62,483	64,332	0.01	0.04	0.03
Private nonfarm employment	49,032	51,749	53,410	0.06	0.09	0.03
Forestry, fishing, and related activities	(D)	226	299			0.32
Mining	(D)	83	161			0.94
Utilities	411	367	445	-0.11	0.08	0.21
Construction	3,058	5,178	6,721	0.69	1.20	0.30

VARIABLE	2004	2006	2013	% CHANGE 2004-13	% CHANGE 2004-13	% CHANGE 2006-13
Manufactur-ing	15,934	14,971	13,536	-0.06	-0.15	-0.10
Wholesale trade	564	526	597	-0.07	0.06	0.13
Retail trade	6,178	6,449	5,657	0.04	-0.08	-0.12
Transpor-tation and warehousing	1,196	1,113	1,119	-0.07	-0.06	0.01
Information	1,306	1,135	698	-0.13	-0.47	-0.39
Finance and insurance	1,474	1,489	1,718	0.01	0.17	0.15
Real estate and rental and leasing	1,539	1,718	1,790	0.12	0.16	0.04
Professional, scientific, and technical services	(D)	2,609	2,552			-0.02
Management of companies and enter-prises	(D)	110	481			3.37
Administrative and waste management services	2,755	3,947	4,083	0.43	0.48	0.03
Educational services	179	199	367	0.11	1.05	0.84
Health care and social assistance	3,792	3,632	4,311	-0.04	0.14	0.19
Arts, enter-tainment, and recreation	605	501	781	-0.17	0.29	0.56
Accommoda-tion and food services	4,005	4,229	4,463	0.06	0.11	0.06

VARIABLE	2004	2006	2013	% CHANGE 2004-13	% CHANGE 2004-13	% CHANGE 2006-13
Other services, except public administration	3,384	3,267	3,631	-0.03	0.07	0.11
Government and government enterprises	12,780	10,734	10,922	-0.16	-0.15	0.02
Federal, civilian	782	774	940	-0.01	0.20	0.21
Military	3,050	1,426	999	-0.53	-0.67	-0.30
State and local	8,948	8,534	8,983	-0.05	0.00	0.05
State government	423	423	435	0.00	0.03	0.03
Local government	8,525	8,111	8,548	-0.05	0.00	0.05

Table 6.2
Means and Changes Over Time for Financial Institutions and
Employment

VARIABLE (NATIONAL DATA AND IN THE KATRINA MICRO AREA.)	OVERALL MEAN	MEAN 1994	MEAN 2004	MEAN 2013	% CHANGE 2004-13	% CHANGE 1994-13
Assets (2013 dollars based on 373,411 observations)	655 m.	309 m.	711 m.	1.18 b.	66	282
Credit Unions	79 m.	35 m.	87 m.	161 m.	85	360
Savings Banks	1.09 b.	676 m.	1.51 b.	1.12 b.	-26	66
Commercial Banks	1.26 b.	554 m.	1.32 b.	2.34 b.	77	322
Giants (Assets over 50 b. $)	209 b.	117 b.	206 b.	283 b.	37	142
Assets in Katrina Micro area(2013 dollars based on 2,147 observations)	372 m.	221 m.	456 m.	536 m.	18	143
Credit Unions	38 m.	17 m.	37 m.	83 m.	124	388
Savings Banks	283 m.	350 m.	269 m.	295 m.	10	-16
Commercial Banks	1.54 b.	986 m.	1.97 b.	1.56 b.	-21	58
Giants (Assets over 50 b. $)	0	0	0	0	0	0
Employment (County level with 368,915 observations)	318,312	307,018	317,869	303,406	-5	-1
Unemployed	21,317	22,645	20,122	26,268	31	16
Unemployment Rate	5.75	5.97	5.57	7.12	28	19
Labor Force	339,630	329,663	337,991	329,674	-3	0
Employment in Katrina Micro area(2,147 observations)	118,785	131,657	132,370	93,410	-29	-29

VARIABLE (NATIONAL DATA AND IN THE KATRINA MICRO AREA.)	OVERALL MEAN	MEAN 1994	MEAN 2004	MEAN 2013	% CHANGE 2004-13	% CHANGE 1994-13
Unemployed	8,652	13,116	7,742	7,566	-2	-42
Unemployment Rate	6.70	8.30	5.64	7.62	35	-8
Labor Force	127,437	144,773	140,113	100,977	-28	-30
Loans (2013 dollars based on 373,411 observations)	385 m.	185 m.	432 m.	635 m.	47	243
Credit Unions	50.6 m.	22.2 m.	55.4 m.	97.7 m.	76	340
Savings Banks	726 m.	431 m.	1.08 b.	691 m.	-36	60
Commercial Banks	722 m.	326 m.	768 m.	1.24 b.	61	280
Giants (Assets over 50 b. $)	112 b.	63.6 b.	118 b.	139 b.	18	119
Loans in Katrina Micro area (2013 dollars based on 2,147 observations)	236 m.	113 m.	312 m.	346 m.	11	206
Credit Unions	23.5 m.	11.3 m.	24.4 m.	44.9 m.	84	297
Savings Banks	175 m.	203 m.	168 m.	196 m.	17	-3
Commercial Banks	980 m.	485 m.	1,360 m.	1,020 m.	-25	110
Giants (Assets over 50 b. $)	0	0	0	0	NA	NA
Return on Assets (373,399 observations)	.0072	.0107	.0074	.0050	-0.32	-0.53
Credit Unions	.0058	.0108	.0049	.0014	-0.71	-0.87
Savings Banks	.0058	.0078	.0079	.0067	-0.15	-0.14
Commercial Banks	.0091	.0113	.0104	.0088	-0.15	-0.22
Giants (Assets over 50 b. $)	.0097	.0088	.0151	.0104	-0.31	0.18

VARIABLE (NATIONAL DATA AND IN THE KATRINA MICRO AREA.)	OVERALL MEAN	MEAN 1994	MEAN 2004	MEAN 2013	% CHANGE 2004-13	% CHANGE 1994-13
Return on Assets in Katrina Micro area(2,147 observations)	.0067	.0130	.0065	.0037	-0.43	-0.72
Credit Unions	.0061	.0130	.0054	.0010	-0.81	-0.92
Savings Banks	.0055	.0107	.0060	.0041	-0.32	-0.62
Commercial Banks	.0095	.0138	.0107	.0093	-0.13	-0.33
Giants (Assets over 50 b. $)	0	0	0	0	0	0
Return on Equity (373,411 observations)	.0687	.1097	.0717	.0449	-0.37	-0.59
Credit Unions	.0501	.1071	.0428	.0182	-0.57	-0.83
Savings Banks	.0564	.0850	.0689	.0338	-0.51	-0.60
Commercial Banks	.0932	.1179	.1067	.0771	-0.28	-0.35
Giants (Assets over 50 b. $)	.1054	.1291	.1534	.0921	-0.40	-0.29
Return on Equity in Katrina Micro area (2,147 observations)	.0592	.1297	.0591	.0353	-0.40	-0.73
Credit Unions	.0464	.1257	.0420	.0106	-0.75	-0.92
Savings Banks	.0462	.1058	.0413	.0314	-0.24	-0.70
Commercial Banks	.1073	.1561	.1238	.0882	-0.29	-0.43
Giants (Assets over 50 b. $)	0	0	0	0	0	0
Assets per Dollar of Salary(373,411 observations)	76.41	71.10	78.02	77.73	0.00	0.09
Credit Unions	64.50	67.00	64.31	65.14	0.01	-0.03
Savings Banks	99.85	102.81	99.43	86.41	-0.13	-0.16

VARIABLE (NATIONAL DATA AND IN THE KATRINA MICRO AREA.)	OVERALL MEAN	MEAN 1994	MEAN 2004	MEAN 2013	% CHANGE 2004-13	% CHANGE 1994-13
Commercial Banks	74.67	66.27	76.00	78.31	0.03	0.18
Giants (Assets over 50 b. $)	79.04	64.58	81.68	81.31	0.00	0.26
Variable	Overall-Mean	Mean1994	Mean2004	Mean2013	Percentage Change 2004-2013	Percentage Change 1994-2013
Assets per Dollar of Salary in Katrina Micro area(2,147 observations)	62.47	58.18	61.54	57.35	-0.07	-0.01
Credit Unions	57.85	59.75	53.45	67.32	0.26	0.13
Savings Banks	68.47	68.95	69.22	62.42	-0.10	-0.09
Commercial Banks	62.54	56.69	61.87	56.17	-0.09	-0.01
Giants (Assets over 50 b. $)	0	0	0	0	0	0
Assets per Dollar of Salary, if Firm has less than $50 million in Assets(183,002 observations)	52.93	57.34	52.07	54.03	0.04	-0.06
Credit Unions	54.73	60.32	54.89	56.55	0.03	-0.06
Savings Banks	41.05	63.88	28.35	35.57	0.25	-0.44
Commercial Banks	51.78	53.95	51.80	51.48	-0.01	-0.05
Giants (Assets over 50 b. $)	NA	NA	NA	NA	NA	NA

VARIABLE (NATIONAL DATA AND IN THE KATRINA MICRO AREA.)	OVERALL MEAN	MEAN 1994	MEAN 2004	MEAN 2013	% CHANGE 2004-13	% CHANGE 1994-13
Assets per Dollar of Salary, if Firm has less than $50 million in Assets, in Katrina Micro area(2,147 observations)	48.67	55.52	47.21	50.14	0.06	-0.10
Credit Unions	49.47	57.06	47.81	50.14	0.05	-0.12
Savings Banks	37.25	20.54	NA	NA	NA	NA
Commercial Banks	42.38	50.21	37.89	NA	NA	NA
Giants (Assets over 50 b. $)	NA	NA	NA	NA	NA	NA

Note that with regard to "Return on Equity (373,411 observations)," the FDIC does not report the return on equity if retained earnings are negative. To maintain comparability across institutional forms, observations greater in absolute value of one were dropped. In order to stay within these same bounds the figures for ROA, 12 observations were dropped.

Credit union breakdown comprises approximately 78 percent of all credit union observations, 13 percent of savings banks, and 21 percent for commercial banks.

APPENDIX B

Supplementary Material

Lessons and Suggestions

Ongoing:

- Insurance: understand with certainty the provisions of your policies covering main buildings, auxiliary structures, buildings, contents, vehicles, boats, and special items. Features to be certain of: perils named, adjustments for depreciation, evidence of ownership, evidence of loss, and schedule of payments. Update regularly.

- Insurance: Photograph spaces and contents exhaustively, so that you can list contents to support a claim if your building is destroyed and contents damaged and washed away. (Even better, keep a spreadsheet with photos and notes, including date of purchase and cost.)

- Insurance: take advantage of insurance underwriter programs to reduce premiums or improve protections.

- Banking: Businesses and other organizations should establish and maintain contingency funds sufficient to meet operating needed during the disaster emergency response period and afterward into recovery. Be able to supplement insurance payments according to their anticipated amounts and timing.

- Information and data required for critical functions: backup in the cloud.

- Pets: insert an electronic identification tag. After storms, pet rescuers routinely use a wand to check for such tags and retrieve the contact information there.

- Community: identify participating agencies and organizations and become familiar with coordinated plans for emergency and disaster response. Participate if possible.

- Community: Become acquainted with businesses, organizations, agencies, and residents in the geographic area in order to inform planning for business continuity after the emergency response phase.

- Community: businesses and organizations should communicate regularly and fully with staff, executives, and other stakeholders concerning readiness. Plan and budget for exercises, from simulations up to particular drills.

Before:

- Evacuate—the elderly, the infirm, and hospitals especially.

- Position nursing homes in areas not as likely to require evacuation.

- Have resources pre-positioned to help with those without their own transportation.

- Allow some shelters to accept pets (helps lessen the anxiety about leaving).

- Build understanding where potential surges may come.

- If not evacuated, have sufficient supplies (e.g., water, batteries, flashlights, and food) to weather a week without assistance.

- Have electronic copies that can be moved quickly or stored away from the area.

- Have cash for after the disaster in case electronic means are unavailable.

- Position potentially environmentally toxic supplies in hardened facilities above potential surges, and make information available as to what toxins are there.

- Position backup power generation and associated circuitry above potential surge levels and test periodically.

- Restore wetlands.

- Have a "weather radio" and stay informed.

- Clearly mark evacuation spots (as New Orleans has started to do with 17 "Evacuspots" around the city [Nola.gov]).

- Integrate command and control for state and federal agencies.

- During:

- Have at least one room with secure equipment above the water line for first responders.

- Have shelters well supplied with food, water, and ice.

- Avoid panic and unfounded rumors, e.g. "You can only say it if you've seen it."

- After:

- Move quickly to provide water, ice, food, and shelter.

- Have a one stop resource center for applying for assistance.

- Avoid panic and unfounded rumors, e.g. "You can only say it if you've seen it."

- Have money for staff to help fill out paper work through FEMA, etc.

- Coordinate distribution of reconstruction funds through participative organizations that are inclusive of different interests, businesses, income groups, and ethnicities.

Charities this book supports

(10 PERCENT OF NET INCOME FROM BOOK SALES DIVIDED EQUALLY AMONG the following):

- The Green Project, New Orleans (http://www.thegreenproject. org)

- The Gulf Restoration Network (http://www.healthygulf.org)

- Lowernine.org (http://www.lowernine.org)

- The National Education Association's Health Information Network's Jerald L. Newberry School Safety Fund.

FROM THE SANDY HOOK SHOOTING TRAGEDY IN NEW ENGLAND TO THE massive tornado outbreak that flattened two schools in Oklahoma City, we've learned all too well that our public schools are vulnerable to disaster and violence. Educators need to be prepared for the unexpected, to respond swiftly to a crisis, and to help their school communities recover in the aftermath. With that in mind, NEA's Health Information Network (NEA HIN) established the Jerald L. Newberry School Safety Fund to promote the health and safety of public education students and employees. https://www.nea.org/grants/55904.htm

Suggested Books and Web resources

Books:

Brinkley, Douglas. The Great Deluge: Hurricane Katrina, New Orleans,and the Mississippi Gulf Coast. New York: Harper Collins, 2006.

Eggers, Dave. *Zeitoun.* New York: Vintage Books, 2010.

Fink, Sheri. Five Days at Memorial: Life and Death in Storm-Ravaged Hospital. New York: Crown Publishing Group, 2013.

Heerden, Ivor Van and Mike Bryan. The Storm: What Went Wrong and Why During Hurricane Katrina: The Inside Story from one Louisiana Scientist. New York: Viking, 2006.

Horne, Jed. Breach of Faith: Hurricane Katrina and the Near Death of a Great American City. New York: Random House, 2006.

Smith, James Patterson. *Hurricane Katrina: The Mississippi Story.* Oxford, MS: UP of Mississippi, 2012.

Websites:

- Mississippi History Now article "Voices of Katrina" by Stephen Sloan: http://mshistorynow.mdah.state.ms.us/articles/253/voices-of-katrina

- Center for Oral History and Cultural Heritage (Katrina oral history transcripts): www.usm.edu/oral-history

- The University of Southern Mississippi's (USM) Libraries Digital Collections http://digilib.usm.edu/cdm/landingpage/collection/coh

- NPR Rebuilding Biloxi documentary: http://americanradioworks.publicradio.org/features/biloxi/

- NOAA Voices From the Fisheries (Deepwater Horizon oil spill) oral histories conducted by the Center for Oral History and Cultural Heritage at USM: https://www.st.nmfs.noaa.gov/humandimensions/voices-from-the-fisheries/index

- Documentary, "A Village Called Versailles" about the Vietnamese community in New Orleans East post-Katrina recovery: http://avillagecalledversailles.com/

- Mary Queen of Vietnam CDC's VEGGI Farmers Cooperative website: http://www.veggifarmcoop.com/

- Institute for Southern Studies http://www.southernstudies.org

- U.S. Census on Hurricane Katrina http://www.census.gov/newsroom/emergencies/hurricane_katrina.html

- Levees.org

- The Data Center, http://www.datacenterresearch.org

- Asian Americans for Change, www.aachange.org

- Boat People, SOS http://www.bpsos.org/mainsite/en/

About the Authors

DR. MARK KLINEDINST IS EMERITUS PROFESSOR OF ECONOMICS AT THE University of Southern Mississippi. He received his doctorate from Cornell University in 1987. He has worked on national and international projects with funding from groups such as the National Science Foundation, World Bank, Filene Research Institute, United Nations and the International Labor Organization and acts as a reviewer for a number of economics journals. He has published in the European Economic Review, Journal of Comparative Economics, Journal of Economic Issues and a number of other outlets. He has taught money and banking, macroeconomics, economic development and related courses. He is a founder of the Hattiesburg Downtown Farmers Market and is President of the Pine Belt Chapter of the Gaining Ground Sustainability Institute of Mississippi.

LAUREN HUDSON WAS BORN AND RAISED ON THE MISSISSIPPI GULF Coast, and is a graduate of the University of Southern Mississippi with a degree in Cultural Anthropology and Music. She resides in the U.S. Virgin Islands, teaching the art of meditation and speaking publicly on the topic. Lauren is a musician focusing on Hindustani and Qawwali music while simultaneously examining its ethnomusicological aspects. Qawwali music is the devotional music of the Chishti Sufis (the mystics of Islam); these studies have led her on a musical journey to shrines through northern India, submersing her in the culture of the music; allowing her to experience and observe the deep devotional practices that correspond with this art form.

MICHAEL MARKS IS A FORMER AMERICA'S OUTSTANDING TEACHER OF the Performing Arts. As instructor of theatre for over 20 years at Hattiesburg High School, he directed over 50 productions including The Wiz, which played at The International Theatre Festival in Edinburgh, Scotland. Under his direction, Music Theatre International selected HHS as America's Best High School Performing Arts Department. As a play-wright, he won critical acclaim for his national docudrama The Katrina Project: Hell and High Water, which toured the continental United States and enjoyed a command performance for Congress at Washington D.C.'s historic Warner Theatre. The show is currently in revival for the 10th Anniversary of Hurricane Katrina (TheKatrinaProject.com). A Speech Communication and Public Relations graduate of The University of Southern Mississippi, he is Historia Films' Local Casting Director for The Hollow and Chair of the Leaf Scholarship Foundation.

CORAL POGUE IS A GRADUATE OF THE UNIVERSITY OF SOUTHERN MISSIS-sippi with a degree in Economics. Originally from Florida's Emerald Coast she now lives in New Orleans, Louisiana, where she is a frequent foster parent of local shelter animals. Coral is the development direc-tor for lowernine.org, a non-profit organization that rebuilds homes for pre-Katrina residents in New Orleans' Lower Ninth Ward.

BETTY PRESS IS A FINE ART PHOTOGRAPHER. SHE IS WELL KNOWN FOR HER photographs taken Africa where she lived and traveled for many years. In 2003 she started teaching photography at the University of Southern Mississippi. Now living in Hattiesburg, Mississippi she has a new project using toy and old cameras about living in Mississippi.

Her photographs have been widely exhibited and collected as well as selected for many juried competitions. In 2011 she published an award winning photobook I Am Because We Are: African Wisdom in Image and Proverb. She captured a stunning, life-affirming portrait of the Afri-can people and culture. In 2012 she received a statewide award in pho-tography, from the Mississippi Institute of Arts & Letters and in 2013 a Mississippi Visual Artist Grant.

She is represented by Panos Pictures, London; Photographic Image Group, Portland, Oregon; International Visions, Washington, DC; Fischer Galleries, Jackson, Mississippi; One Off Contemporary Art Gal-lery, Nairobi.

DAVID REYNOLDS IS A FACILITY MANAGEMENT CONSULTANT BASED IN Jackson, Mississippi. His background is in systems engineering, project management and consulting, serving a variety of commercial and NGO clients and industries. He holds degrees in science, engineering, and allied health areas. David is a member of the International Facility Management Association (IFMA) Consulting and Environmental Health and Safety Councils. His projects engage people, processes, and technology in the built environment. His pro bono work concerns safe and healthy housing, workplace safety, and environmental health. David served in the United States Coast Guard.

LINDA VANZANDT IS AN ORAL HISTORIAN AND FOUNDER OF SOUND SEED Productions. Formerly she was managing editor and special projects director of the Center for Oral History and Cultural Heritage at The University of Southern Mississippi where she co-directed the Hurricane Katrina Oral History Project and co-produced Surviving Katrina: Lost and Found in Mississippi and Mississippi Moments. She received the Special Recognition Award by the Mississippi Humanities Council in 2011 for her work with Vietnamese American communities of the Gulf Coast in the aftermath of Hurricane Katrina. She lives in Pass Christian, Mississippi.

Acknowledgements

THE AUTHORS WOULD LIKE TO THANK ALL OF THE PEOPLE WHO VOLUN-teered to share their experiences. We would also like to thank the employ-ees and CEOs of credit unions and banks in the Katrina impacted area for the time they took to share with the researchers their personal and institutional challenges as they tried to rebuild. Also, the capable research abilities of economists Dennis Bucklin and Coral Pogue helped with a good number of the research tasks. Later sections were supported by the keen research abilities of Laurence Hudson. Earlier versions of portions of this book benefited from the astute comments when presented at the Allied Social Sciences Association meetings in Boston, 2015, and at the International Association for the Economics of Participation conference in Montevideo, Uruguay in 2014. Thanks also to Charles Elliott of the Mississippi Credit Union Association and George A. Hofheimer and Ben Rogers of the Filene Research Institute for astute comments and assis-tance. Charles P. Rock helped out finding appropriate sources and guid-ance. Allison Tharp provided valuable editing guidance on earlier drafts of parts of this book. A big thanks to Adam Robinson for his patient and skillful help in bringing this book to publication. He managed to pull it all together in time for us to get this out before the tenth anniversary. A dear debt of gratitude is owed to our families for putting up with the time demands that this research has entailed.

References

Akers, Joshua M. "Separate and Unequal: The Consumption of Public Education in Post-Katrina New Orleans." *International Journal of Urban and Regional Research 36*.1 (2012): 29-48. Web.

Alpert, Bruce. "Landrieu Urges Health Care Fix—Senator Questions Jindal's Leadership." *The Times-Picayune* [New Orleans, LA] 5 December 2012. Print.

Amy, Jeff. "Regulators Order Kemper Rate Increase End, Plan Refunds." *Hattiesburg American* 8 July 2015. Print.

Anderson, Heather. "CUNA Economist Hampel Warns That a Swift Recovery Is Not On the Way." *Credit Union Times Magazine* 28 Oct. 2009. Web.

Auerbach, Alan. & Yuriy Gorodnichenko. (2012). "Measuring the Output Responses to Fiscal Policy." *American Economic Journal: Economic Policy, 4*(2), 1-27.

Barofsky, Neil. Bailout: An Inside Account of How Washington Abandoned Main Street While   Rescuing Wall Street. New York: Free Press, 2012. Print.

Bergeron, Kat. "A Devastating Dame/Remembering Camille." *Sun Herald* [Biloxi, MS] 2005. Web.

Berry, Deborah Barfield. "Cochran Seeks Ship Funds." *Hattiesburg American* 12 Jul. 2015. Web.

Beven, John., et al. "Annual Summary, Atlantic Hurricane Season of 2005." *Tropical Prediction Center.* NOAA/NWS/National Hurricane Center, 2007. PDF file.

Blinder, Alan, & Mark Zandi. "How the Great Recession Was Brought to an End." 27 Jul. 2010. PDF file.

Bloomberg. "Goldman Sachs Settles with Mississippi Pension Plan in Class Action Over MBS Offering." *Pensions and Investments.* P&I, 18 Jul. 2012.

Boyd, Ezra. Fatalities Due to Hurricane Katrina's Impacts in Louisiana: A Statistical and Spatial Analysis. LAP, 2015. Print.

Brancaccio, David. "How Independent Businesses kept New Orleans Afloat." MarketPlace.org. Web. 10 Aug. 2015.

Breitner, S., et al. "Short-term Effects of Air Temperature on Cause-specific Cardiovascular Mortality in Bavaria, Germany." *Heart, 100*.16 (2014): 1272. Web.

Brinkley, Douglas. The Great Deluge: Hurricane Katrina, New Orleans, and the Mississippi Gulf Coast. New York: Harper Collins, 2006. Print.

Brunkard, Joan, Gonza Namulanda, and Raoult Ratard.. "Hurricane Katrina Deaths, Louisiana, 2005." *Disaster Medicine and Public Health Preparedness* (2008): 215-23. Web.

Brunsma, David L., David Overfelt, and J. Steven Picou. *The Sociology of Katrina: Perspectives   on a Modern Catastrophe*. Lanham, MD: Rowman & Littlefield, 2007. Print.

Bureau of Economic Analysis (BEA). 2014. Retrieved from http://www.bea.gov.

Bureau of Labor Statistics (BLS). 2014. Retrieved from http://www.bls.gov.

Burkett, Paul. "Review of 'Coming to Terms with Nature.'" *Review of Radical Political Economy* (2008). Web.

Campanella, Richard. "Above-Sea-Level New Orleans: The Residential Capacity of Orleans Parish's Higher Ground." *Center for Bioenvironmental Research* (2007). PDF file.

CBS News. "Katrina Housing Funds Go To Port Instead." *CBS News.* Associated Press, 2008.

City of New Orleans. "City Breaks Ground on a Series of Major Projects in Historic Lower Ninth Ward." *Nola.gov.* City of New Orleans, 2013. Web. 6 Mar. 2015.

Chicago Political Economy Group. "CPEG Notes." *CPEG Notes 1*.1 (2015):. 1-10. PDF file.

Chodorow-Reich, G., et al. "Does State Fiscal Relief During Recessions Increase Employment? Evidence from the American Recovery and

Reinvestment Act." *American Economic Journal: Economic Policy*, 4.3 (2012): 118-145.

Clemens, J. & Miran, S. "Fiscal Policy Multipliers on Subnational Government Spending." *American Economic Journal: Economic Policy*, 4.2 (2012): 46-48. Web. 1 Jun. 2015.

Congressional Budget Office (CBO). Estimated Impact of the American Recovery and Reinvestment Act on Employment and Economic Output from January 2012 through March 2012. Congressional Budget Office, 2012. PDF file.

Cooper, Brad. "Gov. Sam Brownback is Cutting Aid to Kansas Schools by $44.5 Million." *Kansas City Star* 5 Feb. 2015. Print.

Cooper, Christopher, and Robert Block. *Disaster: Hurricane Katrina and the Failure of Homeland Security.*" New York: Henry Holt and Company, 2006. Print.

Cooper, Mark. Public Risk, Private Profit, Ratepayer Cost, Utility Imprudence: Advanced Cost Recovery for Reactor Construction Creates Another Nuclear Fiasco, Not a Renaissance. Institute for Energy and the Environment, Vermont Law School, 2013. PDF file.

Corporation for National and Community Service. *Number of Volunteers in Year 2 of Katrina Recovery Exceeds Historic 1st Year.* National Service, 2007. PDF file.

Credit Union National Association (CUNA). Credit Union National Association, 2012.

Crockett, James R. Operation Pretense

Data Center. "Plan for the 21ˢᵗ Century: New Orleans 2030-Neighborhoods and Housing." Greater New Orleans Community Data Center, 2010. PDF file.

Davis, Lynn E., et al. Hurricane Katrina: Lessons for Army Planning and Operations. Rand Corporation, 2007. PDF file.

DeParle, J. "Katrina's Diaspora." *The New York Times.* NYT, 2 Oct. 2005. Web. 1 May 2015.

DePillis, Lydia. "If You Rebuild It, They Might Not Come." *New Republic* 13 Mar. 2013.

Derthick, M. "Where Federalism Didn't Fail." *Public Administration Review 67*.6 (2007): 36-47.

Dolfman, Michael L., Solidelle Fortier Wasser, and Bruce Bergman. *The Effects of Hurricane Katrina on the New Orleans Economy*. BLS Monthly Labor Review, 2007. PDF file.

Dosa, David, et al. "Effects of Hurricane Katrina on Nursing Facility Resident Mortality, Hospitalization, and Functional Decline." *Disaster Medicine and Public Health Preparedness* (2010).

Duffus, Rita. "They Came, and We Are Humbly Thankful." *Sun Herald* [Biloxi, MS] 20 Nov. 2007. Print.

DuPree, Johnny. Interview with David Tisdale. University of Southern Mississippi Katrina Oral History (2006).

Dyer, Scott. "Overflow City." *Planning 72*.4 (2006): 28-31.

Eakin, Sue. The Autobiography of Solomon Northup: Twelve Years a Slave. Eakin Films and Publishing, 2013.

EconSouth. "Southeast Begins the Healing Process." *EconSouth 7*.4 (2005): 11–16.

———."Life after Katrina: Reflecting, Rebuilding Continue on the Gulf Coast." *EconSouth 8.1* (2006): 20–23.

Egan, Timothy. "Uprooted and Scattered Far From the Familiar." *The New York Times*. NYT, 2005. Web. 1 Mar. 2015.

Eggers, Dave. *Zeitoun*. New York: Vintage Books, 2010. Print.

Elie, Lolis Eric.."We Just Like Our Cash Served Cold." *The Times-Picayune* [New Orleans, LA] 2005. Print.

Elliott, Charles. "Written Testimony of Charles Elliott, President and CEO of the Mississippi Credit Union Association on Behalf of the Credit Union National Association on 'Hurricane Katrina: The Financial Institutions Response.'" Credit Union National Association, Inc., 2005. PDF file.

Elliott, David. Interview with James Pat Smith. *University of Southern Mississippi Katrina Oral History* (2009).

Ellis, Blake. "Most Charitable States in America." *CNNMoney*. CNN 12 Jun. 2013. Web. 1 Mar. 2015.

Federal Deposit Insurance Corporation (FDIC). *FDIC,* 2014. Web. 9 Feb. 2015.

Federal Emergency Management Agency. "Six Years after Hurricane Katrina, Mississippi Continues to Recover and Rebuild." *Federal Emergency Management Agency.* FEMA, 2011. Web. 15 Jun. 2015.

Federal Emergency Management Agency. "Louisiana recovery: Eight Years After Hurricanes Katrina and Rita." *Federal Emergency Management Agency.* FEMA, 2013. Web. 15 Jun. 2015.

Finger, Davida. "Stranded and Squandered: Lost on the Road Home." *Seattle Journal for Social Justice 7.*1 (2008): 59-100.

Fink, Sheri. Five Days at Memorial: Life and Death in Storm-Ravaged Hospital. New York: Crown Publishing, 2013. Print.

Forgette, Richard, et al. "Before, Now, and After: Assessing Hurricane Katrina Relief." *Population Research and Policy Review 28.*1 (2009): 31-44. Web. 1 Jun. 2015.

Foster, J., and R. McChesney. The Endless Crisis: How Monopoly-Finance Capital Produces Stagnation and Upheaval from the USA to China. New York: Monthly Review Press, 2012. Print.

Francis, Pope. "Pope's Tweet on 'Profit at Any Cost.'" *NBC News.* NBC, 2 May 2013. Web. 1 May 2015

Friedman, Milton. "What Every American Wants." *Wall Street Journal.* WSJ, 2003.

"Goldman Sachs Mortgage Pass-Through Litigation." *Bernstein Litowitz Berger and Grossman LLP*, BLB&G, 2012.

Grimm, Andy. "Ray Nagin Arrives at Federal Prison in Texas, Station Reports." *Times-Picayune* [New Orleans, LA] 8 Sept. 2014. Print.

Hall, Tamron. "Former New Orleans Mayor Ray Nagin Charged with Katrina-Related Corruption." *NBC News.* NBC, 18 Jan. 2013. Web. 1 Jul. 2015.

Heldman, Caroline. "The Truths of Katrina." *Coffee at Midnight.* Wordpress, 25 Aug. 2010. Web. 1 Aug. 2014.

Hermann, Fritz, et al. "Hurricane Katrina Storm Surge Distribution and Field Observations on the Mississippi Barrier Islands." *Coastal and Shelf Science 74* (2007).

Hiaasen, Carl. "New FEMA Motto, We will bury you." *Sun Herald* [Biloxi, MS] 2005. Print.

Hsu, Spencer S. and Susan B. Glasser. "The Point Man, FEMA Director Singled Out by Response Critics." *Washington Post* 6 Sept. 2005.

Gelles, J. "Bank Transfer Day a Boon to Credit Unions, Small Banks." *Philadelphia Inquirer* 2011.

Gilbert, A. R, et al. "Federal Reserve Lending to Troubled Banks During the Financial Crisis, 2007-10." *Economic Research.* Federal Reserve Bank of St. Louis, 2012. Web. 15 Feb. 2015.

Giroux, Henry A. "Reading Hurricane Katrina: Race, Class, and the Biopolitics of Disposability." *College Literature 33.*3 (2006): 171-196. Web. 15 Jun. 2015.

Global CCS Institute. "The Global Status of CCS." *Global CCS Institute.* Global CCS Institute, 2013.

Goddard J., D. McKillop, and J. Wilson. "Consolidation in the US Credit Union Sector: Determinants of Failure and Acquisition." *Federal Deposit Insurance Corporation.* FDIC, 2008.

Goldman Sachs. *2010 Annual Report.* Goldman Sachs, 2010. PDF file.

Gollott, Richard. Interview with Linda VanZandt. *University of Southern Mississippi Katrina Oral History,* 21 March 2006.

Gratz, Roberta Brandes (2015-06-09). *We're Still Here Ya Bastards: How the People of New Orleans Rebuilt Their City.* Nation Books. Kindle Edition. 9 June 2015.

Greater New Orleans Fair Housing Action Center. "Fair Housing and Civil Rights Groups File Federal Lawsuit in Post-Katrina Housing Discrimination Case." *Greater New Orleans Fair Housing Action Center.* GNO Fair Housing, 2008.

Green, Rodney, Marie Kouassi, and Belinda Mambo. 2013. "Housing, Race, and Recovery from Hurricane Katrina." *The Review of Black Political Economy 40.*2 (2013): 145-163.

Grissett, Sheila. "Securing FEMA Aid Proves Stormy—Cindy Not Yet Declared Disaster." *Times-Picayune* [New Orleans, LA] 2005. Print.

Groen, J. A. & A. E. Polivka. "Going home after Hurricane Katrina: Determinants of Return Migration and Changes in Affected Areas." *Demography,* 47.4 (2010): 821-844. Web. 1 May 2015.

Halary, I. "Cooperatives in Globalization: The Advantages of Networking." In Participation in the Age of Globalization and Information: Advances in the Economic Analysis of Participatory and Labor-Managed Firms, eds. M.A. Klinedinst and P. Kalmi, vol. 9. Amsterdam: Elsevier, 2006.

Heerden, Ivor Van and Mike Bryan. The Storm: What Went Wrong and Why During Hurricane Katrina: The Inside Story from One Louisiana Scientist. New York: Viking, 2006. Print.

Hodge, Megan. "Mississippi Unemployment Highest in Nation." *WDAM* [Hattiesburg, MS] 2014.

Honoré, Retired Lieutenant General Russell. Interview with David Tisdale. *The University of Southern Mississippi Katrina Oral History* 4 Aug. 2010.

Hori, M., Schafer, M., & Bowman, D. "Displacement Dynamics in Southern Louisiana After Hurricanes Katrina and Rita." *Population Research and Policy Review* (2008): 45-65. Web. 1 May 2015.

Horne, Jed. Breach of Faith: Hurricane Katrina and the Near Death of a Great American City. New York: Random House, 2006. Print.

Horvat, B. *Political Economy.* New York: M.E. Sharpe, 1979. Print.

Insurance Information Institute. "The Ten Most Costly World Insurance Losses, 1970–2006." *Insurance Information Institute.* III, 2006.

Insurance Information Institute. "Hurricane Katrina: The Five Year Anniversary." *Insurance Information Institute.* III, 2010.

Insurance Information Institute. "Catastrophes: Insurance Issues." *Insurance Information Institute.* III, 2014.

Jackson, Andrew. "Farewell Address." *The American Presidency Project.* Gerhard Peters and John T. Woolley, 2015.

Jervis, Rick. "Economy Keeps Some Habitat for Humanity Homes Empty." *USA Today* 24 Nov. 2008. Print.

Jurgens, Rick. "Avoiding Home Repair Fraud: Lessons from Hurricane Katrina." National Consumer Law Center. Retrieved from

https://www.nclc.org/images/pdf/pr-reports/report-katrina_repair_
fraud_2008.pdf, 2008.

Kemp, E. "USM, PRCC Confront Utility Rate Hikes." *Hattiesburg
American* 2014. Print.

Khanna, Roma. "Nursing Homes Left Residents With Weak Safety
Net." *Houston Chronicle* 11 Dec. 2005. Print.

King, Noel. "A Small Credit Union Brings Hope to New Orleans."
MarketPlace.org. 5 Aug. 2015.

Klinedinst, M. A. 2007. Cooperative Comebacks: Resilience in the Face
of the Hurricane Katrina Catastrophe. Filene Research Institute,
2007. PDF file.

Knabb R.D., J.R. Rhome, and D. P. Brown. *Tropical Cyclone Report
Hurricane Katrina 23-30 August 2005*. National Hurricane Center,
2011. PDF file.

Koebler, Jason. "Katrina-Like' Hurricanes to Occur More Frequently
Due to Warming." *U.S. News and World Report* 18 Mar. 2013.
Print.

Koliba, Christopher, Russell Mills, and Asim Zia. "Accountability in
Governance Networks: An Assessment of Public, Private, and
Nonprofit Emergency Management Practices Following Hurricane
Katrina." *Public Administration Review 71.*2 (2011): 210-20.

Kromm, Chris and Sue Sturgis. "A Harder Look at Haley Barbour's
Post-Katrina.

Miracle. Mississippi's GOP and Governor Did a Good Job Getting
Cash Out of Republicans in Washington, But is He Really Doing a
Good Job Cleaning up After Katrina?" *Salon*, 25 May 2007.

Landphair, J. "'The Forgotten People of New Orleans': Community,
Vulnerability, and the Lower Ninth Ward." *Journal of American
History* (2007): 837-845. Web. 1 May 2015.

LaFontaine, Ryan. "Condo Moratoriums May Go Up on Coast." *Sun
Herald* [Biloxi, MS] 2005. Print.

Landry, Bin, Whitehead Hindsley, and Kenneth Wilson. "Going Home:
Evacuation-Migration Decisions of Hurricane Katrina Survivors."
*Southern Economic Association 74.*2 (2007): 326-343.

Lawrence, S. Snapshot of Philanthropy's Response to the Gulf Coast Hurricanes. Foundation Center, 2006. PDF file.

Leachman, Michael and Michael Mazerov. "State Personal Income Tax Cuts: Still a Poor Strategy for Economic Growth." *Center on Budget and Policy Priorities.* CBPP, 2015.

Lee, Anita. "Diazes Indicted." *Sun Herald* [Biloxi, MS] 2005. Print.

Levees.org. "Lower Ninth Ward Levee Breaches in 2005." *New Orleans Historical* 2005.

Liu, Betty. "Southern's Fanning Explains Added Kemper Costs." *Bloomberg Business.* Bloomberg, 2013.

Livingston, Dennis. Rebuilding Water-Damaged Homes: A Manual for the Safe,

Healthy, Green, and Low-Cost Restoration of Housing. The Alliance for Healthy Homes, 2009. PDF file.

Louisiana's Office of Community Development. *The Homeowner Assistance Program Situation & Pipeline Report #440.* State of Louisiana Division of Administration, Office of Community Development, 2015. PDF file.

Lott, Trent. *Testimony of The Honorable Trent Lott.* United States Senate Committee on the Judiciary, 7 Mar. 2007. PDF file.

Lugosi, Charles I. "Natural Disaster; Unnatural Deaths: The Killings on the Life

Care Floors at Tenet's Memorial Medical Center in New Orleans During Hurricane Katrina." *Issues in Law & Medicine* (2007): 71-85. Web. 1 May 2015.

Macey, Jonathan R. and Geoffrey P. Miller. "The McCarran-Ferguson Act of 1945: Reconceiving the Federal Role in Insurance Regulation." *Yale Law School Faculty Scholarship Series.* Paper 1605.

Matthews, Chris. "The 10 Most Corrupt States in the U.S." *Fortune* 10 Jun. 2014. Print.

Mathews, Ricky. Interview with David Tisdale. *University of Southern Mississippi*

Katrina Oral History, 25 August 2006.

Maute, Nikki Davis.. "Taylor Says U.S. Needs Exit Plan for War in Iraq." *Hattiesburg American* 2005. Print.

Member Scholars of the Center for Progressive Reform. *An Unnatural Disaster: The Aftermath of Hurricane Katrina*. Center for Progressive Reform, 2005. PDF file.

Meyers, Lisa. "Is the Orleans Levee Board Doing its Job?" *NBC Investigative Unit*. NBC News, 15 Sept. 2005.

Michel-Kerjan, E. "Catastrophe Economics: The National Flood Insurance Program." *Journal of Economic Perspectives 24*.4 (2010): 165-186.

Mississippi Business Journal Staff. "Fitch Gives Mississippi Power a Negative Outlook Due to Kemper Plant." *Mississippi Business Journal*. MBJ, 2014.

Mississippi Department of Education. "Enrollment by Grade. Enrollment by Subgroup." *Mississippi Department of Education*. MDE, 2015.

Moretti, E. "Local multipliers." *American Economic Review: Papers & Proceedings 100* (2010): 373-377. Web. 1 Mar. 2015.

Mowbray, Rebecca. "Casino Says 450-room Hotel being Built Isn't Enough—Harrah's Wants to Up Ante." *Times-Picayune* [New Orleans, LA] 2005. Print.

MIT. "Carbon Capture and Sequestration Technologies." *Massachusetts Institute of Technology*. MIT, 2014. Web. 9 Jan. 2015.

Mississippi Power. "Financial Annual Reports 2000-2013." *Mississippi Power*. Mississippi Power Company, 2014. Web. 1 Feb. 2015.

National Center for Employee Ownership (NCEO). "Data Show Widespread Employee Ownership in U.S." *National Center for Employee Ownership*. NCEO, 2014. Web. 1 Jul. 2015.

National Credit Union Administration (NCUA). *National Credit Union Association,* 2014.

National Educational Association (NEA). "Rankings of the States 2013 and Estimates of School Statistics 2014." *National Education Association*. National Education Association, 2014.

"Neighborhood Statistical Area Data Profiles." *The Data Center.* Non-profit Knowledge Works, 2015. Web. 15 Jun. 2015.

NOAA National Hurricane Center. "Memorable Gulf Coast Hurricanes of the 20th Century." *Atlantic Oceanographic & Meteorological Library.* National Oceanic and Atmospheric Association, 1993. Web. 1 May 2015.

Neal, B. "The Economic Impact Multiplier is Not Seven." *Mississippi Economic Review and Outlook, 21.*1 (2007): 44-46. Web. 15 Mar. 2015.

Nicosia, Francesca. "Ecology, Embodiment and Aesthetics of Death in Hurricane Katrina." *Mortality 14.*1 (2009). Web. 1 Mar. 2015.

Nguyen, Daniel. Interview with Linda VanZandt. *University of Southern Mississippi Deepwater Horizon Oil Disaster Oral History,* 22 February 2011.

Nguyen, Kha Van. Interview with Linda VanZandt. *University of Southern Mississippi Deepwater Horizon Oil Disaster Oral History,* 19 September 2011.

Nguyen-Brown, Sue. Interview with Deanne Nuwer. *University of Southern Mississippi Katrina Oral History,* 8 January 2006.

Nguyen, Tong and Chien. Interview with Linda VanZandt. *University of Southern Mississippi Katrina Oral History,* 21 September 2005

Nguyen, Tuan. Interview with Linda VanZandt. *University of Southern Mississippi Deepwater Horizon Oil Disaster Oral History,* 2 June 2011.

Nguyen,Tung. Interview with Linda VanZandt. *University of Southern Mississippi Katrina Oral History,* 27 March 2006.

Office of Congressman Cedric Richmond. "Richmond on Road Home Discrimination Suit Settlement." *Congressman Cedric Richmond.* Cedric Richmond, 2011.

Pender, Geoff. "A Quarter of Katrina Aid Money Still Unspent." *McClatchy DC.* McClatchy DC, 2010.

Perlstein, Michael and Trymaine Lee. "The Good and the Bad." *NOLA. com.* NOLA.com, 18 Dec. 2005.

Pham, Xuyen Thi. Interview with Linda VanZandt. University of Southern Mississippi *Deepwater Horizon Oil Disaster Oral History*, 25 May 2011.

Phan, Reverend Duc Dong. Interview with Linda VanZandt. *University of Southern Mississippi Katrina Oral History*, 26 September 2005.

Pike, Jennifer. *Spending Federal Disaster Aid: Comparing the Process and Priorities in Louisiana and Mississippi in the Wake of Hurricanes Katrina and Rita.* The Nelson A. Rockefeller Institute of Government and the Public Affairs Research Council of Louisiana, 2007. PDF file.

Plyer, Allison. "Facts for Features: Katrina Impact." *The Data Center.* The Data Center, 2014.

Plyer, Allison and Mack Vicki. "Neighborhood Recovery Rates: Growth Continues Through 2015 in New Orleans Neighborhoods." *The Data Center.* Nonprofit Knowledge Works, 2015. Web. 15 Jun, 2015.

Public Service Commission of Wisconsin (PSCW). "Shaping Utility Regulation in Wisconsin." *Public Service Commission of Wisconsin.* PSC, 2014.

Quigley, Bill. "New Orleans Katrina Pain Index at 10: Who Was Left Behind." *The Huffington Post.* The Huffington Post, 2015. Web. 1 Aug. 2015.

Ramey, V. A. "Can Government Purchases Stimulate the Economy? *Journal of Economic Literature, 49.*3 (2011): 673-685.

Road Home. *FAQ : What is the Homeowner Assistance program?* The Road Home, 2007. PDF file.

Roberts, Patrick S. "FEMA After Katrina." *Policy Review 137* (2006): 15-35. Web. 10 Aug. 2015.

Rubenstein, Jim. "BTD Founder Christian Thanks Industry." *Credit Union Times.* CUTimes, 14 Jun. 2012. Web. 1 Aug. 2015.

Russell, Gordan and James Varney. "From Blue Tarps to Debris Removal, Layers of Contractors Drive Up the Cost of Recovery, Critics Say. Top-tier Contractors Say It's the Only Way to Get the Work Done." *Times-Picayune* [New Orleans, LA] 29 Dec. 2005. Print.

Sastry, N. and Gregory, J. "The Location of Displaced New Orleans Residents in the Year After Hurricane Katrina." *Demography* *51*(2014): 753-775.

Sayre, Alan. "Gulf Lease Sale Today Draws Strong Interest." *Sun Herald* [Biloxi, MS] 2005. Print.

Schleifstein, Mark. "Judge: Corps' MR-GO 'Took' Value of Properties in St. Bernard, Lower 9th Ward." *The Times-Picayune* [New Orleans, LA] 2015. Print.

Schloegel, George. Interview with James Pat Smith. *University of Southern Mississippi Katrina Oral History* 14 Aug. 2008.

"September 11th Fast Facts." *CNN*. Cable News Network, 27 Mar. 2015.

Shane, Scott and Thom Shanker. "When Storm Hit, National Guard Was Deluged Too." *The New York Times*. NYT, 28 Sept. 2005.

SIGTARP. *Quarterly Report to Congress*. Office of the Special Inspector General for the Troubled Asset Relief Program, 2012. PDF file.

Simon, Stephanie. "Katrina's Aftermath; Far from Home, They Feel They've Arrived; in Shelters Across the Nation, Grateful New Orleans Evacuees Aren't Looking Back. Instead They're Relishing the Chance for a Fresh Start in a New City." *Los Angeles Times* 2005.

Smith, James Patterson. *Hurricane Katrina: The Mississippi Story*. Oxford, MS: UP of Mississippi, 2012.

Smith, R. "Southern Co. to Take $380 Million Charge for Kemper Coal Plant." *The Wall Street Journal*. Dow Jones & Company, Inc., 29 Apr. 2014.

Solomon, John and Spencer S. Hsu. "Most Katrina Aid From Overseas Went Unclaimed," *Washington Post* 29 Apr. 2007.

State News Service. "Gov. Jindal: We Won't Allow President Obama to Bully

Louisiana Into Expanding Obamacare." *Louisiana State News Service*. Louisiana State News Service, 8 Nov. 2013.

Stephens, K. U., et al. "Excess Mortality in the Aftermath of Hurricane Katrina: A Preliminary Report."_*Disaster Med Public Health Prep* *1*.1 (2007):15-20.

Steenhuysen, Julie. "Mississippi Blues: The Cost of Rejecting Medicaid Expansion." *Reuters*. Thomson Reuters, 4 Oct. 2013.

Stigler, George. The Theory of Economic Regulation." *The Bell Journal of Economics and Management Science* 2 (1971): 3-21.

Stone, Daniel. "Rising Temperatures May Cause More Katrinas: Small Increases in Temperature Found to Add Power to Storms in the Atlantic." *National Geographic* 19 Mar. 2013.

Stringfield, Jonathan. "Higher Ground: An Exploratory Analysis of Characteristics Affecting Returning Populations after Hurricane Katrina." *Population & Environment vol. 31*.1-3 (2009): n.p.

Strout, Lawrence N. *Pass Christian and the Gazebo Gazette: A Gulf Community's Post-Katrina Triumph*. Charleston, SC: History Press, 2015. Print.

Sturgis, Sue. "Mississippi Gov. Barbour's Relative Committed Katrina Fraud, Court Rules." *The Institute for Southern Studies*. The Institute for Southern Studies, 1 Sept. 2011.

Swarzenki, Christopher M. *The Gulf Intracoastal Waterway as a Distributary of Mississippi River Water to Coastal Louisiana Wetlands*. US Geological Survey Baton Rouge, n.d. PDF file.

Swenson, D. *Statewide Economic Impacts of Disaster-Related Payments to Support Household and Private and Public Sector Recovery in Iowa*. The RIO Iowa Project, 2010. PDF file.

Taibbi, Matt. *Griftopia: A Story of Bankers, Politicians, and the most Audacious Power Grab in American History*. New York: Speigel and Grau, 2010. Print.

Taibbi, Matt. "Secrets and Lies of the Bailout." *Rolling Stone Magazine*, 2013.

Taylor, Congressman Gene. 2008. Interview with Dariusz Grabka and Alanna Tobia. *University of Southern Mississippi Katrina Oral History*, 21 Sept. 2008.

Thevenot, Brian and Gordon Russell. "Rape. Murder. Gunfights." *Times-Picayune* [New Orleans, LA] 26 Sept. 2005. Print.

Thiede, B & Brown, D. "Hurricane Katrina: Who Stayed and Why?" *Popular Research and Policy Review* 32.6 (2013): 803-824.

Thomas, Greg. "Deal May Trump New Orleans—Big Apple Mogul's Firm has Interest in Big Easy." *Times-Picayune* [New Orleans, LA] 2005.

Tiner, Stan.. "Condo Boom Will Change Us, But How?" *Sun Herald* [Biloxi, MS] 2005. Print.

Trinh, Trina. Interview with Linda VanZandt. *University of Southern Mississippi Katrina Oral History,* 29 October 2005.

Truong, Dac. Interview with Linda VanZandt. Biloxi Oil Spill Claims Fair, 8 July 2010.

U. S. Bureau of Economic Analysis. "Total Gross Domestic Product by State for Louisiana." *Federal Reserve Economic Data.* Federal Reserve, 2014.

U. S. Bureau of Economic Analysis. "Per Capita Personal Income in Mississippi." *Federal Reserve Economic Data.* Federal Reserve, 2014.

U. S. Bureau of Labor Statistics. "May 2013 State Occupational Employment and   Wage Estimates for Mississippi." *Bureau of Labor Statistics.* United States Department of Labor, 2014.

U.S. Bureau of Labor Statistics, 2014. "Quarterly Census of Employment and Wages. The

QCEW NAICS-Based Data Files (1975-2013)." *Bureau of Labor Statistics.* United States Department of Labor, 2014.

U.S. Census. "State and County QuickFacts." *United States Census Bureau.* United States Census Bureau, 2014.

U.S. Census. "2010 Census Interactive Population Search." *United States Census Bureau.* United States Census Bureau, 2015. Web. 1 Aug. 2015.

U.S. Department of Housing and Urban Development. *Recovery Snapshot:*

Louisiana Road Home—Homeowner Compensation and Incentives. Housing and Urban Development, 2008. PDF file.

U.S. Department of Housing and Urban Development's Office of Policy Development and Research. "Current Housing Unite Damage Estimate Hurricanes Katrina, Rita, and Wilma." *Housing and Urban Development.* Housing and Urban Development, 2008.

U.S. Energy Information Administration. "Electric Power Monthly." *Energy Information Administration.* EIA, 2014.

U.S. House of Representatives Select Bipartisan Committee to Investigate the Preparation for and Response to Katrina. "A Failure of Initiative: The Final Report of the Select Bipartisan Committee to Investigate the Preparation for and Response to Hurricane Katrina." *U.S. House of Representatives.* Katrina.house.gov., 2006.

U.S. Government Accountability Office (GAO). *Testimony Before the Subcommittee on Energy and Water Development, Committee on Appropriations.* Government Accountability Office, 2005. PDF file.

U.S. Senate Committee on Homeland Security and Governmental Affairs. *Hurricane Katrina: A Nation Still Unprepared.* The Government Publishing Office, 2006. PDF file.

United States Senate. "Wall Street and the Financial Crisis: Anatomy of a Financial Collapse, Washington." *U.S. Senate Committee on Homeland Security and Governmental Affairs.* HSGAC, 2011.

Uyen, Kim. Interview with Linda VanZandt. *University of Southern Mississippi Katrina Oral History,* 20 August 2009.

Vander, Robin. "Five Years and Beyond: Reflections on Recovery in Post-Katrina New Orleans." *The Review of Black Political Economy* 38.4 (2011): 271-278.

Vanek, J. *The General Theory of Labor- Managed Market Economies.* New York: Cornell University Press, 1970. Print.

Waller, M. "Hurricane Katrina Eight Years Later, a Statistical Snapshot of the New Orleans Area" *The Times- Picayune* [New Orleans, LA] 2013. Print.

Watkins, John P. "Economic Institutions Under Disaster Situations: The Case of Hurricane Katrina." *Journal of Economic Issues 41.2* (2007): 477-83.

Weldon, Nick. "Biloxi's Crude Deal: Oil Spill Reparations are Funding a Baseball Stadium in Mississippi." *Vice Sports* 28 May 2015.

Wilcox, James A., and Luis G. Dopico. "Credit Union Mergers: Efficiencies and Benefits." *Federal Reserve Bank of San Francisco.* Federal Reserve Bank of San Francisco, 2011.

Wilemon, Tom. "Competition Breeds Added Benefits." *Sun Herald* [Biloxi, MS] 2005. Print.

Williams, Andrea. "Lignite Coal Plant Latest." *WTOK News Center.* WTOK, 2005. Web. 1 Jun, 2015.

Wilson, D. J. "Fiscal Spending Jobs and Multipliers: Evidence from the 2009 American Recovery and Reinvestment Act." *American Economic Journal: Economic Policy, 4.*3 (2012): 251-282.

WLOX. "State Farm Writing New Policies in Mississippi, But Not the Coast." *WLOX.* WLOX, 9 Jun. 2009.

Women of the Storm. "Personal Impacts." *Women of the Storm: A Gulf Coast Coalition.* Women of the Storm, 2015. 1 Aug. 2015.

Worth, J., B. Hampel, and M. Schenk. "The 2012 Economy: 'Good, not Great.'" *CreditUnion Magazine* 2012.

Yang, Tse-Chuan, et al. "Using Quantile Regression to Examine the Effects of Inequality Across the Mortality Distribution in the U.S. Counties." *Social Science & Medicine 74.*12 (2012): 1900-1910.

Yang, W., Fidrmuc, Jan, & Ghosh, S. *Government Spending Shocks and the Multiplier: New evidence from the U. S. Based on Natural Disasters.* Economics and Finance Working Papers Series, Working Paper 12-24, Nov. 2012. PDF file.

Zenger, T.R., et al. "Informal and Formal Organization in New Institutional Economics." *School of Business, Washington University.* Research Gate, 2001.

Zimmermann, Kim Ann. "Hurricane Katrina: Facts, Damage & Aftermath." *Live Science.* Live Science, 2012.

Zissimopoulos, J. & Karoly, L. A. "Employment and Self-employment in the Wake of Hurricane Katrina." *Demography, 47.*2 (2010): 345-367.

Please visit www.katrinatenyearsafter.com for additional material.

www.ingramcontent.com/pod-product-compliance
Lightning Source LLC
Chambersburg PA
CBHW030108300326
41934CB00034B/608